ENTREPRENEUR LINE

ARVIND UPADHYAY

Imagine a life where all your time is spent on the things you want to do. Imagine giving your greatest attention to a project you create yourself, instead of working as a cog in a machine that exists to make other people rich. Imagine handing a letter to your boss that reads, "Dear Boss, I'm writing to let you know that your services are no longer required. Thanks for everything, but I'll be doing things my own way now." Imagine that today is your final day of working for anyone other than yourself. What if—very soon, not in some distant, undefined future—you prepare for work by firing up a laptop in your home office, walking into a storefront you've opened, phoning a client who trusts you for helpful advice, or otherwise doing what you want instead of what someone tells you to do? All over the world, and in many different ways, thousands of people are doing exactly that. They are rewriting the rules of work, 20/617 becoming their own bosses, and creating a new future. This new model of doing business is well under way for these unexpected entrepreneurs, most of whom have never thought of themselves as businessmen and businesswomen. It's a microbusiness revolution—a way of earning a good living while crafting a life of independence and purpose. Other books chronicle the rise of Internet startups, complete with rants about venture capital and tales of in-house organic restaurants. Other guides tell you how to write eighty-page business plans that no one will ever read and that don't resemble how an actual business operates anyway. This book is different, and it has two key themes: freedom and value. Freedom is what we're all looking for, and value is the way to achieve it.Make no mistake: The blueprint does not tell you how to do less work; it tells you how to do better work. The goal isn't to get rich quickly but to build something that other people will value enough to pay for. You're not just creating a job for yourself; you're crafting a legacy. This blueprint does not involve secrets, shortcuts, or gimmicks. There are no visualization exercises here. If you think you can manifest your way to money simply by thinking about it, put this book down and spend your time doing that. Instead, this book is all about practical things you can do to take responsibility for your own future. Read it if you want to build something beautiful on the road to freedom. Can you transition to a meaningful life oriented toward something you love to do? Yes. Can you make money doing it? Yes, and here are the stories of people who have led the way. Is there a path you can follow for your 32/617 own escape plan? Yes—here is the path. Follow it to create the freedom you crave.

Contents

Foreword

I've been hearing stories about unconventional businesses for at least a decade, even 49/617 as I've been operating a series of them myself. Through my work as a writer and entrepreneur, I had access to a wide circle of microbusiness case studies: profitable businesses typically run solely by one person without much in the way of startup capital. In preparing for a comprehensive study, I began by checking with many of my friends and colleagues, but I didn't stop there. In 2017 I produced a series of workshops on low-budget business ideas . The first time we announced a workshop, it sold out in ninety minutes. We then offered spots in another workshop that wouldn't be held for several months, and it sold out before lunchtime. Since it was clear we had found a demand for this information, I dug deeper. While hosting the workshops, I became interested in the "follow-your-passion" model—the idea that successful small businesses.are often built on the pursuit of a personal hobby or interest. I conducted interviews with entrepreneurs all over the world and documented their stories for an online course called the Empire Building Kit. The course was the inspiration for launching the project on a wider scale and then for writing this book. I had a number of case studies in mind at the outset, but in preparation for writing the book, I cast the net much wider. I drew respondents from online and offline, collecting data through a Google form that grew to thousands of data points. As I traveled to sixty-three cities in North America on a book tour, I kept meeting and hearing about more unconventional, accidental entrepreneurs. When I finally closed the nomination process, I had more than 1,500 respondents to choose from. All of the respondents met at least four of the following six criteria: 51/617 • Follow-your-passion model. Many people are interested in building a business that is based on a hobby or activity they are especially enthusiastic about. As we'll see, not every passion leads to big bank deposits, but some certainly do. • Low startup cost. I was interested in businesses that required less than $1,000 in startup capital, especially those that cost almost nothing (less than $100) to begin. • At least $50,000 a year in net income. I wanted profitable businesses that earned at least as much as the average North American income. As we go along, you'll notice that the range varies considerably, with many businesses earning healthy six-figure incomes or higher, but a baseline profitability level of at least $50,000 a year was required. 52/

617 • No special skills. Since we were looking at ordinary people who created a successful business, I had a bias toward businesses that anyone can operate. This point can be hard to define, but there's a key distinction: Many businesses require specialized skills of some kind, but they are skills that can be acquired through a short period of training or independent study. You could learn to be a coffee roaster on the job, for example, but hopefully not a dentist. • Full financial disclosure. Respondents for the study agreed to disclose their income projection for the current year and actual income for at least the previous two years. Furthermore, they had to be willing to discuss income and expenses in specific terms. 53/ 617 • Fewer than five employees. For the most part, I was interested in unexpected or accidental entrepreneurs who deliberately chose to remain small. Many of the case studies are from businesses operated strictly by one person, which closely relates to the goal of personal freedom that so many respondents identified. I excluded businesses that were in "adult" or quasi-legal markets, and in most cases also excluded businesses that were highly technical or required special skills to operate. The baseline test was, "Could you explain what you do to your grandmother, and would you be willing to?" Next, I wanted to look at businesses started by people all over the world. About half of our stories come from the United States, and half come from the rest of the world. From Silicon Valley to Atlanta, the U.S. is a hub for entrepreneurship, both in terms of 54/617 values and ease of startup. But as we'll see, people from all over the world are creating their own microbusinesses, sometimes following the U.S. model and other times doing it independently. Finally, in making the last selections for the studies presented here, I had a bias toward "interesting" stories. Not every business needs to be sexy or trendworthy—in fact, many of the ones here aren't—but I liked stories that highlighted originality and creativity. Two years ago in Minneapolis, Lisa Sellman attracted my attention by telling me about her dog care business. At first, I didn't think much of it. How profitable could a dog care business be? But then Lisa told me how much money she made: $88,000 the previous year and on track to clear six figures the next. All of a sudden I was interested. How did Lisa do it ... and what lessons could we learn from her? 55/617 Each case study subject completed several detailed surveys about his or her business, including financial data and demographics, in addition to dozens of open-ended questions. The group surveys were followed up with further individual questions in hundreds of emails, phone calls, Skype video calls, and in-person meetings in fifteen

cities around the world. My goal was to create a narrative by finding common themes among a diverse group. The collected data would be enough for several thick books by itself, but I've tried to present only the most important information here.In other studies, books, and media coverage, two kinds of business models get most of the attention. Business model number one is old-school: An inventor gets an idea and 56/617 persuades the bank to lend her money for a growing operation, or a company spins off a division to create another company. Most corporations traded on the stock market fit this category. Business model number two is the investment-driven startup, which is typically focused on venture capital, buyouts, advertising, and market share. The business is initiated by a founder or small group of partners, but often run by a management team, reporting to a board of directors who seek to increase the business's valuation with the goal of "going public" or being acquired. Each of the older models has strengths, weaknesses, and various other characteristics. In both of them, there is no shortage of success and failure stories. But these models and their stories are not our concern here. While business models number one and number two have been getting all the attention, something else has been happening quietly—something completely different. 57/617 Our story is about people who start their own microbusinesses without investment, without employees, and often without much of an idea of what they're doing. They almost never have a formal business plan, and they often don't have a plan at all besides "Try this out and see what happens." More often than not, the business launches quickly, without waiting for permission from a board or manager. Market testing happens on the fly. "Are customers buying?" If the answer is yes, good. If no, what can we do differently? Like Michael's progression from corporate guy to mattress bicyclist, many of our case studies started businesses accidentally after experiencing a hardship such as losing a job. In Massachusetts, Jessica Reagan Salzman's husband called from work to say he was coming home early—and he wouldn't be going back to the office the next day. The unexpected layoff catapulted Jessica, new mother to a three-week-old, into action. Her part58/617 time bookkeeping "hobby" became the family's full-time income. In Pennsylvania, Tara Gentile started her business with the goal of being able to work from home while caring for her children; the business grew so quickly that her husband ended up staying home too. Across the Atlantic, David Henzell was a director for the largest advertising agency outside London. He left in part because he was bored with the work, and in part because of a diagnosis of chronic fatigue syndrome that left him struggling with "chronic director responsibilities." In his new company, Lightbulb Design, he makes the rules. "For a while the illness managed me," he said, "but now I manage it. Lightbulb started as a way for me to make a living on my terms. It's still on my terms, but now we are kicking ass!" The people we'll meet vary considerably in the ways they chose to structure their projects. Some eventually opted for expansion, 59/617 either by hiring or building teams of "virtual assistants." Erica Cosminsky grew her transcription team to seventeen people at one point, but by working with contractors instead of hiring employees, she retained the freedom to keep things simple. The Tom Bihn luggage factory in Seattle grew to a seven-figure operation, while remaining completely independent and turning down offers to sell its line to big-box stores. Others pursued partnerships that allowed each person to focus on what he or she was best at. Fresh out of design school and disillusioned with their entry-level jobs, Jen Adrion and Omar Noory began selling custom-made maps out of an apartment in Columbus, Ohio. Patrick McCrann and Rich Strauss were competitors who teamed up to create a community for endurance athletes. Several of our stories are about married couples or partners building a business together. 60/617 But many others chose to go it alone, with the conviction that they would find freedom by working primarily by themselves. Charlie Pabst was a successful architect with a "dream job" as a store designer for Starbucks. But the desire for autonomy overcame the comfort of the dream job and the free lattes: "One day I drove to work and realized I couldn't do it anymore, called in sick, drafted my two-week notice, and the rest is history." Charlie still works as a designer, but now he works from home for clients of his choosing. We'll view these stories as an ensemble: a group of individual voices that, when considered together, comprise an original composition. In sharing how different people have set themselves free from corporate misery, the challenge is to acknowledge their courage without exaggerating their skills. Most of them aren't geniuses or natural-born entrepreneurs; they are ordinary people who 61/617 made a few key decisions that changed their lives. Very few of our case studies went to business school, and more than half had no previous business experience whatsoever. Several dropped out of college, and others never went in the first place.* In sharing these stories, the goal is to provide a blueprint for freedom, a plan you can use to apply their lessons to your own escape plan. Throughout the case studies, three lessons of micro-entrepreneurship emerge. We'll focus on these lessons in various ways throughout the book.EVERY MOMENT IN BUSINESS happens only once. The next Bill Gates will not build an operating system. The next Larry Page or Sergey Brin won't make a search engine. And the next Mark Zuckerberg won't create a social network. If you are copying these guys, you aren't learning from them. Of course, it's easier to copy a model than to make something new. Doing what we already know how to do takes the world from 1 to n, adding more of something familiar. But every time we create something new, we go from 0 to 1. The act of creation is singular, as is the moment of creation, and the result is something fresh and strange. Unless they invest in the difficult task of creating new things, American companies will fail in the future no matter how big their profits remain today. What happens when we've gained everything to be had from fine-tuning the old lines of business that we've inherited? Unlikely as it sounds, the answer threatens to be far worse than the crisis of 2008. Today's "best practices" lead to dead ends; the best paths are new and untried. In a world of gigantic administrative bureaucracies both public and private, searching for a new path might seem like hoping for a miracle. Actually, if American business is going to succeed, we are going to need hundreds, or even thousands, of miracles. This would be depressing but for one crucial fact: humans are distinguished from other species by our ability to work miracles. We call these miracles technology. Technology is miraculous because it allows us to do more with less, ratcheting up our fundamental capabilities to a higher level. Other animals are instinctively driven to build things like dams or honeycombs, but we are the only ones that can invent new things and better ways of making them. Humans don't decide what to build by making choices from some cosmic catalog of options given in advance; instead, by creating new technologies, we rewrite the plan of the world. These are the kind of elementary truths we teach to second graders, but they are easy to forget in a world where so much of what we do is repeat what has been done before.

Preface

We have something new to say about building, running, and growing (or not growing) a business. This book isn't based on academic theories. It's based on our experience. We've been in business for more than six years. Along the way, we've seen two recessions, one burst bubble, business-model shifts, and doom-and-gloom predictions come and go--and we've remained profitable through it all. We're an intentionally small company that makes software to help small companies and groups get things done the easy way. More than 3 million people around the world use our products. We started out in 1999 as a three-person Web-design consulting firm. In 2004, we weren't happy with the project-management software used by the rest of the industry, so we created our own: Basecamp. When we showed the online tool to clients and colleagues, they all said the same thing: "We need this for our business too." Five years later, Basecamp generates millions of dollars a year in profits. We now sell other online tools too. Highrise, our contact manager and simple CRM (customer relationship management) tool, is used by tens of thousands of small businesses to keep track of leads, deals, and more than 10 million contacts. More than 500,000 people have signed up for Backpack, our intranet and knowledge-sharing tool. And people have sent more than 100 million messages using Campfire, our real-time business chat tool. We also invented and open-sourced a computer-programming framework called Ruby on Rails that powers much of the Web 2.0 world. Some people consider us an Internet company, but that makes us cringe. Internet companies are known for hiring compulsively, spending wildly, and failing spectacularly. That's not us. We're small (sixteen people as this book goes to press), frugal, and profitable. A lot of people say we can't do what we do. They call us a fluke. They advise others to ignore our advice. Some have even called us irresponsible, reckless, and--gasp!- -unprofessional. These critics don't understand how a company can reject growth, meetings, budgets, boards of directors, advertising, salespeople, and "the real world," yet thrive. That's their problem, not ours. They say you need to sell to the Fortune 500. Screw that. We sell to the Fortune 5,000,000. They don't think you can have employees who almost never see each other spread out across eight cities on two continents. They say you can't succeed without making financial projections and five-year plans. They're wrong

CHAPTER ONE

Startup

"Catch a man a fish, and you can sell it to him. Teach a man to fish, and you ruin a wonderful business opportunity." —KARL MARX Along with some of the other stories mentioned . we'll return to the Jamestown Coffee Company as we go along. But first, let's consider a key principle of building your way to freedom through a microbusiness based on a skill, hobby, or passion. The hard way to start a business is to fumble along, uncertain whether your big idea will resonate with customers. The easy way is to find out what people want and then find a way to give it to them. Another way to consider it is to think about fish. Picture this scenario: It's Friday night, and you head out to a nice restaurant after a long week of work. While you're relaxing over a glass of wine, the waiter comes over and informs you of the special. "We have a delicious salmon risotto tonight," he says. "That sounds perfect," you think, so you order the dish. The waiter jots it down and heads back 79/617 toward the kitchen as you continue your wine and conversation. So far, so good, right? But then the chef comes out and walks over to your table. "I understand you've ordered the salmon risotto," she says as you nod in affirmation. "Well, risotto is a bit tricky, and it's important we get the salmon right, too ... Have you ever made it before?" Before you can respond, the chef turns around. "Tell you what, I'll go ahead and get the olive oil started.... You wash up and meet me back in the kitchen." I'm guessing this experience has never happened to you, and I'm also guessing that you probably wouldn't enjoy it if it did. After getting past the initial surprise (Does the chef really want me to come back into the kitchen and help prepare the food?), you'd probably find it very odd. You know that the food in the restaurant costs much more than it would in the grocery store—you're paying a 80/617 big premium for atmosphere and service. If you wanted to make salmon risotto yourself, you would have done so. You didn't go to the restaurant to learn to make a new dish; you went to relax and have people do everything for you. What does this scenario have to do with starting a microbusiness and plotting a course toward freedom? Here's the problem: Many businesses are modeled on the idea that customers should come back to the kitchen and make their own dinner. Instead of giving people what they really want, the business owners have the idea that it's better to involve customers behind the scenes … because that's what they think customers want. It's all the fault of the old saying: "Give a man a fish and he'll eat for a day. Teach a man to fish and he'll eat for a lifetime." This might be a good idea for hungry fishermen, but it's usually a terrible idea in business. Most customers don't want to learn how to 81/617 fish. We work all week and go to the restaurant so that someone can take care of everything for us. We don't need to know the details of what goes on in the kitchen; in fact, we may not even want to know the details. A better way is to give people what they actually want, and the way to do that lies in understanding something very simple about who we are. Get this point right, and a lot of other things become much easier. For fifteen years, John and Barbara Varian were furniture builders, living on a ranch in Parkfield, California, a tiny town where the welcome sign reads "Population 18." The idea for a side business came about by accident after a group of horseback riding enthusiasts asked if they could pay a fee to ride on the ranch. They would need to eat, too—could John and Barbara do something about that? Yes, they could. 82/617 In the fall of 2006, a devastating fire burned down most of their inventory, causing them to reevaluate the whole operation. Instead of rebuilding the furniture business (no pun intended), they decided to change course. "We had always loved horses," Barbara said, "so we decided to see about having more groups pay to come to the ranch." They built a bunkhouse and upgraded other buildings, putting together specific packages for riding groups that included all meals and activities. John and Barbara reopened as the V6 Ranch, situated on 20,000 acres exactly halfway between Los Angeles and San Francisco. Barbara's story stood out to me because of something she said. I always ask business owners what they sell and why their customers buy from them, and the answers are often insightful in more ways than one. Many people answer the question directly—"We sell widgets, and people buy them because 83/617 they need a widget"—but once in a while, I hear a more astute response. "We're not selling horse rides," Barbara said emphatically. "We're offering freedom. Our work helps our guests escape, even if just for a moment in time, and be someone they may have never even considered before." The difference is crucial. Most people who visit the V6 Ranch have day jobs and a limited number of vacation days. Why do they choose to visit a working ranch in a tiny town instead of jetting off to lie on a beach in Hawaii? The answer lies in the story and messaging behind John and Barbara's offer. Helping their clients "escape and be someone else" is far more valuable than offering horse rides. Above all else, the V6 Ranch is selling happiness. On the other side of the country, Kelly Newsome was a straight-A student and an 84/617 ambitious Washington, D.C., career climber. By the time she started college, she already had the goal of big career achievement in mind. From the top of her class at the University of Virginia School of Law, she went on to a high-paying job as a Manhattan lawyer—her dream for more than six years. Alas, Kelly soon discovered that dutifully checking the company's filings for compliance with the Securities Act day in and day out wasn't exactly what she had hoped for back in law school. After the high of scoring her dream job wore off and the reality of being a well-paid paper pusher set in, Kelly wanted a change. Abandoning her $240,000-a-year corporate law gig five years in, Kelly left for a new position at Human Rights Watch, the international charity. This job was more fulfilling than the moneymaking job, but it also helped her realize that she really wanted to be on her own. Before the next change, Kelly took 85/617 time off and traveled the world. Yoga had always been a passion for her, and during her time away, she underwent a two-hundredhour training course, followed by teaching in Asia and Europe. The next step was Higher Ground Yoga, a private practice she founded back in Washington, D.C. There were plenty of yoga studios in D.C., but Kelly wanted to focus on a specific market: busy women, usually executives, ages thirty to forty-five and often with young children or expecting. In less than a year, Kelly built the business to the $50,000+ level, and she's now on track for more than $85,000 a year. The practice has its weaknesses—during a big East Coast "snowpocalypse," Kelly was unable to drive to her appointments for nearly three weeks, losing income for much of that time. Despite the lower salary and the problem of losing business during bad weather, Kelly says she wouldn't return to her old career. Here's how she put it: "One 86/617 time when I was a lawyer, having just worked with an outstanding massage therapist, I said to her, 'It must be so great to make people so happy.' And it is." Like Barbara and John in California, Kelly discovered that the secret to a meaningful new career was directly related to making people feel good about themselves. Where Do Ideas Come From? As you begin to think like an entrepreneur, you'll notice that business ideas can come from anywhere. When you go to the store, pay attention to the way they display the signage. Check the prices on restaurant menus not just for your own budget but also to compare them with the prices at other places. When you see an ad, ask yourself: What is the most important message the company is trying to communicate? While thinking like this, you'll notice opportunities for microbusiness projects 87/617 everywhere you go. Here are a few common sources of inspiration. An inefficiency in the marketplace. Ever notice when something isn't run the way it should be, or you find yourself looking for something that doesn't exist? Chances are, you're not the only one frustrated, and you're not the only one who wants that nonexistent thing. Make what you want to buy yourself, and other people will probably want it too. New technology or opportunity. When everyone started using smart phones, new markets cropped up for app developers, case manufacturers, and so on. But the obvious answer isn't the only one: Makers of nice journals and paper notebooks also saw an uptick in sales, perhaps in part because of 88/617 customers who didn't want everything in their lives to be electronic. A changing space. As we saw with Michael's example in Chapter 1, car dealerships were going out of business, and he was able to rent his first temporary mattress space on the cheap. Not everyone would have thought of locating a mattress shop in a former car dealership, but Michael grabbed the opportunity. A spin-off or side project. One business idea can lead to many others. Whenever something is going well, think about offshoots, spin-offs, and side projects that could also bring in income. Brandon Pearce, whom we'll see more of in Chapter 4, founded Studio Helper as a side project to his main business of Music Teacher's Helper. It 89/617 now brings in more than $100,000 a year on its own. Tip: When thinking about different business ideas, also think about money. Get in the habit of equating "money stuff" with ideas. When brainstorming and evaluating different projects, money isn't the sole consideration—but it's an important one. Ask three questions for every idea: a. How would I get paid with this idea? b. How much would I get paid from this idea? c. Is there a way I could get paid more than once? We'll look at money issues more in Chapters 10 and 11. 90/617 What Is Value? The stories of the V6 Ranch and Higher Ground Yoga are good examples of how freedom and value are related. In California, John and Barbara found a way to pursue the outdoor lives they wanted by inviting guests to make the ranch their escape. Meanwhile, even though Kelly makes less money (at least for now) in her new career, her health is better and she does work she enjoys—a trade-off she was happy to make. Freedom was Kelly's primary motivation in making the switch, but the key to her success is the value she provides her clients. Let's stop for a moment and look at the concept of value, a word that is often used without much exploration. What is value, exactly? Here's a basic definition: 91/617 val-ue: something desirable and of worth, created through exchange or effort In our context, an even easier way to think about it is: Value means helping people. If you're trying to build a microbusiness and you begin your efforts by helping people, you're on the right track. When you get stuck, ask yourself: How can I give more value? Or more simply: How can I help my customers more? Freedom and value have a direct relationship: You can pursue freedom for yourself while providing value for others. As we saw in the discussion of convergence, a business ultimately succeeds because of the value it provides its end users, customers, or clients. More than anything else, value relates to emotional needs. Many business owners talk about their work in terms of the features it offers, but it's much more powerful to talk 92/617 about the benefits customers receive. A feature is descriptive; a benefit is emotional. Consider the difference in the stories we've looked at in the chapter thus far. The V6 Ranch helps people "escape and be someone new." Isn't that more powerful than just offering a horse ride? Kelly's private classes help busy female executives prepare for their day in a quiet setting, a much more meaningful and tailor-made experience than going to the gym with hundreds of other people. We can apply the same thinking to the examples we briefly reviewed in Chapter 1. At its most basic level, we could say that Jaden Hair (founder of Steamy Kitchen) offers recipes on her website, but plenty of websites have recipes. A much stronger benefit, and the one that Jaden puts forward, is that her work helps families spend quality time making and enjoying delicious food. Similarly, Megan Hunt makes dresses, but that's not the point: She also helps brides share in the 93/617 anticipation, celebration, and memories of a perfect day. Who wouldn't pay for that? The list below provides a contrast between features and benefits.* This kind of analysis applies even to businesses that you might think of as boring or commodity-based. Michael Hanna (the mattress guy) talked with me about selling a mattress to a family with an infant and then seeing them return two years later with their three-year-old, who now needed to upgrade 94/617 to her first bed. This kind of story, which Michael tries to communicate frequently, is much more interesting than talking about box springs or mattress ratings. Overall, the more a business can focus on core benefits instead of boring features, the more customers will connect ... and purchase. As you think about how to apply the $100 Startup model to your own quest for freedom, these three strategies will help. Strategy 1: Dig Deeper to Uncover Hidden Needs You might think it's obvious that restaurant patrons don't want to wander back to the kitchen and make their own meals, but sometimes what people say they want and what they actually want are different things. Kyle Hepp, a wedding photographer who travels the world from her home base in Santiago, Chile, learned that sometimes you have to look deeper. Kyle's clients tend to be young 95/ 617 and hip, and they're drawn to her work because it is non-traditional. Sometimes they even say they don't want any traditional wedding shots. "We're not into old-school," was how one couple put it. Kyle agrees and spends her time at the wedding getting fun, candid shots that she knows the couple will like. But that's not all. Having done this for a while, Kyle knows that what her clients want and what they say they want may be different—and she also knows that the families of the bride and groom may have preferences of their own. Here's how she handles these competing desires: On the day of the wedding, I'll grab them and say, "Let's get your family and just do a couple of traditional shots." I'll make it quick and painless. I make sure everyone is laughing and having a good time and it's not those awful, everybodystare-at-the-camera-and-look-miserable 96/617 kinds of shots. And then after the wedding, when I deliver those photos, either the bride and groom's parents will be thrilled to have those pictures (which in turn makes the couple happy), or the bride and groom themselves will end up saying they're so happy that we did those shots. Kyle goes above and beyond by giving her photography clients what they really want ... even if they hadn't realized it themselves. Strategy 2: Make Your Customer a Hero In India I heard from Purna Duggirala, who said that he operates a training business to "help people become awesome at Microsoft Excel." Microsoft Excel doesn't interest me much, but Purna's financial details caught my attention: In the "Last Year's Net 97/617 Income" column on my survey form, he had written $136,000. A salary like that is impressive where I live, but I've traveled enough to know that in India it's huge. What's more, Purna was on track to earn more than $200,000 the next year, his third year of operation. His customers were big fans. When I Googled him, I found a comment that said he was one user's "BFF for Excel," his best friend forever. What was he doing to attract such a response from spreadsheet users? Purna started his website several years back, but for a while it only contained posts about his family and life in India. In 2009, he settled in and got more serious, chronicling a series of tips and tutorials about using Excel to become more productive. Crucially, he didn't target Indians, but instead reached out to interested prospects all over the world. He also didn't depend on advertising revenue, something that very few people in our 98/617 study mentioned. Instead, he created products and services himself, offering downloadable guides and an ongoing training school. He was also a good copywriter. Updating spreadsheets can sound like incredibly tedious work, but Purna positioned the core benefit away from numbers and toward something far more powerful: "Our training programs make customers a hero in front of their bosses or colleagues." Not only would their work become easier, Purna said, but other people would recognize and appreciate them for simplifying a complicated process. A former business analyst, Purna quit his job when it became apparent that he would earn much more money with the new business. Despite having such a high income in India, Purna and his wife continue to live frugally. "We are in a position where we would not have to worry about money for lots of years to come," he says. Even better, 99/617 new customers arrive every day from Google searches, mainstream media coverage, and hundreds of links. "If I wanted to turn it off," he told me, "it would be very difficult." Take it from Purna: If spreadsheets can be made sexy, surely any business can find a way to communicate a similar message. Strategy 3: Sell What People Buy In deciding what to sell, the best approach is to sell what people buy—in other words, think more about what people really want than about what you think they need. Perhaps a story of my own failure-to-success progression will help illustrate this principle. Early in the life of my business, I created a project called Travel Ninja. Since I've been to more than 150 countries and regularly fly more than 200,000 miles a year, I've learned a lot about getting from place to place on a budget. Travel Ninja would be a guide to illustrate how it all works—how to book 100/617 round-the-world tickets, how to take advantage of airline mistake fares, and so on. As I surveyed my audience, the initial response was encouraging. Plenty of people said they were excited and wanted to learn about these topics. A previous launch for another product had sold five hundred copies right off the bat, so on the big day I dutifully got up early and updated the site to make it live. Then I waited ... and waited. Orders came in, but at a much slower rate than I expected. At the end of the launch day,

I had sold only a hundred copies—not terrible, but not great either. For several weeks, I was puzzled by the low response. The feedback from the customers who purchased Travel Ninja was almost unanimously positive, but so few people had purchased that I knew something was wrong with the messaging. Finally I figured it out: Most people don't care about the intricacies of how airlines work; they just 101/617 want to know how to get cheap tickets. My prospects who didn't buy felt overwhelmed by the details and complexities. Like the overeager chef at the beginning of the chapter, I was trying to take them into the kitchen with me, not just giving them the meal they wanted. Ah-ha. Lesson learned. I regrouped a year later with another travel product. This one was called Frequent Flyer Master, and I did everything I could to make it more accessible. I even used the previous experience as part of the sales copy: "Maybe you don't want to travel to twenty countries a year like I do. But if you could go to one place for nearly free, where would it be?" This product did much better, selling five hundred copies on launch day and going on to produce more than $50,000 in net income over the next year. The success was also quite a relief, because for almost a year I had wondered whether people would buy 102/617 information about travel. Thankfully, they will—if it's packaged properly in a way that meets their needs. Another year later, I applied the lesson even further: The most frequent request from Frequent Flyer Master owners, who otherwise loved the product, was for more updates on late-breaking travel opportunities. With that in mind, I created the Travel Hacking Cartel to tell people exactly what to do to take advantage of deals all over the world. The careful message this time was: Don't worry about the details; just do what we say and you'll regularly earn enough miles for free plane tickets every year. This launch did the best of all—more than three thousand customers joined on the first day. I had finally figured out how to give my customers what they wanted.As I learned from my early mistakes, homing in on what customers really want from a business is critical. Simply put, we want more of some things and less of others. In the "More" column are things such as love, money, acceptance, and free time. We all want more of those things, right? In the "Less" column are the undesirables: things such as stress, long commutes, and bad relationships. If your business focuses on giving people more of what they want or taking away something they don't want (or both), you're on the right track. 107/617 A spa takes away stress while making guests feel loved and accepted. A popular message is, "We'll do everything for you—relax and leave the details to us." This is also the message that a good restaurant sends, not, "Come back into the kitchen and make your own dinner." Brooke Snow, an artist and musician, struggled to make a living by teaching classes in her small Utah town. She got by without working a real job and paid for college without going into debt, which could be considered a success on its own, but making 108/617 ends meet was a continual battle. One day she realized the obvious: Instead of putting up flyers in Logan, Utah, and hoping for enough phone calls, what if she could teach anywhere in the world? The change happened by accident, ironically after one of the worst days of her initial business. "I had to cancel a class due to underenrollment," Brooke says. "At the time my husband was starting graduate school, and we had an eight-month-old baby and a new home." Needless to say, the pressure was mounting. When she phoned Micah, one of the few students who had enrolled, to notify him of the cancellation, it turned out he was a doctoral candidate in instructional technology with an emphasis on distance education. Brooke describes herself as a good photographer and teacher but not highly technical. Happily, she is also good at bartering—and in this case, she offered private lessons to 109/ 617 Micah in exchange for his help in setting up an online course. Since it was almost perfectly in line with what he was studying, Micah was thrilled to help Brooke make the online transition. In the last year Brooke taught all her classes locally, she made $30,000. In the first year she offered the class online, she made more than $60,000. Nice! Going from offline to online helped a lot, but Brooke also attributes the successful transition to something else: the idea of always being willing to share. Early in her career, she went to a seminar where she heard someone say, "If you make your business about helping others, you'll always have plenty of work." Here's what happened next: That statement changed my life. I was in an over-saturated market of photographers competing for portrait work, all of whom were very closed about sharing any trade secrets. I let go of fear 110/617 and embraced the concept of helping others (so I could have "plenty of work"!) and decided to start teaching classes on photography in my basement. One family skeptic cautioned me that I would be "training my competition." Thankfully, making my business about helping others has proved itself over and over. We'll return to Brooke's theme several times throughout the book. I call it the freely receive, freely give approach. When all else fails, ask yourself how you can help people more. What do people really, really want? At the end of the day, they want to be happy, and businesses that help their customers be happy are well-positioned to succeed. The V6 Ranch creates modern cowboys. Kelly's yoga practice helps busy executives prepare for their day in peace. The restaurant we went to at the end of a stressful week—when it's not 111/617 making its customers pop back into the kitchen—helps its patrons relax and decompress over a glass of wine and great service. Conversations with the group returned to this theme many times in different ways. The common theme was to figure out what people want and then find a way to give it to them. This is the road map to a successful, profitable business. As you build your escape plan, keep your eyes on the prize: creating real value by giving people what they really want. KEY POINTS Value means "helping people." Our unexpected entrepreneurs discovered that when they focused on providing value above all else, their businesses were successful. Give people what they really want, not just what you think they should have. Give them the fish! 112/617 The more you can market a core benefit instead of a list of features, the easier it will be to profit from your idea. Core benefits usually relate to emotional needs more than physical needs. Most people want more of some things (money, love, attention) and less of other things (stress, anxiety, debt). Always focus on what you can add or take away to improve someone's life ... and then prepare to get paid.Like many of us, Gary Leff begins his day with email. As a CFO for two university research centers in northern Virginia, he's in touch with colleagues from morning to night. It's a good job that he enjoys, and he has no plans to leave. But the "early early" morning email traffic comes from another source: Gary's part-time business as a specific kind of consultant. Like me, Gary is an active "travel hacker," earning hundreds of thousands of frequent flyer miles every year through various airline promotions. Many executives also earn plenty of miles, usually from business credit card charges, but earning miles and redeeming them for actual vacations are two different things. The executives typically have no idea how the process works and don't have 117/617 the time to learn. How many miles do you need for any specific trip? What if the airline tells you no seats are available? If you don't know what you're doing, it's easy to get frustrated and give up. That's where Gary comes in. For a fee (currently $250 for up to two passengers with the same itinerary), Gary will set up the trip of your dreams based on preferences you select. Clients tell Gary where they want to go, which airline their miles are coming from, and any restrictions they have on their travel dates. Then Gary gets to work, combing databases to check on availability, phoning the airlines, and taking advantage of every loophole.

It may sound strange to pay $250 for something you could do on your own for free, but the value Gary provides through the service is immense: Many of the trips he arranges would otherwise cost $5,000 or more. He specializes in first- and business-class 118/617 itineraries, and some of them feature as many as six airlines on a single award ticket. You want a free stopover in Paris en route to Johannesburg? No problem. You want to allow plenty of time to visit the Lufthansa firstclass terminal in Frankfurt before continuing on to Singapore? Done. If he's not successful in booking your trip, you don't pay—the business succeeds only when it provides real value to clients. In addition to executives, Gary's clients are often retirees headed for cruises and couples planning a once-in-a-lifetime trip: basically anyone who has a bunch of miles but doesn't want to go through the hassle of figuring out how to use them. Business picked up after he was featured in Condé Nast Traveler, but aside from calling the airlines to book the tickets, Gary manages communications entirely by email. The part-time job brought in $75,000 last year and is on track to top six figures annually. Since he has the full-time 119/617 CFO gig and other business ventures, Gary invests the money instead of spending it. "I honestly do this because it's fun," he says. Meanwhile, he cashes in miles from his own bulging mileage accounts to travel the world with his wife, squeezing in luxury trips to the Philippines and Thailand between financial planning meetings back home. Gary's business, like many others we'll look at, can be described as a follow-your-passion business. Gary was passionate about travel and had found a number of creative ways to enjoy first-class trips around the world at economy prices. He started helping people do the same thing, first as a volunteer community member for several travel forums, then on a blog, and then on an individual basis for people he knew. Word got around—"Hey, Gary, I'd like to take my wife to Europe and I have all these miles ... What 120/617 do I do?"—and before he knew it, he had more requests for help than he could handle. The next logical step was to start charging. He built a very basic website and set up shop in a short period of time, not entirely sure what would happen next. Would anyone purchase this unusual service? Well, yes, they would—and even though Gary is content in his day job and has no plans to leave, he no longer depends on it. If something changed at work, he'd have no problem living off the funds from his side business or ramping it up to something bigger. Gary's story is inspiring but not all that uncommon. As I foraged for case studies and went from interview to interview, I learned to stop being surprised when I heard that a coupon-clipping website run by a single mom brought in $60,000 part-time or that a handmade toy business was closing in on $250,000 and hiring multiple employees. 121/617 Instant Consultant Biz Gary's business is great, and no one cares that his website looks like it was made ten years ago. He also didn't wait for someone to accredit or endorse him for his business. There is no "consulting school" or degree. You can start a new business as a consultant in about one day, if not sooner. Follow these two basic rules: 1. Pick something specific as opposed to something general. Don't be a "business consultant" or a "life coach"—get specific about what you can really do for someone. 2. No one values a $15-an-hour consultant, so do not underprice your service. Since you probably won't have forty hours of billable work every week, charge at least $100 an hour or a comparable fixed rate for the benefit you provide.When we think about the future, we hope for a future of progress. That progress can take one of two forms. Horizontal or extensive progress means copying things that work—going from 1 to n. Horizontal progress is easy to imagine because we already know what it looks like. Vertical or intensive progress means doing new things—going from 0 to 1. Vertical progress is harder to imagine because it requires doing something nobody else has ever done. If you take one typewriter and build 100, you have made horizontal progress. If you have a typewriter and build a word processor, you have made vertical progress.At the macro level, the single word for horizontal progress is globalization—taking things that work somewhere and making them work everywhere. China is the paradigmatic example of globalization; its 20-year plan is to become like the United States is today. The Chinese have been straightforwardly copying everything that has worked in the developed world: 19th-century railroads, 20th-century air conditioning, and even entire cities. They might skip a few steps along the way— going straight to wireless without installing landlines, for instance—but they're copying all the same. The single word for vertical, 0 to 1 progress is technology. The rapid progress of information technology in recent decades has made Silicon Valley the capital of "technology" in general. But there is no reason why technology should be limited to computers. Properly understood, any new and better way of doing things is technology.globalization and technology are different modes of progress, it's possible to have both, either, or neither at the same time. For example, 1815 to 1914 was a period of both rapid technological development and rapid globalization. Between the First World War and Kissinger's trip to reopen relations with China in 1971, there was rapid technological development but not much globalization. Since 1971, we have seen rapid globalization along with limited technological development, mostly confined to IT. This age of globalization has made it easy to imagine that the decades ahead will bring more convergence and more sameness. Even our everyday language suggests we believe in a kind of technological end of history: the division of the world into the so-called developed and developing nations implies that the "developed" world has already achieved the achievable, and that poorer nations just need to catch up. But I don't think that's true. My own answer to the contrarian question is that most people think the future of the world will be defined by globalization, but the truth is that technology matters more. Without technological change, if China doubles its energy production over the next two decades, it will also double its air pollution. If every one of India's hundreds of millions of households were to live the way Americans already do—using only today's tools—the result would be environmentally catastrophic. Spreading old ways to create wealth around the world will result in devastation, not riches. In a world of scarce resources, globalization without new technology is unsustainable. New technology has never been an automatic feature of history. Our ancestors lived in static, zerosum societies where success meant seizing things from others. They created new sources of wealth only rarely, and in the long run they could never create enough to save the average person from an extremely hard life. Then, after 10,000 years of fitful advance from primitive agriculture to medieval windmills and 16th-century astrolabes, the modern world suddenly experienced relentless technological progress from the advent of the steam engine in the 1760s all the way up to about 1970. As a result, we have inherited a richer society than any previous generation would have been able to imagine. Any generation excepting our parents' and grandparents', that is: in the late 1960s, they expected this progress to continue. They looked forward to a four-day workweek, energy too cheap to meter, and vacations on the moon. But it didn't happen. The smartphones that distract us from our surroundings also distract us from the fact that our surroundings are strangely old: only computers and communications have improved dramatically since midcentury. That doesn't mean our parents were wrong to imagine a better future—they were only wrong to expect it as something automatic. Today our challenge is to both imagine and create the new technologies that can make the 21st century more peaceful and prosperous than the 20th.

New technology tends to come from new ventures—startups. From the Founding Fathers in politics to the Royal Society in science to Fairchild Semiconductor's "traitorous eight" in business, small groups of people bound together by a sense of mission have changed the world for the better. The easiest explanation for this is negative: it's hard to develop new things in big organizations, and it's even harder to do it by yourself. Bureaucratic hierarchies move slowly, and entrenched interests shy away from risk. In the most dysfunctional organizations, signaling that work is being done becomes a better strategy for career advancement than actually doing work (if this describes your company, you should quit now). At the other extreme, a lone genius might create a classic work of art or literature, but he could never create an entire industry. Startups operate on the principle that you need to work with other people to get stuff done, but you also need to stay small enough so that you actually can. Positively defined, a startup is the largest group of people you can convince of a plan to build a different future. A new company's most important strength is new thinking: even more important than nimbleness, small size affords space to think. This book is about the questions you must ask and answer to succeed in the business of doing new things: what follows is not a manual or a record of knowledge but an exercise in thinking. Because that is what a startup has to do: question received ideas and rethink business from scratch.—What important truth do very few people agree with you on?—is difficult to answer directly. It may be easier to start with a preliminary: what does everybody agree on? "Madness is rare in individuals—but in groups, parties, nations, and ages it is the rule," Nietzsche wrote (before he went mad). If you can identify a delusional popular belief, you can find what lies hidden behind it: the contrarian truth. Consider an elementary proposition: companies exist to make money, not to lose it. This should be obvious to any thinking person. But it wasn't so obvious to many in the late 1990s, when no loss was too big to be described as an investment in an even bigger, brighter future. The conventional wisdom of the "New Economy" accepted page views as a more authoritative, forward-looking financial metric than something as pedestrian as profit. Conventional beliefs only ever come to appear arbitrary and wrong in retrospect; whenever one collapses, we call the old belief a bubble. But the distortions caused by bubbles don't disappear when they pop. The internet craze of the '90s was the biggest bubble since the crash of 1929, and the lessons learned afterward define and distort almost all thinking about technology today. The first step to thinking clearly is to question what we think we know about the past.

S Introduction top me if you've heard this one before. Brilliant college kids sitting in a dorm are inventing the future. Heedless of boundaries, possessed of new technology and youthful enthusiasm, they build a new company from scratch. Their early success allows them to raise money and bring an amazing new product to market. They hire their friends, assemble a superstar team, and dare the world to stop them. Ten years and several startups ago, that was me, building my !rst company. I particularly remember a moment from back then: the moment I realized my company was going to fail. My cofounder and I were at our wits' end. The dot-com bubble had burst, and we had spent all our money. We tried desperately to raise more capital, and we could not. It was like a breakup scene from a Hollywood movie: it was raining, and we were arguing in the street. We couldn't even agree on where to walk next, and so we parted in anger, heading in opposite directions. As a metaphor for our company's failure, this image of the two of us, lost in the rain and drifting apart, is perfect. It remains a painful memory. The company limped along for months afterward, but our situation was hopeless. At the time, it had seemed we were doing everything right: we had a great product, a brilliant team, amazing technology, and the right idea at the right time. And we really were on to something. We were building a way for college kids to create online pro!les for the purpose of sharing ... with employers. Oops. But despite a promising idea, we were nonetheless doomed from day one, because we did not know the process we would need to use to turn because we did not know the process we would need to use to turn our product insights into a great company. If you've never experienced a failure like this, it is hard to describe the feeling. It's as if the world were falling out from under you. You realize you've been duped. The stories in the magazines are lies: hard work and perseverance don't lead to success. Even worse, the many, many, many promises you've made to employees, friends, and family are not going to come true. Everyone who thought you were foolish for stepping out on your own will be proven right. It wasn't supposed to turn out that way. In magazines and newspapers, in blockbuster movies, and on countless blogs, we hear the mantra of the successful entrepreneurs: through determination, brilliance, great timing, and—above all—a great product, you too can achieve fame and fortune. There is a mythmaking industry hard at work to sell us that story, but I have come to believe that the story is false, the product of selection bias and after-the-fact rationalization. In fact, having worked with hundreds of entrepreneurs, I have seen firsthand how often a promising start leads to failure. The grim reality is that most startups fail. Most new products are not successful. Most new ventures do not live up to their potential. Yet the story of perseverance, creative genius, and hard work persists. Why is it so popular? I think there is something deeply appealing about this modern-day rags-to-riches story. It makes success seem inevitable if you just have the right stuff. It means that the mundane details, the boring stuff, the small individual choices don't matter. If we build it, they will come. When we fail, as so many of us do, we have a ready-made excuse: we didn't have the right stuff. We weren't visionary enough or weren't in the right place at the right time. After more than ten years as an entrepreneur, I came to reject that line of thinking. I have learned from both my own successes and failures and those of many others that it's the boring stuff that matters the most. Startup success is not a consequence of good genes or being in the right place at the right time. Startup success can be engineered by following the right process, which means it can be engineered by following the right process, which means it can be learned, which means it can be taught. Entrepreneurship is a kind of management. No, you didn't read that wrong. We have wildly divergent associations with these two words, entrepreneurship and management. Lately, it seems that one is cool, innovative, and exciting and the other is dull, serious, and bland. It is time to look past these preconceptions. Let me tell you a second startup story. It's 2004, and a group of founders have just started a new company. Their previous company had failed very publicly. Their credibility is at an all-time low. They have a huge vision: to change the way people communicate by using a new technology called avatars (remember, this was before James Cameron's blockbuster movie). They are following a visionary named Will Harvey, who paints a compelling picture: people connecting with their friends, hanging out online, using avatars to give them a combination of intimate connection and safe anonymity. Even better, instead of having to build all the clothing, furniture, and accessories these avatars would need to accessorize their digital lives, the customers would be enlisted to build those things and sell them to one another. The engineering challenge before them is immense: creating virtual worlds, user-generated content, an online commerce engine, micropayments, and—last but not least—the three-dimensional avatar technology that can run on anyone's PC. I'm in this second story, too. I'm a cofounder and chief technology officer of this company, which is called IMVU. At this point in our careers, my cofounders and I are determined to make new mistakes. We do everything wrong: instead of spending years perfecting our technology, we build a minimum viable product, an early product that is terrible, full of bugs and crash-your-computer-yes-really stability problems. Then we ship it to customers way before it's ready. And we charge money for it. After securing initial customers, we change the product constantly—much too fast by traditional standards—shipping new versions of our product dozens of times every single day. We really did have customers in those early days—true visionary early adopters—and we often talked to them and asked for their early adopters—and we often talked to them and asked for their feedback. But we emphatically did not do what they said. We viewed their input as only one source of information about our product and overall vision. In fact, we were much more likely to run experiments on our customers than we were to cater to their whims. Traditional business thinking says that this approach shouldn't work, but it does, and you don't have to take my word for it. As you'll see throughout this book, the approach we pioneered at IMVU has become the basis for a new movement of entrepreneurs around the world. It builds on many previous management and product development ideas, including lean manufacturing, design thinking, customer development, and agile development. It represents a new approach to creating continuous innovation. It's called the Lean Startup. Despite the volumes written on business strategy, the key attributes of business leaders, and ways to identify the next big thing, innovators still struggle to bring their ideas to life. This was the frustration that led us to try a radical new approach at IMVU, one characterized by an extremely fast cycle time, a focus on what customers want (without asking them), and a scienti!c approach to making decisions. ORIGINS OF THE LEAN STARTUP I am one of those people who grew up programming computers, and so my journey to thinking about entrepreneurship and management has taken a circuitous path. I have always worked on the product development side of my industry; my partners and bosses were managers or marketers, and my peers worked in engineering and operations. Throughout my career, I kept having the experience of working incredibly hard on products that ultimately failed in the marketplace. At !rst, largely because of my background, I viewed these as technical problems that required technical solutions: better architecture, a better engineering process, better discipline, focus, or architecture, a better engineering process, better discipline, focus, or product vision. These supposed !xes led to still more failure. So I read everything I could get my hands on and was blessed to have had some of the top minds in Silicon Valley as my mentors. By the time I became a cofounder of IMVU, I was hungry for new ideas about how to build a company. I was fortunate to have cofounders who were willing to experiment with new approaches. They were fed up—as I was—by the failure of traditional thinking. Also, we were lucky to have Steve Blank as an investor and adviser. Back in 2004, Steve had just begun preaching a new idea: the business and marketing functions of a startup should be considered as important as engineering and product development and therefore deserve an equally rigorous methodology to guide them. He called that methodology Customer Development, and it o/ered insight and guidance to my daily work as an entrepreneur. Meanwhile, I was building IMVU's product development team, using some of the unorthodox methods I mentioned earlier. Measured against the traditional theories of product development I had been trained on in my career, these methods did not make sense, yet I could see !rsthand that they were working. I struggled to explain the practices to new employees, investors, and the founders of other companies. We lacked a common language for describing them and concrete principles for understanding them. I began to search outside entrepreneurship for ideas that could help me make sense of my experience. I began to study other industries, especially manufacturing, from which most modern theories of management derive. I studied lean manufacturing, a process that originated in Japan with the Toyota Production System, a completely new way of thinking about the manufacturing of physical goods. I found that by applying ideas from lean manufacturing to my own entrepreneurial challenges—with a few tweaks and changes—I had the beginnings of a framework for making sense of them. This line of thought evolved into the Lean Startup: the application of lean thinking to the process of innovation. IMVU became a tremendous success. IMVU customers have IMVU became a tremendous success. IMVU customers have created more than 60 million avatars. It is a pro!table company with annual revenues of more than $50 million in 2011, employing more than a hundred people in our current o;ces in Mountain View, California. IMVU's virtual goods catalog—which seemed so risky years ago—now has more than 6 million items in it; more than 7,000 are added every day, almost all created by customers. As a result of IMVU's success, I began to be asked for advice by other startups and venture capitalists. When I would describe my experiences at IMVU, I was often met with blank stares or extreme skepticism. The most common reply was "That could never work!" My experience so Kew in the face of conventional thinking that most people, even in the innovation hub of Silicon Valley, could not wrap their minds around it. Then I started to write, !rst on a blog called Startup Lessons Learned, and speak—at conferences and to companies, startups, and venture capitalists—to anyone who would listen. In the process of being called on to defend and explain my insights and with the collaboration of other writers, thinkers, and entrepreneurs, I had a chance to re!ne and develop the theory of the Lean Startup beyond its rudimentary beginnings. My hope all along was to !nd ways to eliminate the tremendous waste I saw all around me: startups that built products nobody wanted, new products pulled from the shelves, countless dreams unrealized. Eventually, the Lean Startup idea blossomed into a global movement. Entrepreneurs began forming local in-person groups to discuss and apply Lean Startup ideas. There are now organized communities of practice in more than a hundred cities around the world.1 My travels have taken me across countries and continents. Everywhere I have seen the signs of a new entrepreneurial renaissance. The Lean Startup movement is making entrepreneurship accessible to a whole new generation of founders who are hungry for new ideas about how to build successful companies. Although my background is in high-tech software entrepreneurship, the movement has grown way beyond those entrepreneurship, the movement has grown way beyond those roots. Thousands of entrepreneurs are putting Lean Startup principles to work in every conceivable industry. I've had the chance to work with entrepreneurs in companies of all sizes, in di/erent industries, and even in government.This journey has taken me to places I never imagined I'd see, from the world's most elite venture capitalists, to Fortune 500 boardrooms, to the Pentagon. The most nervous I have ever been in a meeting was when I was attempting to explain Lean Startup principles to the chief information o;cer of the U.S. Army, who is a three-star general (for the record, he was extremely open to new ideas, even from a civilian like me). Pretty soon I realized that it was time to focus on the Lean Startup movement full time. My mission: to improve the success rate of new innovative products worldwide. The result is the book you are reading. THE LEAN STARTUP METHOD This is a book for entrepreneurs and the people who hold them accountable. The !ve principles of the Lean Startup, which inform all three parts of this book, are as follows: 1. Entrepreneurs are everywhere. You don't have to work in a garage to be in a startup. The concept of entrepreneurship includes anyone who works within my de!nition of a startup: a human institution designed to create new products and services under conditions of extreme uncertainty. That means entrepreneurs are everywhere and the Lean Startup approach can work in any size company, even a very large enterprise, in any sector or industry. 2. Entrepreneurship is management. A startup is an institution, not just a product, and so it requires a new kind of management speci!cally geared to its context of extreme uncertainty. In fact, as I will argue later, I believe "entrepreneur" should be considered a will argue later, I believe "entrepreneur" should be considered a job title in all modern companies that depend on innovation for their future growth. 3. Validated learning. Startups exist not just to make stu/, make money, or even serve customers. They exist to learn how to build a sustainable business. This learning can be validated scienti!cally by running frequent experiments that allow entrepreneurs to test each element of their vision. 4. Build-Measure-Learn. The fundamental activity of a startup is to turn ideas into products, measure how customers respond, and then learn whether to pivot or persevere. All successful startup processes should be geared to accelerate that feedback loop. 5. Innovation accounting. To improve entrepreneurial outcomes and hold innovators accountable, we need to focus on the boring stu/: how to measure progress, how to set up milestones, and how to prioritize work. This requires a new kind of accounting designed for startups—and the people who hold them accountable. Why Startups Fail Why are startups failing so badly everywhere we look? The !rst problem is the allure of a good plan, a solid strategy, and thorough market research. In earlier eras, these things were indicators of likely success. The overwhelming temptation is to apply them to startups too, but this doesn't work, because startups operate with too much uncertainty. Startups do not yet know who their customer is or what their product should be. As the world becomes more uncertain, it gets harder and harder to predict the future. The old management methods are not up to the task. Planning and forecasting are only accurate when based on a long, stable operating history and a relatively static environment. Startups stable operating history and a relatively static environment. Startups have neither. The second problem is that after seeing traditional management fail to solve this problem, some entrepreneurs and investors have thrown up their hands and adopted the "Just Do It" school of startups. This school believes that if management is the problem, chaos is the answer. Unfortunately, as I can attest !rsthand, this doesn't work either. It may seem counterintuitive to think that something as disruptive, innovative, and chaotic as a startup can be managed or, to be accurate, must be managed. Most people think of process and management as boring and dull, whereas startups are dynamic and exciting. But what is actually exciting is to see startups succeed and change the world.The passion, energy, and vision that people bring to these new ventures are resources too precious to waste. We can— and must—do better.This book is about how.ENTREPRENEURIAL MANAGEMENT uilding a startup is an exercise in institution building; thus, it necessarily involves management. This often comes as a surprise to aspiring entrepreneurs, because their associations with these two words are so diametrically opposed. Entrepreneurs are rightly wary of implementing traditional management practices early on in a startup, afraid that they will invite bureaucracy or stifle creativity. Entrepreneurs have been trying to)t the square peg of their unique problems into the round hole of general management for decades. As a result, many entrepreneurs take a "just do it" attitude, avoiding all forms of management, process, and discipline. Unfortunately, this approach leads to chaos more often than it does to success. I should know: my)rst startup failures were all of this kind. The tremendous success of general management over the last century has provided unprecedented material abundance, but those management principles are ill suited to handle the chaos and uncertainty that startups must face. I believe that entrepreneurship requires a managerial discipline to harness the entrepreneurial opportunity we have been given. There are more entrepreneurs operating today than at any previous time in history. This has been made possible by dramatic previous time in history. This has been made possible by dramatic changes in the global economy. To cite but one example, one often hears commentators lament the loss of manufacturing jobs in the United States over the previous two decades, but one rarely hears about a corresponding loss of manufacturing capability. That's because total manufacturing output in the United States is increasing (by 15 percent in the last decade) even as jobs continue to be lost (see the charts below). In e4ect, the huge productivity increases made possible by modern management and technology have created more productive capacity than)rms know what to do with.1 We are living through an unprecedented worldwide entrepreneurial renaissance, but this opportunity is laced with peril. Because we lack a coherent management paradigm for new innovative ventures, we're throwing our excess capacity around with wild abandon. Despite this lack of rigor, we are)nding some ways to make money, but for every success there are far too many failures: products pulled from shelves mere weeks after being launched, high-pro)le startups lauded in the press and forgotten a few months later, and new products that wind up being used by nobody. What makes these failures particularly painful is not just the economic damage done to individual employees, companies, and investors; they are also a colossal waste of our civilization's most precious resource: the time, passion, and skill of its people. The Lean Startup movement is dedicated to preventing these failures. THEROOTS OF THE LEAN STARTUP The Lean Startup takes its name from the lean manufacturing revolution that Taiichi Ohno and Shigeo Shingo are credited with developing at Toyota. Lean thinking is radically altering the way supply chains and production systems are run. Among its tenets are drawing on the knowledge and creativity of individual workers, the shrinking of batch sizes, just-in-time production and inventory control, and an acceleration of cycle times. It taught the world the di4erence between value-creating activities and waste and showed how to build quality into products from the inside out. The Lean Startup adapts these ideas to the context of entrepreneurship, proposing that entrepreneurs judge their progress di4erently from the way other kinds of ventures do. Progress in di4erently from the way other kinds of ventures do. Progress in manufacturing is measured by the production of high-quality physical goods. As we'll see in Chapter 3, the Lean Startup uses a di4erent unit of progress, called validated learning. With scientific learning as our yardstick, we can discover and eliminate the sources of waste that are plaguing entrepreneurship. A comprehensive theory of entrepreneurship should address all the functions of an early-stage venture: vision and concept, product development, marketing and sales, scaling up, partnerships and distribution, and structure and organizational design. It has to provide a method for measuring progress in the context of extreme uncertainty. It can give entrepreneurs clear guidance on how to make the many trade-o4 decisions they face: whether and when to invest in process; formulating, planning, and creating infrastructure; when to go it alone and when to partner; when to respond to feedback and when to stick with vision; and how and when to invest in scaling the business. Most of all, it must allow entrepreneurs to make testable predictions. For example, consider the recommendation that you build crossfunctional teams and hold them accountable to what we call learning milestones instead of organizing your company into strict functional departments (marketing, sales, information technology, human resources, etc.) that hold people accountable for performing well in their specialized areas (see Chapter 7). Perhaps you agree with this recommendation, or perhaps you are skeptical. Either way, if you decide to implement it, I predict that you pretty quickly will get feedback from your teams that the new process is reducing their productivity. They will ask to go back to the old way of working, in which they had the opportunity to "stay e?cient" by working in larger batches and passing work between departments. It's safe to predict this result, and not just because I have seen it many times in the companies I work with. It is a straightforward prediction of the Lean Startup theory itself. When people are used to evaluating their productivity locally, they feel that a good day is one in which they did their job well all day. When I worked as a programmer, that meant eight straight hours of programming without interruption. That was a good day. In contrast, if I was without interruption. That was a good day. In contrast, if I was interrupted with questions, process, or—heaven forbid—meetings, I felt bad. What did I really accomplish that day? Code and product features were tangible to me; I could see them, understand them, and show them off. Learning, by contrast, is frustratingly intangible. The Lean Startup asks people to start measuring their productivity di4erently. Because startups often accidentally build something nobody wants, it doesn't matter much if they do it on time and on budget. The goal of a startup is to)gure out the right thing to build—the thing customers want and will pay for—as quickly as possible. In other words, the Lean Startup is a new way of looking at the development of innovative new products that emphasizes fast iteration and customer insight, a huge vision, and great ambition, all at the same time. Henry Ford is one of the most successful and celebrated entrepreneurs of all time. Since the idea of management has been bound up with the history of the automobile since its)rst days, I believe it is)tting to use the automobile as a metaphor for a startup. An internal combustion automobile is powered by two important and very di4erent feedback loops. The)rst feedback loop is deep inside the engine. Before Henry Ford was a famous CEO, he was an engineer. He spent his days and nights tinkering in his garage with the precise mechanics of getting the engine cylinders to move. Each tiny explosion within the cylinder provides the motive force to turn the wheels but also drives the ignition of the next explosion. Unless the timing of this feedback loop is managed precisely, the engine will sputter and break down. Startups have a similar engine that I call the engine of growth. The markets and customers for startups are diverse: a toy company, a consulting)rm, and a manufacturing plant may not seem like they have much in common, but, as we'll see, they operate with the same engine of growth. Every new version of a product, every new feature, and every Every new version of a product, every new feature, and every new marketing program is an attempt to improve this engine of growth. Like Henry Ford's tinkering in his garage, not all of these changes turn out to be improvements. New product development happens in)ts and starts. Much of the time in a startup's life is spent tuning the engine by making improvements in product, marketing, or operations. The second important feedback loop in an automobile is between the driver and the steering wheel. This feedback is so immediate and automatic that we often don't think about it, but it is steering that di4erentiates driving from most other forms of transportation. If you have a daily commute, you probably know the route so well that your hands seem to steer you there on their own accord. We can practically drive the route in our sleep. Yet if I asked you to close your eyes and write down exactly how to get to your o?ce—not the street directions but every action you need to take, every push of hand on wheel and foot on pedals—you'd)nd it impossible. The choreography of driving is incredibly complex when one slows down to think about it. By contrast, a rocket ship requires just this kind of in-advance calibration. It must be launched with the most precise instructions on what to do: every thrust, every)ring of a booster, and every change in direction. The tiniest error at the point of launch could yield catastrophic results thousands of miles later. Unfortunately, too many startup business plans look more like they are planning to launch a rocket ship than drive a car. They prescribe the steps to take and the results to expect in excruciating detail, and as in planning to launch a rocket, they are set up in such a way that even tiny errors in assumptions can lead to catastrophic outcomes. One company I worked with had the misfortune of forecasting signi)cant customer adoption—in the millions—for one of its new products. Powered by a splashy launch, the company successfully executed its plan. Unfortunately, customers did not Cock to the product in great numbers. Even worse, the company had invested in massive infrastructure, hiring, and support to handle the inCux of customers it expected. When the customers failed to materialize, the customers it expected. When the customers failed to materialize, the company had committed itself so completely that they could not adapt in time. They had "achieved failure"—successfully, faithfully, and rigorously executing a plan that turned out to have been utterly flawed. The Lean Startup method, in contrast, is designed to teach you how to drive a startup. Instead of making complex plans that are based on a lot of assumptions, you can make constant adjustments with a steering wheel called the Build-Measure-Learn feedback loop. Through this process of steering, we can learn when and if it's time to make a sharp turn called a pivot or whether we should persevere along our current path. Once we have an engine that's revved up, the Lean Startup o4ers methods to scale and grow the business with maximum acceleration. Throughout the process of driving, you always have a clear idea of where you're going. If you're commuting to work, you don't give up because there's a detour in the road or you made a wrong turn. You remain thoroughly focused on getting to your destination. Startups also have a true north, a destination in mind: creating a thriving and world-changing business. I call that a startup's vision. To achieve that vision, startups employ a strategy, which includes a business model, a product road map, a point of view about partners and competitors, and ideas about who the customer will be. The product is the end result of this strategy (see the chart on this page). Products change constantly through the process of optimization, what I call tuning the engine. Less frequently, the strategy may have to change (called a pivot). However, the overarching vision rarely changes. Entrepreneurs are committed to seeing the startup through to that destination. Every setback is an opportunity for learning how to get where they want to go (see the chart below). In real life, a startup is a portfolio of activities. A lot is happening simultaneously: the engine is running, acquiring new customers and serving existing ones; we are tuning, trying to improve our product, marketing, and operations; and we are steering, deciding if and when to pivot. The challenge of entrepreneurship is to balance all these activities. Even the smallest startup faces the challenge of supporting existing customers while trying to innovate. Even the most established company faces the imperative to invest in innovation lest it become obsolete. As companies grow, what changes is the mix of these activities in the company's portfolio of work. Entrepreneurship is management. And yet, imagine a modern manager who is tasked with building a new product in the context of an established company. Imagine that she goes back to her company's chief)nancial o?cer (CFO) a year later and says, "We have failed to meet the growth targets we predicted. In fact, we have almost no new customers and no new revenue. However, we have learned an incredible amount and are on the cusp of a breakthrough new line of business. All we need is another year." Most of the time, this would be the last report this intrapreneur would give her employer. The reason is that in general management, a failure to deliver results is due to either a failure to plan adequately or a failure to execute properly. Both are signi)cant lapses, yet new product development in our modern economy routinely requires exactly this kind of failure on the way to greatness. In the Lean Startup movement, we have come to realize that these internal innovators are actually entrepreneurs, too, and that entrepreneurial management can help them succeed.an entrepreneur, nothing plagued me more than the question of whether my company was making progress toward creating a successful business. As an engineer and later as a manager, I was accustomed to measuring progress by making sure our work proceeded according to plan, was high quality, and cost about what we had projected. After many years as an entrepreneur, I started to worry about measuring progress in this way. What if we found ourselves building something that nobody wanted? In that case what did it matter if we did it on time and on budget? When I went home at the end of a day's work, the only things I knew for sure were that I had kept people busy and spent money that day. I hoped that my team's e&orts took us closer to our goal. If we wound up taking a wrong turn, I'd have to take comfort in the fact that at least we'd learned something important. Unfortunately, "learning" is the oldest excuse in the book for a failure of execution. It's what managers fall back on when they fail to achieve the results we promised. Entrepreneurs, under pressure to succeed, are wildly creative when it comes to demonstrating what we have learned. We can all tell a good story when our job, career, or reputation depends on it. However, learning is cold comfort to employees who are following an entrepreneur into the unknown. It is cold comfort to the investors who allocate precious money, time, and energy to entrepreneurial teams. It is cold comfort to the organizations—large entrepreneurial teams. It is cold comfort to the organizations—large and small—that depend on entrepreneurial innovation to survive. You can't take learning to the bank; you can't spend it or invest it. You cannot give it to customers and cannot return it to limited partners. Is it any wonder that learning has a bad name in entrepreneurial and managerial circles? Yet if the fundamental goal of entrepreneurship is to engage in organization building under conditions of extreme uncertainty, its most vital function is learning. We must learn the truth about which elements of our strategy are working to realize our vision and which are just crazy. We must learn what customers really want, not what they say they want or what we think they should want. We must discover whether we are on a path that will lead to growing a sustainable business. In the Lean Startup model, we are rehabilitating learning with a concept I call validated learning. Validated learning is not after-thefact rationalization or a good story designed to hide failure. It is a rigorous method for demonstrating progress when one is embedded in the soil of extreme uncertainty in which startups grow. Validated learning is the process of demonstrating empirically that a team has discovered valuable truths about a startup's present and future business prospects. It is more concrete, more accurate, and faster than market forecasting or classical business planning. It is the principal antidote to the lethal problem of achieving failure: successfully executing a plan that leads nowhere. VALIDATED LEARNING AT IMVU Let me illustrate this with an example from my career. Many audiences have heard me recount the story of IMVU's founding and the many mistakes we made in developing our 8rst product. I'll now elaborate on one of those mistakes to illustrate validated learning clearly. Those of us involved in the founding of IMVU aspired to be serious strategic thinkers. Each of us had participated in previous ventures that had failed, and we were loath to repeat that ventures that had failed, and we were loath to repeat that experience. Our main concerns in the early days dealt with the following questions: What should we build and for whom? What market could we enter and dominate? How could we build durable value that would not be subject to erosion by competition? 1 Brilliant Strategy We decided to enter the instant messaging (IM) market. In 2004, that market had hundreds of millions of consumers actively participating worldwide. However, the majority of the customers who were using IM products were not paying for the privilege. Instead, large media and portal companies such as AOL, Microsoft, and Yahoo! operated their IM networks as a loss leader for other services while making modest amounts of money through advertising. IM is an example of a market that involves strong network effects. Like most communication networks, IM is thought to follow Metcalfe's law: the value of a network as a whole is proportional to the square of the number of participants. In other words, the more people in the network, the more valuable the network. This makes intuitive sense: the value to each participant is driven primarily by how many other people he or she can communicate with. Imagine a world in which you own the only telephone; it would have no value. Only when other people also have a telephone does it become valuable. In 2004, the IM market was locked up by a handful of incumbents. The top three networks controlled more than 80 percent of the overall usage and were in the process of consolidating their gains in market share at the expense of a number of smaller players.2 The common wisdom was that it was more or less impossible to bring a new IM network to market without spending an extraordinary amount of money on marketing. The reason for that wisdom is simple. Because of the power of network e&ects, IM products have high switching costs. To switch from one network to another, customers would have to convince from one network to another, customers would have to convince their friends and colleagues to switch with them. This extra work for customers creates a barrier to entry in the IM market: with all consumers locked in to an incumbent's product, there are no customers left with whom to establish a beachhead. At IMVU we settled on a strategy of building a product that would combine the large mass appeal of traditional IM with the high revenue per customer of three-dimensional (3D) video games and virtual worlds. Because of the near impossibility of bringing a new IM network to market, we decided to build an IM add-on product that would interoperate with the existing networks. Thus, customers would be able to adopt the IMVU virtual goods and avatar communication technology without having to switch IM providers, learn a new user interface, and—most important—bring their friends with them. In fact, we thought this last point was essential. For the add-on product to be useful, customers would have to use it with their existing friends. Every communication would come embedded with an invitation to join IMVU. Our product would be inherently viral, spreading throughout the existing IM networks like an epidemic.To achieve that viral growth, it was important that our add-on product support as many of the existing IM networks as possible and work on all kinds of computers. Six Months to Launch With this strategy in place, my cofounders and I began a period of intense work. As the chief technology oDcer, it was my responsibility, among other things, to write the software that would support IM interoperability across networks. My cofounders and I worked for months, putting in crazy hours struggling to get our 8rst product released. We gave ourselves a hard deadline of six months —180 days—to launch the product and attract our 8rst paying customers. It was a grueling schedule, but we were determined to launch on time. The add-on product was so large and complex and had so many The add-on product was so large and complex and had so many moving parts that we had to cut a lot of corners to get it done on time. I won't mince words: the 8rst version was terrible. We spent endless hours arguing about which bugs to 8x and which we could live with, which features to cut and which to try to cram in. It was a wonderful and terrifying time: we were full of hope about the possibilities for success and full of fear about the consequences of shipping a bad product. Personally, I was worried that the low quality of the product would tarnish my reputation as an engineer. People would think I didn't know how to build a quality product. All of us feared tarnishing the IMVU brand; after all, we were charging people money for a product that didn't work very well. We all envisioned the damning newspaper headlines: "Inept Entrepreneurs Build Dreadful Product." As launch day approached, our fears escalated. In our situation, many entrepreneurial teams give in to fear and postpone the launch date. Although I understand this impulse, I am glad we persevered, since delay prevents many startups from getting the feedback they need. Our previous failures made us more afraid of another, even worse, outcome than shipping a bad product: building something that nobody wants. And so, teeth clenched and apologies at the ready, we released our product to the public. Launch And then—nothing happened! It turned out that our fears were unfounded, because nobody even tried our product. At 8rst I was relieved because at least nobody was 8nding out how bad the product was, but soon that gave way to serious frustration. After all the hours we had spent arguing about which features to include and which bugs to 8x, our value proposition was so far o& that customers weren't getting far enough into the experience to 8nd out how bad our design choices were. Customers wouldn't even download our product. Over the ensuing weeks and months, we labored to make the Over the ensuing weeks and months, we labored to make the product better. We brought in a steady Gow of customers through our online registration and download process. We treated each day's customers as a brand-new report card to let us know how we were doing. We eventually learned how to change the product's positioning so that customers at least would download it. We were making improvements to the underlying product continuously, shipping bug 8xes and new changes daily. However, despite our best e&orts, we were able to persuade only a pathetically small number of people to buy the product. In retrospect, one good decision we made was to set clear revenue targets for those early days. In the 8rst month we intended to make $300 in total revenue, and we did—barely. Many friends and family members were asked (okay, begged). Each month our small revenue targets increased, 8rst to $350 and then to $400. As they rose, our struggles increased. We soon ran out of friends and family; our frustration escalated. We were making the product better every day, yet our customers' behavior remained unchanged: they still wouldn't use it. Our failure to move the numbers prodded us to accelerate our e&orts to bring customers into our oDce for in-person interviews and usability tests. The quantitative targets created the motivation to engage in qualitative inquiry and guided us in the questions we asked; this is a pattern we'll see throughout this book. I wish I could say that I was the one to realize our mistake and suggest the solution, but in truth, I was the last to admit the problem. In short, our entire strategic analysis of the market was utterly wrong. We 8gured this out empirically, through experimentation, rather than through focus groups or market research. Customers could not tell us what they wanted; most, after all, had never heard of 3D avatars. Instead, they revealed the truth through their action or inaction as we struggled to make the product better. Talking to Customers Out of desperation, we decided to talk to some potential customers. We brought them into our oDce, and said, "Try this new product; it's IMVU." If the person was a teenager, a heavy user of IM, or a tech early adopter, he or she would engage with us. In constrast, if it was a mainstream person, the response was, "Right. So exactly what would you like me to do?" We'd get nowhere with the mainstream group; they thought IMVU was too weird. Imagine a seventeen-year-old girl sitting down with us to look at this product. She chooses her avatar and says, "Oh, this is really fun." She's customizing the avatar, deciding how she's going to look. Then we say, "All right, it's time to download the instant messaging add-on," and she responds, "What's that?" "Well, it's this thing that interoperates with the instant messaging client." She's looking at us and thinking, "I've never heard of that, my friends have never heard of that, why do you want me to do that?" It required a lot of explanation; an instant messaging add-on was not a product category that existed in her mind. But since she was in the room with us, we were able to talk her into doing it. She downloads the product, and then we say, "Okay, invite one of your friends to chat." And she says, "No way!" We say, "Why not?" And she says, "Well, I don't know if this thing is cool yet. You want me to risk inviting one of my friends? What are they going to think of me? If it sucks, they're going to think I suck, right?" And we say, "No, no, it's going to be so much fun once you get the person in there; it's a social product." She looks at us, her face 8lled with doubt; you can see that this is a deal breaker. Of course, the 8rst time I had that experience, I said, "It's all right, it's just this one person, send her away and get me a new one." Then the second customer comes in and says the same thing. Then the third customer comes in, and it's the same thing. You start to see patterns, and no matter how stubborn you are, there's obviously something wrong. Customers kept saying, "I want to use it by myself. I want to try it out 8rst to see if it's really cool before I invite a friend." Our team was from the video game industry, so we understood what that meant: single-player mode. So we built a single-player version. meant: single-player mode. So we built a single-player version. We'd bring new customers into our oDce. They'd customize the avatar and download the product like before. Then they would go into single-player mode, and we'd say, "Play with your avatar and dress it up; check out the cool moves it can make." Followed by, "Okay, you did that by yourself; now it's time to invite one of your friends."You can see what's coming.They'd say, "No way! This isn't cool." And we'd say, "Well, we told you it wasn't going to be cool! What is the point of a single-player experience for a social product?" See, we thought we should get a gold star just for listening to our customers. Except our customers still didn't like the product.They would look at us and say, "Listen, old man, you don't understand. What is the deal with this crazy business of inviting friends before I know if it's cool?" It was a total deal breaker. Out of further desperation, we introduced a feature called ChatNow that allows you to push a button and be randomly matched with somebody else anywhere in the world. The only thing you have in common is that you both pushed the button at the same time. All of a sudden, in our customer service tests, people were saying, "Oh, this is fun!" So we'd bring them in, they'd use ChatNow, and maybe they would meet somebody they thought was cool. They'd say, "Hey, that guy was neat; I want to add him to my buddy list. Where's my buddy list?" And we'd say, "Oh, no, you don't want a new buddy list; you want to use your regular AOL buddy list." Remember, this was how we planned to harness the interoperability that would lead to network e&ects and viral growth. Picture the customer looking at us, asking, "What do you want me to do exactly?" And we'd say, "Well, just give the stranger your AIM screen name so you can put him on your buddy list." You could see their eyes go wide, and they'd say, "Are you kidding me? A stranger on my AIM buddy list?" To which we'd respond, "Yes; otherwise you'd have to download a whole new IM client with a new buddy list." And they'd say, "Do you have any idea how many IM clients I already run?" "No. One or two, maybe?" That's how many clients each of us in the oDce used. To which the teenager would say, "Duh! I run the oDce used. To which the teenager would say, "Duh! I run eight." We had no idea how many instant messaging clients there were in the world. We had the incorrect preconception that it's a challenge to learn new software and it's tricky to move your friends over to a new buddy list. Our customers revealed that this was nonsense. We wanted to draw diagrams on the whiteboard that showed why our strategy was brilliant, but our customers didn't understand concepts like network e&ects and switching costs. If we tried to explain why they should behave the way we predicted, they'd just shake their heads at us, bewildered. We had a mental model for how people used software that was years out of date, and so eventually, painfully, after dozens of meetings like that, it started to dawn on us that the IM add-on concept was fundamentally flawed.3 Our customers did not want an IM add-on; they wanted a standalone IM network. They did not consider having to learn how to use a new IM program a barrier; on the contrary, our early adopters used many di&erent IM programs simultaneously. Our customers were not intimidated by the idea of having to take their friends with them to a new IM network; it turned out that they enjoyed that challenge.Even more surprising, our assumption that customers would want to use avatar-based IM primarily with their existing friends was also wrong. They wanted to make new friends, an activity that 3D avatars are particularly well suited to facilitating. Bit by bit, customers tore apart our seemingly brilliant initial strategy. Throwing My Work Away Perhaps you can sympathize with our situation and forgive my obstinacy. After all, it was my work over the prior months that needed to be thrown away. I had slaved over the software that was required to make our IM program interoperate with other networks, which was at the heart of our original strategy. When it came time to pivot and abandon that original strategy, almost all of came time to pivot and abandon that original strategy, almost all of my work—thousands of lines of code—was thrown out. I felt betrayed. I was a devotee of the latest in software development methods (known collectively as agile development), which promised to help drive waste out of product development. However, despite that, I had committed the biggest waste of all: building a product that our customers refused to use. That was really depressing. I wondered: in light of the fact that my work turned out to be a waste of time and energy, would the company have been just as well o& if I had spent the last six months on a beach sipping umbrella drinks? Had I really been needed? Would it have been better if I had not done any work at all? There is, as I mentioned at the beginning of this chapter, always one last refuge for people aching to justify their own failure. I consoled myself that if we hadn't built this 8rst product—mistakes and all—we never would have learned these important insights about customers. We never would have learned that our strategy was Gawed. There is truth in this excuse: what we learned during those critical early months set IMVU on a path that would lead to our eventual breakout success. For a time, this "learning" consolation made me feel better, but my relief was short-lived. Here's the question that bothered me most of all: if the goal of those months was to learn these important insights about customers, why did it take so long? How much of our e&ort contributed to the essential lessons we needed to learn? Could we have learned those lessons earlier if I hadn't been so focused on making the product "better" by adding features and fixing bugs? VALUE VS. WASTE In other words, which of our e&orts are value-creating and which are wasteful? This question is at the heart of the lean manufacturing revolution; it is the 8rst question any lean manufacturing adherent is trained to ask. Learning to see waste and then systematically is trained to ask. Learning to see waste and then systematically eliminate it has allowed lean companies such as Toyota to dominate entire industries. In the world of software, the agile development methodologies I had practiced until that time had their origins in lean thinking. They were designed to eliminate waste too. Yet those methods had led me down a road in which the majority of my team's efforts were wasted. Why? The answer came to me slowly over the subsequent years. Lean thinking de8nes value as providing bene8t to the customer; anything else is waste. In a manufacturing business, customers don't care how the product is assembled, only that it works correctly. But in a startup, who the customer is and what the customer might 8nd valuable are unknown, part of the very uncertainty that is an essential part of the de8nition of a startup. I realized that as a startup, we needed a new de8nition of value. The real progress we had made at IMVU was what we had learned over those 8rst months about what creates value for customers. Anything we had done during those months that did not contribute to our learning was a form of waste. Would it have been possible to learn the same things with less e&ort? Clearly, the answer is yes. For one thing, think of all the debate and prioritization of e&ort that went into features that customers would never discover. If we had shipped sooner, we could have avoided that waste. Also consider all the waste caused by our incorrect strategic assumptions. I had built interoperability for more than a dozen di&erent IM clients and networks. Was this really necessary to test our assumptions? Could we have gotten the same feedback from our customers with half as many networks? With only three? With only one? Since the customers of all IM networks found our product equally unattractive, the level of learning would have been the same, but our effort would have been dramatically less. Here's the thought that kept me up nights: did we have to support any networks at all? Is it possible that we could have discovered how Gawed our assumptions were without building anything? For example, what if we simply had o&ered customers anything? For example, what if we simply had o&ered customers the opportunity to download the product from us solely on the basis of its proposed features before building anything? Remember, almost no customers were willing to use our original product, so we wouldn't have had to do much apologizing when we failed to deliver. (Note that this is di&erent from asking customers what they want. Most of the time customers don't know what they want in advance.) We could have conducted an experiment, o&ering customers the chance to try something and then measuring their behavior. Such thought experiments were extremely disturbing to me because they undermined my job description. As the head of product development, I thought my job was to ensure the timely delivery of high-quality products and features. But if many of those features were a waste of time, what should I be doing instead? How could we avoid this waste? I've come to believe that learning is the essential unit of progress for startups. The e&ort that is not absolutely necessary for learning what customers want can be eliminated. I call this validated learning because it is always demonstrated by positive improvements in the startup's core metrics. As we've seen, it's easy to kid yourself about what you think customers want. It's also easy to learn things that are completely irrelevant. Thus, validated learning is backed up by empirical data collected from real customers. WHERE DO YOU FIND VALIDATION? As I can attest, anybody who fails in a startup can claim that he or she has learned a lot from the experience. They can tell a compelling story. In fact, in the story of IMVU so far, you might have noticed something missing. Despite my claims that we learned a lot in those early months, lessons that led to our eventual success, I haven't o&ered any evidence to back that up. In hindsight, it's easy to make such claims and sound credible (and you'll see some evidence later in the book), but imagine us in IMVU's early months evidence later in the book), but imagine us in IMVU's early months trying to convince investors, employees, family members, and most of all ourselves that we had not squandered our time and resources. What evidence did we have? Certainly our stories of failure were entertaining, and we had fascinating theories about what we had done wrong and what we needed to do to create a more successful product. However, the proof did not come until we put those theories into practice and built subsequent versions of the product that showed superior results with actual customers. The next few months are where the true story of IMVU begins, not with our brilliant assumptions and strategies and whiteboard gamesmanship but with the hard work of discovering what customers really wanted and adjusting our product and strategy to meet those desires. We adopted the view that our job was to 8nd a synthesis between our vision and what customers would accept; it wasn't to capitulate to what customers thought they wanted or to tell customers what they ought to want. As we came to understand our customers better, we were able to improve our products. As we did that, the fundamental metrics of our business changed. In the early days, despite our e&orts to improve the product, our metrics were stubbornly Gat. We treated each day's customers as a new report card. We'd pay attention to the percentage of new customers who exhibited product behaviors such as downloading and buying our product. Each day, roughly the same number of customers would buy the product, and that number was pretty close to zero despite the many improvements. However, once we pivoted away from the original strategy, things started to change. Aligned with a superior strategy, our product development e&orts became magically more productive—not because we were working harder but because we were working smarter, aligned with our customers' real needs. Positive changes in metrics became the quantitative validation that our learning was real. This was critically important because we could show our stakeholders—employees, investors, and ourselves—that we were making genuine progress, not deluding ourselves. It is also the right way to think about productivity in a startup: not in terms of how way to think about productivity in a startup: not in terms of how much stu& we are building but in terms of how much validated learning we're getting for our efforts.4 For example, in one early experiment, we changed our entire website, home page, and product registration Gow to replace "avatar chat" with "3D instant messaging." New customers were split automatically between these two versions of the site; half saw one, and half saw the other. We were able to measure the di&erence in behavior between the two groups. Not only were the people in the experimental group more likely to sign up for the product, they were more likely to become long-term paying customers. We had plenty of failed experiments too. During one period in which we believed that customers weren't using the product because they didn't understand its many bene8ts, we went so far as to pay customer service agents to act as virtual tour guides for new customers. Unfortunately, customers who got that VIP treatment were no more likely to become active or paying customers. Even after ditching the IM add-on strategy, it still took months to understand why it hadn't worked. After our pivot and many failed experiments, we 8nally 8gured out this insight: customers wanted to use IMVU to make new friends online. Our customers intuitively grasped something that we were slow to realize. All the existing social products online were centered on customers' real-life identity. IMVU's avatar technology, however, was uniquely well suited to help people get to know each other online without compromising safety or opening themselves up to identity theft. Once we formed this hypothesis, our experiments became much more likely to produce positive results. Whenever we would change the product to make it easier for people to 8nd and keep new friends, we discovered that customers were more likely to engage. This is true startup productivity: systematically8guring out the right things to build. These were just a few experiments among hundreds that we ran week in and week out as we started to learn which customers would use the product and why. Each bit of knowledge we would use the product and why. Each bit of knowledge we gathered suggested new experiments to run, which moved our metrics closer and closer to our goal. THE AUDACITY OF ZERO Despite IMVU's early success, our gross numbers were still pretty small. Unfortunately, because of the traditional way businesses are evaluated, this is a dangerous situation. The irony is that it is often easier to raise money or acquire other resources when you have zero revenue, zero customers, and zero traction than when you have a small amount. Zero invites imagination, but small numbers invite questions about whether large numbers will ever materialize. Everyone knows (or thinks he or she knows) stories of products that achieved breakthrough success overnight. As long as nothing has been released and no data have been collected, it is still possible to imagine overnight success in the future. Small numbers pour cold water on that hope. This phenomenon creates a brutal incentive: postpone getting any data until you are certain of success. Of course, as we'll see, such delays have the unfortunate e&ect of increasing the amount of wasted work, decreasing essential feedback, and dramatically increasing the risk that a startup will build something nobody wants. However, releasing a product and hoping for the best is not a good plan either, because this incentive is real. When we launched IMVU, we were ignorant of this problem. Our earliest investors and advisers thought it was quaint that we had a $300-per-month revenue plan at 8rst. But after several months with our revenue hovering around $500 per month, some began to lose faith, as did some of our advisers, employees, and even spouses. In fact, at one point, some investors were seriously recommending that we pull the product out of the market and return to stealth mode. Fortunately, as we pivoted and experimented, incorporating what we learned into our product development and marketing e&orts, our numbers started to improve. our numbers started to improve.

In 2004, three college sophomores arrived in Silicon Valley with their edgling college social network. It was live on a handful of college campuses. It was not the market-leading social network or even the &rst college social network; other companies had launched sooner and with more features. With 150,000 registered users, it made very little revenue, yet that summer they raised their &rst $500,000 in venture capital. Less than a year later, they raised an additional $12.7 million. Of course, by now you've guessed that these three college sophomores were Mark Zuckerberg, Dustin Moskovitz, and Chris Hughes of Facebook. Their story is now world famous. Many things about it are remarkable, but I'd like to focus on only one: how Facebook was able to raise so much money when its actual usage was so small.1 By all accounts, what impressed investors the most were two facts about Facebook's early growth.The first fact was the raw amount of time Facebook's active users spent on the site. More than half of the users came back to the site every single day.2 This is an example of how a company can validate its value hypothesis—that customers &nd the product valuable. The second impressive thing about Facebook's early traction was the rate at which it had taken over its &rst few college campuses. The rate of growth was staggering: Facebook launched on February 4, 2004, and by the end of that month almost three-quarters of Harvard's undergraduates were using it, without a dollar of marketing or advertising having been using it, without a dollar of marketing or advertising having been spent. In other words, Facebook also had validated its growth hypothesis. These two hypotheses represent two of the most important leap-of-faith questions any new startup faces.3 At the time, I heard many people criticize Facebook's early investors, claiming that Facebook had "no business model" and only modest revenues relative to the valuation o?ered by its investors. They saw in Facebook a return to the excesses of the dot-com era, when companies with little revenue raised massive amounts of cash to pursue a strategy of "attracting eyeballs" and "getting big fast." Many dot-com-era startups planned to make money later by selling the eyeballs they had bought to other advertisers. In truth, those dot-com failures were little more than middlemen, effectively paying money to acquire customers' attention and then planning to resell it to others. Facebook was different, because it employed a different engine of growth. It paid nothing for customer acquisition, and its high engagement meant that it was accumulating massive amounts of customer attention every day. There was never any question that attention would be valuable to advertisers; the only question was how much they would pay. Many entrepreneurs are attempting to build the next Facebook, yet when they try to apply the lessons of Facebook and other famous startup success stories, they quickly get confused. Is the lesson of Facebook that startups should not charge customers money in the early days? Or is it that startups should never spend money on marketing? These questions cannot be answered in the abstract; there are an almost infinite number of counterexamples for any technique. Instead, as we saw in Part One, startups need to conduct experiments that help determine what techniques will work in their unique circumstances. For startups, the role of strategy is to help figure out the right questions to ask. STRATEGY IS BASED ON ASSUMPTIONS Every business plan begins with a set of assumptions. It lays out a strategy that takes those assumptions as a given and proceeds to strategy that takes those assumptions as a given and proceeds to show how to achieve the company's vision. Because the assumptions haven't been proved to be true (they are assumptions, after all) and in fact are often erroneous, the goal of a startup's early efforts should be to test them as quickly as possible. What traditional business strategy excels at is helping managers identify clearly what assumptions are being made in a particular business. The first challenge for an entrepreneur is to build an organization that can test these assumptions systematically. The second challenge, as in all entrepreneurial situations, is to perform that rigorous testing without losing sight of the company's overall vision. Many assumptions in a typical business plan are unexceptional. These are well-established facts drawn from past industry experience or straightforward deductions. In Facebook's case, it was clear that advertisers would pay for customers' attention. Hidden among these mundane details are a handful of assumptions that require more courage to state—in the present tense—with a straight face: we assume that customers have a signi&cant desire to use a product like ours, or we assume that supermarkets will carry our product. Acting as if these assumptions are true is a classic entrepreneur superpower. They are called leaps of faith precisely because the success of the entire venture rests on them. If they are true, tremendous opportunity awaits. If they are false, the startup risks total failure. Most leaps of faith take the form of an argument by analogy. For example, one business plan I remember argued as follows: "Just as the development of progressive image loading allowed the widespread use of the World Wide Web over dial-up, so too our progressive rendering technology will allow our product to run on low-end personal computers." You probably have no idea what progressive image loading or rendering is, and it doesn't much matter.But you know the argument (perhaps you've even used it): Previous technologyX was used to win market Y because of attribute Z. We have a new technology X2 that will enable us to win marketY2 because we too have attribute Z. The problem with analogies like this is that they obscure the true leap of faith. That is their goal: to make the business seem less risky. They are used to persuade investors, employees, or partners to sign on. Most entrepreneurs would cringe to see their leap of faith written this way: Large numbers of people already wanted access to the World Wide Web.They knew what it was, they could a?ord it, but they could not get access to it because the time it took to load images was too long. When progressive image loading was introduced, it allowed people to get onto the World Wide Web and tell their friends about it. Thus, companyX won marketY. Similarly, there is already a large number of potential customers who want access to our product right now. They know they want it, they can a?ord it, but they cannot access it because the rendering is too slow. When we debut our product with progressive rendering technology, they will ock to our software and tell their friends, and we will win marketY2. There are several things to notice in this revised statement. First, it's important to identify the facts clearly. Is it really true that progressive image loading caused the adoption of the World Wide Web, or was this just one factor among many? More important, is it really true that there are large numbers of potential customers out there who want our solution right now? The earlier analogy was designed to convince stakeholders that a reasonable &rst step is to build the new startup's technology and see if customers will use it. The restated approach should make clear that what is needed is to do some empirical testing &rst: let's make sure that there really are hungry customers out there eager to embrace our new technology. Analogs and Antilogs There is nothing intrinsically wrong with basing strategy on comparisons to other companies and industries. In fact, that approach can help you discover assumptions that are not really leaps of faith. For example, the venture capitalist Randy Komisar, whose book Getting to Plan B discussed the concept of leaps of faith in great detail, uses a framework of "analogs" and "antilogs" to plot strategy. He explains the analog-antilog concept by using the iPod as an example. "If you were looking for analogs, you would have to look at the Walkman," he says. "It solved a critical question that Steve Jobs never had to ask himself: Will people listen to music in a public place using earphones? We think of that as a nonsense question today, but it is fundamental. When Sony asked the question, they did not have the answer. Steve Jobs had [the answer] in the analog [version]" Sony's Walkman was the analog. Jobs then had to face the fact that although people were willing to download music, they were not willing to pay for it. "Napster was an antilog. That antilog had to lead him to address his business in a particular way," Komisar says. "Out of these analogs and antilogs come a series of unique, unanswered questions.Those are leaps of faith that I, as an entrepreneur, am taking if I go through with this business venture. They are going to make or break my business. In the iPod business, one of those leaps of faith was that people would pay for music." Of course that leap of faith turned out to be correct.4 Beyond "The Right Place at the RightTime" There are any number of famous entrepreneurs who made millions because they seemed to be in the right place at the right time. However, for every successful entrepreneur who was in the right place in the right time, there are many more who were there, too, in that right place at the right time but still managed to fail. Henry Ford was joined by nearly &ve hundred other entrepreneurs in the early twentieth century. Imagine being an automobile entrepreneur, trained in state-of-the-art engineering, on the ground oor of one of trained in state-of-the-art engineering, on the ground oor of one of the biggest market opportunities in history. Yet the vast majority managed to make no money at all.5 We saw the same phenomenon with Facebook, which faced early competition from other collegebased social networks whose head start proved irrelevant. What di?erentiates the success stories from the failures is that the successful entrepreneurs had the foresight, the ability, and the tools to discover which parts of their plans were working brilliantly and which were misguided, and adapt their strategies accordingly. Value and Growth As we saw in the Facebook story, two leaps of faith stand above all others: the value creation hypothesis and the growth hypothesis. The &rst step in understanding a new product or service is to &gure out if it is fundamentally value-creating or value-destroying. I use the language of economics in referring to value rather than pro&t, because entrepreneurs include people who start not-for-pro&t social ventures, those in public sector startups, and internal change agents who do not judge their success by pro&t alone. Even more confusing, there are many organizations that are wildly profitable in the short term but ultimately value-destroying, such as the organizers of Ponzi schemes, and fraudulent or misguided companies (e.g.,Enron and Lehman Brothers). A similar thing is true for growth. As with value, it's essential that entrepreneurs understand the reasons behind a startup's growth. There are many value-destroying kinds of growth that should be avoided. An example would be a business that grows through continuous fund-raising from investors and lots of paid advertising but does not develop a value-creating product. Such businesses are engaged in what I call success theater, using the appearance of growth to make it seem that they are successful. One of the goals of innovation accounting, which is discussed in depth in Chapter 7, is to help di?erentiate these false startups from true innovators. Traditional accounting judges new ventures by the same standards it uses for established companies, but these same standards it uses for established companies, but these indications are not reliable predictors of a startup's future prospects. Consider companies such as Amazon.com that racked up huge losses on their way to breakthrough success. Like its traditional counterpart, innovation accounting requires that a startup have and maintain a quantitative &nancial model that can be used to evaluate progress rigorously. However, in a startup's earliest days, there is not enough data to make an informed guess about what this model might look like. A startup's earliest strategic plans are likely to be hunch- or intuition-guided, and that is a good thing. To translate those instincts into data, entrepreneurs must, in Steve Blank's famous phrase, "get out of the building" and start learning. GENCHI GEMBUTSU The importance of basing strategic decisions on &rsthand understanding of customers is one of the core principles that underlies the Toyota Production System. At Toyota, this goes by the Japanese term genchi gembutsu, which is one of the most important phrases in the lean manufacturing vocabulary. In English, it is usually translated as a directive to "go and see for yourself" so that business decisions can be based on deep &rsthand knowledge. Je?rey Liker, who has extensively documented the "Toyota Way," explains it this way: In my

Toyota interviews, when I asked what distinguishes the Toyota Way from other management approaches, the most common &rst response was genchi gembutsu —whether I was in manufacturing, product development, sales, distribution, or public a?airs. You cannot be sure you really understand any part of any business problem unless you go and see for yourself &rsthand. It is unacceptable to take anything for granted or to rely on the reports of others.6 To demonstrate, take a look at the development of Toyota's Sienna minivan for the 2004 model year. At Toyota, the manager responsible for the design and development of a new model is called the chief engineer, a cross-functional leader who oversees the entire process from concept to production. The 2004 Sienna was assigned to Yuji Yokoya, who had very little experience in North America, which was the Sienna's primary market. To &gure out how to improve the minivan, he proposed an audacious entrepreneurial undertaking: a road trip spanning all &fty U.S. states, all thirteen provinces and territories of Canada, and all parts of Mexico. In all, he logged more than 53,000 miles of driving. In small towns and large cities, Yokoya would rent a current-model Sienna, driving it in addition to talking to and observing real customers. From those &rsthand observations, Yokoya was able to start testing his critical assumptions about what North American consumers wanted in a minivan. It is common to think of selling to consumers as easier than selling to enterprises, because customers lack the complexity of multiple departments and di?erent people playing di?erent roles in the purchasing process.Yokoya discovered this was untrue for his customers: "The parents and grandparents may own the minivan. But it's the kids who rule it. It's the kids who occupy the rear twothirds of the vehicle. And it's the kids who are the most critical— and the most appreciative of their environment. If I learned anything in my travels, it was the new Sienna would need kid appeal." 7 Identifying these assumptions helped guide the car's development. For example,Yokoya spent an unusual amount of the Sienna's development budget on internal comfort features, which are critical to a long-distance family road trip (such trips are much more common in America than in Japan). The results were impressive, boosting the Sienna's market share dramatically. The 2004 model's sales were 60 percent higher than those in 2003. Of course, a product like the Sienna is a classic sustaining innovation, the kind that the world's best-managed established companies, such as Toyota, excel at. Entrepreneurs face established companies, such as Toyota, excel at. Entrepreneurs face a di?erent set of challenges because they operate with much higher uncertainty. While a company working on a sustaining innovation knows enough about who and where their customers are to use genchi gembutsu to discover what customers want, startups' early contact with potential customers merely reveals what assumptions require the most urgent testing. GET OUT OF THE BUILDING Numbers tell a compelling story, but I always remind entrepreneurs that metrics are people, too. No matter how many intermediaries lie between a company and its customers, at the end of the day, customers are breathing, thinking, buying individuals. Their behavior is measurable and changeable. Even when one is selling to large institutions, as in a business-to-business model, it helps to remember that those businesses are made up of individuals. All successful sales models depend on breaking down the monolithic view of organizations into the disparate people that make them up. As Steve Blank has been teaching entrepreneurs for years, the facts that we need to gather about customers, markets, suppliers, and channels exist only "outside the building." Startups need extensive contact with potential customers to understand them, so get out of your chair and get to know them. The &rst step in this process is to con&rm that your leap-of-faith questions are based in reality, that the customer has a signi&cant problem worth solving.8 When ScottCook conceived Intuit in 1982, he had a vision—at that time quite radical—that someday consumers would use personal computers to pay bills and keep track of expenses. When Cook left his consulting job to take the entrepreneurial plunge, he didn't start with stacks of market research or in-depth analysis at the whiteboard. Instead, he picked up two phone books: one for Palo Alto, California, where he was living at the time, and the other for Winnetka, Illinois. Calling people at random, he inquired if he could ask them a few questions about the way they managed their &nances. Those early questions about the way they managed their &nances. Those early conversations were designed to answer this leap-of-faith question: do people &nd it frustrating to pay bills by hand? It turned out that they did, and this early validation gave Cook the con&rmation he needed to get started on a solution.9 Those early conversations did not delve into the product features of a proposed solution; that attempt would have been foolish. The average consumers at that time were not conversant enough with personal computers to have an opinion about whether they'd want to use them in a new way. Those early conversations were with mainstream customers, not early adopters. Still, the conversations yielded a fundamental insight: if Intuit could &nd a way to solve this problem, there could be a large mainstream audience on which it could build a significant business. Design and the Customer Archetype The goal of such early contact with customers is not to gain definitive answers. Instead, it is to clarify at a basic, coarse level that we understand our potential customer and what problems they have. With that understanding, we can craft a customer archetype, a brief document that seeks to humanize the proposed target customer. This archetype is an essential guide for product development and ensures that the daily prioritization decisions that every product team must make are aligned with the customer to whom the company aims to appeal. There are many techniques for building an accurate customer archetype that have been developed over long years of practice in the design community. Traditional approaches such as interaction design or design thinking are enormously helpful. To me, it has always seemed ironic that many of these approaches are highly experimental and iterative, using techniques such as rapid prototyping and in-person customer observations to guide designers' work. Yet because of the way design agencies traditionally have been compensated, all this work culminates in a monolithic deliverable to the client. All of a sudden, the rapid monolithic deliverable to the client. All of a sudden, the rapid learning and experimentation stops; the assumption is that the designers have learned all there is to know. For startups, this is an unworkable model. No amount of design can anticipate the many complexities of bringing a product to life in the real world. In fact, a new breed of designers is developing brand-new techniques under the banner of Lean User Experience (Lean UX). They recognize that the customer archetype is a hypothesis, not a fact. The customer pro&le should be considered provisional until the strategy has shown via validated learning that we can serve this type of customer in a sustainable way.10 ANALYSIS PARALYSIS There are two ever-present dangers when entrepreneurs conduct market research and talk to customers. Followers of the just-do-it school of entrepreneurship are impatient to get started and don't want to spend time analyzing their strategy. They'd rather start building immediately, often after just a few cursory customer conversations. Unfortunately, because customers don't really know what they want, it's easy for these entrepreneurs to delude themselves that they are on the right path.Packing a carry-on bag with running shoes and two changes of clothes, I head out into the world via a short connection from Portland to Vancouver International Airport. Later that evening, the twelve-hour Cathay Pacific flight to Hong Kong gives me two hours to watch a movie, six hours to sleep, and four hours to write emails. Arriving in Asia, I clear immigration (no bags to claim), check my wallet to see if I still have local currency from the last trip here, and settle into a concourse chair before jumping on the train into the city. I flip open the laptop, connect to "HKG-Free-WiFi," and log onto the world. Whoosh ... out go all the emails I wrote on the plane, and in come 150 more that arrived during the night. I check in with Reese, my designer, about a project we've been working on. I answer customer support requests—a page on our site is down, someone needs a login, and so on—and write a quick update to customers. I 148/617 review reader comments from my latest blog post and quickly check my daily list of email signups, the only metric I monitor on a frequent basis. (If all's going well with new subscribers, everything else should be OK.) I often stay in guest houses and hostels, but later tonight I have a conference call scheduled for the bleary hour of 2 a.m.—it's daytime in North America—so I head to the Conrad Hotel. Fortunately, I slept enough on the plane that I'm good to go after a shower, so I set up shop in my "office" for the next two days. A few hours later, the host on the call is saying "good afternoon" to everyone, and I try to refrain from mentioning the local time while looking out at the Hong Kong skyline. On this trip I'm headed on to Vietnam and Laos, but I could be going anywhere. After I adjust to the time difference over the next couple of days, I settle into a routine of morning work and afternoon exploration. At 149/617 least one week a month, I live in this dream world of travel, work, and frequent coffee breaks. The business is structured around my life, not the other way around. I know what some people think: It sounds like a fantasy. Well ... it really is happening, on a broad scale, for thousands of people all over the world. My example is just one of many; let's hear about a few others. Case Study 1: The Music Teacher In 2009, Brandon Pearce was living in Utah and working as a successful piano teacher, meaning that he got by and paid the rent while doing something he enjoyed. But Brandon was also intensely curious, and wanted to combine an interest in technology with his passion for music education. As he thought 150/617 about colleagues he knew, he found the convergence point between his skill and what they needed. "Music teachers don't want to deal with business administration; they want to teach music," he said. "But in the typical music teacher's workday, they have to spend much of their time dealing with administrative tasks." Scheduling, rescheduling, sending reminders—in addition to time, all these things take up a lot of attention and distract from teaching. Furthermore, many music teachers aren't making all the money they should, since payments are sometimes overlooked and students fail to show up. Brandon didn't intend to create a business at first; he just wanted to solve what he called the "disorganized music teacher problem" for himself. The answer was Music Teacher's Helper, an interface that Brandon created for personal use before turning it into a one-stop platform for music teachers of 151/617 all kinds. The teachers could create their own websites (without having any technical skills) and handle all aspects of scheduling and billing, thus enabling them to focus on the actual teaching they enjoyed. Was this a market in search of a solution? Yes, and the market was substantial. Was Brandon giving them the fish? Yes, and because music teachers are often on a low budget, Brandon made sure to highlight the fact that paying for Music Teacher's Helper might actually save them money over time, but to ensure the business's profitability, he didn't skimp on the price. The service is available in several different versions, including a free version for limited use and going up to a $588-a-year version depending on the number of students.* Three years later, Brandon's life is quite different. Instead of living in Utah, he now wakes up in sunny Escazú, Costa Rica, where he lives with his wife and three young 152/617 daughters. He has ten employees living in different places around the world. He carefully tracks his time and estimates that he spends eight to fifteen hours a week directly related to the business. The rest of his time is spent with his family and on various side projects that he pursues for fun. Brandon and his family used to live in Utah and now they live in Costa Rica, but that's not the whole story; the whole story is that they could live anywhere they want. When they needed to do a visa run, they went over to Guatemala for eight days, and since Brandon and his wife are "unschooling" their children and can easily take them anywhere, there's no telling where they'll end up next. (A tentative plan involves moving to Asia.) Oh, and one more thing: Music Teacher's Helper is currently on track to earn at least $360,000 a year. Because his customers commit for the long term and pay monthly, 153/617 it's unlikely that this number will ever go down. Instead, it will continue to increase as more and more music teachers join the ranks. Case Study 2: The Accidental Worldwide Photographer Originally from Michigan, Kyle Hepp is an "accidental" entrepreneur in the literal sense. Having relocated to Chile with her husband, Seba, Kyle made ends meet by working on side projects for AOL while she looked for a job in her planned field of sports management. The South American lifestyle was great, but Seba's job as a construction engineer was far from secure, and the company started to go under. One Friday afternoon, 154/617 he received notice that his salary was being cut 20 percent. He declined to sign a new contract and was immediately let go. Two days after learning of the layoff, Kyle was out jogging when tragedy struck in the form of a pickup truck that ran into her at a crowded intersection, sending her flying a hundred feet from the point of impact. Her injuries weren't life-threatening or permanent, but as you'd expect, Kyle was badly hurt. After a week in the hospital, she spent several more weeks at home, unable to walk and with so many bruises that she couldn't even type—thus ending the side gig with AOL, which was done on a contract basis. "Between my husband's layoff and getting run over by the car," Kyle told me with a straight face, "it was kind of a bad weekend." Kyle and Seba had been married for nearly three years at that point and hadn't ever had a real honeymoon, so they decided they might as well take vacation time while they 155/617 could. Instead of looking for work, they booked flights to Italy and spent several weeks seeing Europe for the first time. Before the accident, Kyle had been dabbling in wedding photography. She had never really tried to make a career of it, but before flying out she updated her website and announced that she was accepting new bookings. A request came in right away, giving Kyle confidence that she might be able to make some kind of career out of it. When they returned to Chile, Kyle and Seba decided to try photography full-time, "at least until the bookings stopped coming and the money ran out." To their surprise, request after request arrived in Kyle's inbox, and the schedule quickly filled up. Two years later, they were making $90,000 a year and were fully booked another year in advance. They now work all over the world, doing weddings in Argentina, Spain, England, and the United States. You might wonder what 156/617 the big deal is with Kyle's work—since there is no shortage of other good photographers available locally, why do clients fly her from country to country? Kyle says that her clients are usually well traveled themselves, and aren't afraid of hiring someone from afar. "They know that the world is a small place," she says, "and they like our work because we build relationships over time.""Business opportunities are like buses; there's always another one coming." —RICHARD BRANSON The frequent references to customers and clients lead to a good question: Who are they? And just as important, where are they and how do you find them? As you consider these questions, it may help to fit your ideal customers into traditional demographics—things such as age, gender, income—or it may not. While I was writing my first book, different people in the publishing industry asked me about the "target market" for the community that was rapidly growing. I'd been in business for a while, so I knew what they meant, but I couldn't figure out how to explain the diverse group of people who read my blog. We had artists, travelers, high 183/617 school students trying to decide whether to go to college or strike out on their own, retired people making plans for a new chapter in their lives, and everyone in between. There were a number of entrepreneurs and self-employed folks but also a lot of people in traditional jobs. The gender ratio was split almost evenly between men and women. Finally, I realized that the target market had nothing to do with demographics in a traditional sense—the group simply consisted of people from all backgrounds who wanted to live unconventional, remarkable lives. They were "pro-change" and interested in pursuing a big dream while also making the world a better place for others. In other words, I didn't have to segment or label them according to irrelevant categories. You may not want to be a writer, but as you explore different possibilities on the road to freedom and value, it helps to think clearly about the people you plan to serve. 184/617 There are now at least two ways to group them together. Traditional Demographics: New Demographics: Age, Location, Sex/ Gender, Interests, Passions, Skills, Race/Ethnicity, Income Beliefs, Values* In Arcata, California, the husband and wife team of Mark Ritz and Charlie Jordan own the Kinetic Koffee Company. KKC is a gourmet "microroaster" that makes great coffee ... but these days there is no shortage of great coffee, so they needed something more. KKC found its legs and became profitable by targeting a specific group: cyclists, skiers, backpackers, and "pretty much anyone who enjoys the outdoor lifestyle." By focusing on enthusiasts, they immediately set KKC apart in a crowded market. 185/617 Mark and Charlie's connection to the outdoors is natural. Before starting the business, Mark had spent most of his career working in the cycling industry. Charlie was vice president of a kayak company, and both of them were active in the local racing and recreational communities. They were also coffee addicts, so combining the two passions seemed like the right approach. "We weren't the first coffee company to target the cycling market," Mark told me, "but we were the first to look at the market from the perspective of the bicycle shops and outdoor dealers. We have now outlived a number of betterfinanced companies who have since left the market." Outdoor enthusiasts are KKC's people, but to reach them, Mark and Charlie work with bicycle shops and outdoor stores. Maintaining good relationships with the distributors ensures access to almost every store in the country, and Mark complements this 186/617 strategy by visiting trade shows and consumer events. Donating 10 percent of profits to outdoor causes every year, KKC is a lowsix-figure business. The Internet has made it much easier to connect with people through shared values and ideals, but it's not strictly an online phenomenon. More than thirty years ago, long before Facebook, a band with an underground following figured this out. Here's what Jerry Garcia said about the Grateful Dead's followers: There's a lot of that stuff with people bringing their kids, kids bringing their parents, people bringing their grandparents—it's gotten to be really stretched out now. It was never my intention to say, this is the demographics of our audience. It just happened. Tom Bihn, a bag manufacturer from Seattle, Washington, gives us a similar idea: 187/617 "We're consistently and pleasantly surprised by the diversity of our customers. People have a natural desire to categorize and quantify, but we've always felt doing so with our customers would be pointless. They're students, artists, businesspeople, teachers, scientists, programmers, photographers, parents, designers, farmers, and philanthropists." (Read more of Tom's story in Chapter 13.) Changing the "Who" A busy working mother from Hudson, Ohio, Kris Murray saw an opportunity in helping child care providers run their businesses more effectively. For years she dutifully worked at building relationships one by one with day-care centers, only to get frustrated 188/617 with their low prices and lack of interest in developing the business. Despite the challenges, Kris knew it could be a good business. Families will always need child care, and child care providers are usually more focused on providing quality service than on managing the business side of things. How could Kris break through with a successful offer, and how could she boost her income as she served her clients? The early days were discouraging. She was exhausted, overwhelmed, and ready to quit. Then something changed. First, she streamlined her services, making them more oriented to what her clients clearly wanted—she learned to give them the fish. But the second change was also important. In Kris's words, she found a way to "change the WHO": the clients she worked with. Many day-care centers were microbusinesses themselves, run by one or two people. Although these centers may provide good child 189/617 care, they tend to be wary of investing in services and therefore aren't the best fit for Kris's consulting practice. Pivoting to a more desirable market, Kris created a new division of products and services targeted to multilocation center owners. These owners had a much larger investment in their businesses and could afford to pay more for marketing help. The change made a huge difference on the bottom line. Kris went from "doing OK" to making more than $20,000 a month. In the early days, she tried to sell something that her clients weren't ready for. She fixed the problem by changing two things: what she offered and to whom she offered it. Disaster and Recovery: CULTURE SHOCK EDITION Ridlon Kiphart, AKA Sharkman, has one of those jobs everyone envies—he's a self-titled CAO, or chief adventure officer, of a small 190/617 company called Live Adventurously. After previous career stints as a trapeze artist, divemaster, charity founder, and "watersports dude" on a cruise ship, he now runs his own show, hosting trips to exotic locations. I asked Sharkman about his greatest challenge in the new business, and here's how he tells the story of a misadventure in the South Pacific. The best and worst days were the same day. We had finished the first half of the first trip in Fiji, and the guests were raving. We returned from a day spent diving turquoise waters to find a long white linen-draped dinner table sitting on the sand at water's edge. It was surrounded by tiki torches and set beautifully. With the sun setting and island music playing in the warm air, we gathered with our friends for one of the most spectacular dinners in 191/617 history ... right up until the phone call came in. The experience was like listening to a beautiful song and then abruptly hearing the needle from the record player rip across the album. The news was that the paramount chief from the neighboring island we had planned to visit the next day had died, and the mourning ritual required that everything be shut down for the next 100 (!) nights. We had nine exultant guests and nowhere to go. This was when doing our research earlier and really knowing the area paid off. We managed to extend our stay where we were by one night and spent the time feverishly cobbling together plans. We chartered an aircraft (dubbed the flying coffin for self-explanatory reasons); contacted numerous hotels, resorts, and dive operators; 192/617 got recommendations; did some more research; and booked the group into a newly opened property on a remote island. The transition went smoothly, the entire rest of the trip came off without a hitch, and it was as if it had been planned that way the entire time. In the end, the resort we were originally booked into kept half our money despite being in breach of contract. Their attitude was if you want us, you'll have to come and get us. That showed us how worthless contracts can be overseas. Our guests rallied to us and offered to pay the additional money, but we declined and ate the loss. It wasn't our guests' fault, and they shouldn't have to pay. It was a hell of a way to start a new business—taking a big financial hit—but it was the right thing to do. That's the way we've chosen 193/617 to operate, and I believe it always pays off. How can you follow in the footsteps of Tom Bihn, the Kinetic Koffee Company, Kris Murray, and even the Grateful Dead? Strategy 1: Latch on to a Popular Hobby, Passion, or Craze Popular diet plans come and go, but a few of them stick around. The Paleo diet, which encourages its followers to eat a lot of some things (meat and uncooked vegetables) and very little or none of other things (grains, dairy, sugars, etc.) looks like it's here to stay. Like all strict diets, Paleo attracts a passionate following in addition to a passionate group on the other side that questions its scientific basis. Situations like these—an industry or movement with lots of lovers and 194/617 haters—always present a good business opportunity. Enter Jason Glaspey, who had adopted the lifestyle after reading The Paleo Diet, a popular manual for Paleo followers. Jason noticed a big difficulty with trying to follow the diet: It was complicated. "Eat natural food and avoid grains" sounds simple enough, but adhering to the whole diet requires a fair amount of ongoing planning. This is another sign of a good business opportunity: when lots of people are interested in something but have a hard time implementing it in their daily lives. Jason got to work creating a solution. He understood that the demographics for hardcore Paleo followers were more male than female and tended to fall in the age range of twenty-five to thirty-five. More important, however, Jason noticed that people of various backgrounds were attracted to the Paleo lifestyle but weren't sure they could devote 195/617 much of their time to planning for it. Thus the opportunity: Provide a comprehensive resource that "gave them the fish" (no pun intended, although Paleo followers do eat a lot of fish) by telling them exactly what to buy, cook, and eat each week. Jason started Paleo Plan, a one-man business, in three weeks with $1,500. Within a year, the business grew to earn recurring income of more than $6,000 a month, requiring a grand total of two hours' work to update the site each week. Strategy 2: Sell What People Buy (and Ask Them If You're Not Sure) As you focus on getting to know "your people," keep this important principle in mind: Most of us like to buy, but we don't like to be sold. Old-school marketing is based on persuasion; new marketing is based on invitation. With persuasion marketing, you're trying to convince people of 196/617 something, whether it's the need for your service in general or why your particular offering is better than the competition's. A persuasion marketer is like a door-to-door vacuum cleaner salesman: If he knocks on enough doors, he might eventually sell a vacuum cleaner … but at great personal cost and much rejection. Persuasion marketing is still around and always will be, but now there's an alternative. If you don't want to go door to door with a vacuum cleaner in hand, consider how the people in our study have created businesses that customers desperately want to be a part of. What do you sell? Remember the lesson from Chapter 2: Find out what people want and find a way to give it to them. As you build a tribe of committed fans and loyal customers, they'll eagerly await your new offers, ready to pounce as soon as they go live. This way isn't just new; it's also better. 197/617 When you're brainstorming different ideas and aren't sure which one is best, one of the most effective ways to figure it out is simply to ask your prospects, your current customers (if you have them), or anyone you think might be a good fit for your idea. It helps to be specific; asking people if they "like" something isn't very helpful. Since you're trying to build a business, not just a hobby, a better method is to ask if they'd be willing to pay for what you're selling. This separates merely "liking" something from actually paying for it.

IF YOUR MISSION STATEMENT IS MUCH LONGER THAN THIS SENTENCE, IT COULD BE TOO LONG. "Plans are only good intentions unless they immediately degenerate into hard work." —PETER F. DRUCKER Jen Adrion and Omar Noory graduated from the Columbus (Ohio) College of Art and Design in 2008. They both began freelancing as designers, in addition to Jen teaching at their alma mater and Omar taking a design job at a studio in town. Based in a tiny apartment, they were making ends meet and working jobs related to their degrees, but just one year after graduation, the feeling of burnout from the world of commercial design was inescapable. "Should I have gone to med school?" Jen wondered. "What if accounting would have been a better fit? It was strange to be feeling this way only a year into our careers." On a drive back from Chicago, they talked about other things: an upcoming 219/617 trip to New York and a plan that they hoped would lead to other travels. When they got home, Omar looked around for a nice map to help chart their upcoming adventures. Long story short, they couldn't find one that they loved, so they decided to make their own. They stayed up late at night, working on their ideal map while talking about all the places they hoped to visit. When they finished the design, there was just one problem: The printer they wanted to use had a minimum order of fifty units for a cost of $500. It was a lot to spend when they only needed one map, but the project had come to mean more than just a print, so Jen and Omar each put down $250. They loved the final result and hung one of the maps on the wall ... leaving forty-nine maps with no obvious purpose. They gave a few out to friends ... and still had forty-four. Finally, Omar asked a crazy question: Would anyone want to buy the remaining prints? 220/617 They made a one-page website, added a PayPal button, and went to bed. The morning after making their work available for purchase, they woke up to their first sale. Then they made another sale, and then another. Thanks to a surprise mention on a popular design forum, they sold out of their first print run in ten minutes and had tons of messages begging for a reprint. Could this be the answer to designer burnout? Over the next few months, Jen and Omar introduced more styles and acted on new ideas: a New York City subway map, for example, and a neighborhood-themed map of San Francisco. The plan was to grow steadily but not introduce new products without a valid reason. As good designers, they understood that everything in the store had to be essential. They also understood that although some customers would make more than one purchase, the best way the 221/617 customers could help was by referring other buyers and fans. Nine months in, both of them had quit their day jobs to work full-time on the business. "This project has totally restored our passion for design," says Omar. "It feels so liberating to have creative control. It's been an incredible opportunity for us to grow as designers. I feel like our work has progressed more in the past year than it ever has." Jen and Omar began with an idea, kept costs low, and didn't wait long before stepping forward with a product. Then they adapted to the marketplace response (make more maps!) and built each new product carefully. "It's funny, because we're both obsessive planners," Jen told me. "But this project had almost no planning whatsoever in the beginning, and now it's our full-time work." 222/617 The Action Bias Plan? What plan? Many of our case studies showed a pattern similar to Jen and Omar's: Get started quickly and see what happens. There's nothing wrong with planning, but you can spend a lifetime making a plan that never turns into action. In the battle between planning and action, action wins. Here's how you do it. SELECT A MARKETABLE IDEA. In Jen and Omar's case, the idea was as follows: Maybe we're not the only ones who like nice maps. Would other people like them enough to buy one from us? A marketable idea doesn't have to be a big, groundbreaking idea; it just has to provide a solution to a problem or be useful enough that other people are willing to 223/617 pay for it. Don't think innovation; think usefulness. * When you're just getting started, how do you know if an idea is marketable? Well, you don't always know for sure—that's why you start as soon as you can and avoid spending much money. But for more ideas, check out "Seven Steps to Instant Market Testing" on the next page. Seven Steps to Instant Market Testing† 1. You need to care about the problem you are going to solve, and there has to be a sizable number of other people who also care. Always remember the lesson of convergence: the way your idea intersects with what other people value. 2. Make sure the market is big enough. Test the size by checking the number 224/617 and relevancy of Google keywords—the same keywords you would use if you were trying to find your product. Think about keywords that people would use to find a solution to a problem. If you were looking for your own product online but didn't know it existed, what keywords would you search for? Pay attention to the top and right sides of the results pages, where the ads are displayed. 3. Focus on eliminating "blatant admitted pain." The product needs to solve a problem that causes pain that the market knows it has. It's easier to sell to someone who knows they have a problem and are convinced they need a solution than it is to persuade someone that they have a problem that needs solving. 4. Almost everything that is being sold is for either a deep pain or a deep desire. 225/617 For example, people buy luxury items for respect and status, but on a deeper level they want to be loved. Having something that removes pain may be more effective then realizing a desire. You need to show people how you can help remove or reduce pain. 5. Always think in terms of solutions. Make sure your solution is different and better. (Note that it doesn't need to be cheaper—competing on price is usually a losing proposition.) Is the market frustrated with the current solution? Being different isn't enough; differentiation that makes you better is what's required. There's no point in introducing something if the market is already satisfied with the Solution—your solution must be different or better. It's significance, not size, that matters. 226/617 6. Ask others about the idea but make sure the people you ask are your potential target market. Others may provide insignificant data and are therefore biased and uninformed. Therefore, create a persona: the one person who would benefit the most from your idea. Examine your whole network—community, friends, family, social networks—and ask yourself if any of these people match your persona. Take your idea to this person and discuss it with him or her in detail. This will get you much more relevant data than talking to just anyone. 7. Create an outline for what you are doing and show it to a subgroup of your community. Ask them to test it for free in return for feedback and confidentiality. As a bonus, the subgroup feels involved and will act as evangelists. Giving builds trust and value and 227/617 also gives you an opportunity to offer the whole solution. Use a blog to build authority and expertise on a subject. Leave comments on blogs where your target audience hangs out.

THE STEP-BY-STEP GUIDE TO CREATING A KILLER OFFER. "I have nothing to offer but blood, toil, tears, and sweat." —WINSTON CHURCHILL Scott McMurren sat in his office at a TV station in Anchorage, Alaska, looking out at Mount McKinley. The day job was in media sales, where he knocked on doors around town, recruiting advertisers for the station. He also hosted a travel show, something he enjoyed but didn't expect to lead to a fulltime gig. Gary Blakely, a buddy of Scott's, had been pestering him for a while about a business idea, but Scott wasn't into it. When two years of Gary's hammering merged with Scott's fatigue from doing the same thing every day, he finally gave in and said, "OK, let's give it a try." The idea was to create coupon books for independent travelers coming to Alaska. Every year, more than a million visitors show up on the state's doorstep, eager to see Denali National Park and other attractions. Some tourists arrive on cruise ships or guided tours, but many more put together their own trip. As is often the case, the consumer 251/617 problem and the business opportunity are related: Alaska is a nice place during the summer, but costs are always high. Almost everything in the state is more expensive than the rest of the U.S. to start with, and some travel companies charge even higher prices to visitors. (A common joke is "Welcome to Alaska ... please hand over your wallet.") The coupon book would be an antidote to high prices, but it would have to provide real value instead of offering the typical, minor discounts available elsewhere. That's where Scott came in. Since he already had the state contacts through his day job in media sales, all he had to do was get them to commit to a discounted offer, typically a two-for-one deal in which the second night or second person was free. A natural salesman, Scott positioned every deal to grow into another one. When he encountered resistance from a vendor who was reluctant to discount, Scott pointed out that 252/617 other companies were going along without objection. The implied message was, "Everyone else is doing this. You don't want to be left out." Once they had proved the benefit to the vendors, the next step was to prove it to the people who would buy the coupon books. You might think Scott and Gary would price the books low to sell as many as possible (comparable products in other places sold for $20 to $25, usually supported by advertising or kickbacks from the vendors), but they had a better idea: price the books at $99.95 and make the value proposition extremely clear. The books contained deals for helicopter flights and tours that cost as much as several hundred dollars, as well as hotels that retailed at more than $100 a night. Why wouldn't people pay $99.95 for a product like that? It was the ultimate follow-your-passion business, combined with a perfect transfer of 253/617 skills from a job to a microbusiness. Scott had the insider knowledge about the local travel industry, along with a way to leverage the deals to ensure they were all high value. Gary was the production guy, handling everything associated with getting the product together in addition to all the Internet work and the banking. For fifteen years and counting, the TourSaver coupon books have been their primary business and source of income. Why is the TourSaver offer so compelling? Because it delivers immediate benefits superior to its cost, with an attractive pitch: "Buy this coupon book, use it once, get your money back. Then you have more than a hundred other uses as a bonus." Scott frames it like this: "Just do the math! Using a single one of the 130+ coupons in the book will save you more than the cost of the book itself." 254/617 Another way to think of it is like this: Scott and Gary created an offer you can't refuse. If you were traveling to Alaska and planned to enjoy some kind of sight-seeing opportunity, there's almost no reason why you wouldn't want one of their books. The Orange and the Donut A few years ago, I ran my first marathon in Seattle. I'd love to tell you I ran strong to the finish, but by mile 18 I was wiped out, focusing entirely on putting one foot in front of the other. As I trudged along in the final hour, I spotted a volunteer handing out fresh orange slices on the side of the road ahead of me. Tired as I was, I made sure to change my position, slow down, and gratefully accept the gift. The piece of fresh orange was an offer I couldn't refuse—even though it was free, 255/617 I would have gladly paid for it if I had the money and was in the right frame of mind to make a transaction. Two miles ahead, I saw another volunteer handing out a different gift: halves of Krispy Kreme donuts. Unfortunately, this offer did not excite me (or any other runners I saw) at all. I'm no puritan and have eaten more than my share of donuts over the years, but three hours into the longest race of my life was bad timing for a sugar rush. The offer was unattractive and a poor fit for the context.* A compelling offer is like a slice of orange at mile 18. It's a marriage proposal from the guy or girl you've been waiting for your whole life. An offer you can't refuse is like the $20,000 Bonderman Fellowship offered every year to graduating seniors at the University of Washington. The fellowship has very strict rules: Take our money in cash and travel the world on your own; don't come back for eight months. Oh, and once in 256/617 a while send us a quick note so we can tell your parents you're alive. If you guessed that hundreds of students compete for the fellowship every year, you'd be right. How can you construct an offer that your prospects won't refuse? Remember, first you need to sell what people want to buy—give them the fish. Then make sure you're marketing to the right people at the right time. Sometimes you can have the right crowd at the wrong time; marathon runners are happy to eat donuts after the race, but not at mile 18. Then you take your product or service and craft it into a compelling pitch ... an offer they can't refuse. Here's how you do it. 1. Understand that what we want and what we say we want are not always the same thing. The next time you get on a crowded plane and head to your cramped middle seat in the 257/617 back, with a screaming infant seated behind you at no extra charge, remember this principle. For years travelers have been complaining about crowded planes and cramped seats, and for years airlines have been ignoring them. Every once in a while, an airline creates a campaign to respond to the concern: "We're giving more legroom in coach!" It sounds great, but a few months later they inevitably reverse course and remove the extra inches of space. Why? Because despite what they say, most travelers don't value the extra legroom enough to pay for it; instead, they value the lowest-priced flights above any other concerns. Airlines have figured this out, so they give people what they want—not what they say they want. A good offer has to be what people actually want and are willing to pay for.Jonathan Fields, a hedge fund lawyer turned fitness entrepreneur, owned a Manhattan yoga studio that sought to be at the top of the market. A single class cost $18, and membership cost $119 a month. Toward the end of summer, the studio saw a significant dropoff in business, but when October rolled around, people got back to their routine and started coming in more often. Jonathan wanted to find a way to inspire people to come back earlier than expected and get as much commitment from them as possible. He had an idea for an offer they couldn't refuse: Starting September 1, firsttime members could get unlimited classes through the end of the year for $180. This was essentially four months of yoga for the price of 45 days, or 62 percent off the normal price. Two additional factors were added to make it even more interesting: First, the sooner a new member signed up, the more 262/617 classes he or she could attend, thus creating instant urgency. Second, the offer could be withdrawn at any time; if someone came in on September 3 and wasn't sure about committing to the rest of the year, the staff made sure to let that person know that the offer might not be available later in the week. Thanks to New Year's resolutions, most fitness centers take in the bulk of their new members in January. Jonathan's strategy helped his business gain a big increase in September, traditionally a difficult month. Also, September was close enough to January that by the time the new year rolled around, many of the members were committed enough to transfer to a monthly plan—at the regular price. EXAMPLE 2: THE INEFFICIENT BUSINESS MODEL (MARKET INEFFICIENCY = BUSINESS OPPORTUNITY) 263/617 Whenever something is more complicated than it should be or any time you spot an inefficiency in the market, you can also find a good business idea. Priceline.com took advantage of hotel inefficiencies by creating a system that allowed consumers to book rooms at name-brand hotels for much less than the retail rates. Then other companies took advantage of Priceline's lack of transparency by creating a business model that allows travelers to know which hotels Priceline works with. Each of these models includes a compelling offer: Priceline's compelling offer: Save 40 percent or more on name-brand hotels, guaranteed. Third-party compelling offer: Learn exactly which hotel you'll get with Priceline ... and save even more when you know exactly how much to bid. 264/617 You can also derive a powerful business model from traditional systems that lack transparency. If you want to make a traditional real estate agent mad, ask the agent about Redfin, the Seattle-based service that splits commissions with home buyers. I learned this lesson when one agent told me that Redfin "should be illegal" and that I was doing a disservice to hardworking people by endorsing it. Why are (some) agents so testy, and why should it be illegal to save consumers money? Oh, because the money is coming from the pockets of real estate agents, who are used to receiving full, hefty commissions regardless of the amount of work they perform. Redfin has succeeded by challenging gatekeepers and addressing a huge inefficiency in the marketplace. Speaking of home owners, the DirectBuy franchise was started in order to offer "ordinary people" (i.e., non-contractors) access to retailer pricing on appliances and home 265/ 617 electronics. To get around the concerns of retailers and manufacturers, DirectBuy structured its business model on charging a flat fee for consumers to join. The compelling offer is: Invest in our membership, and you'll save thousands on home remodeling.† EXAMPLE 3: THE GRAPHIC FACILITATOR I'll invite you to meet Brandy Agerbeck in these pages, but you can "meet" her first by examining the mindmap she made for us below.‡ 266/617 Brandy runs a business of one, with the philosophy "never have a boss, never be a boss." Creating graphical representations of ideas—usually those expressed in meetings, retreats, or conferences—is Brandy's fulltime work. Over the last fifteen years, she's worked with hundreds of clients at all kinds of events. It's a beautiful business model from a talented artist, but it also raises a 267/617 question: How do you nudge or win over executives who don't get it at first? From countless interactions about the valuable service she provides, here's what Brandy learned. She starts every initial conversation by saying, "I have a fantastic, strange job." This creates curiosity and also serves to make the other person not feel bad if he or she is unfamiliar with the world of graphic facilitation. Next, Brandy learned that her target market may be the executives or meeting leaders she serves, but they aren't necessarily the ones who hire her. "I am most often hired by facilitators, acting as their visual silent partners," she says. "They can focus entirely on their client knowing their process, and progress is documented." 268/617 Perceived Value and the Expensive Starbucks Run After nearing the end of a five-hour drive from Boise to Salt Lake City, I stopped off at a Starbucks about twenty minutes away from the bookstore I was speaking at that evening. On the way inside, I grabbed something from the trunk and left the keys inside. Nice move, Chris. It was even worse because I didn't realize my mistake until I had finished my latte and email session an hour later, shortly before I was due to arrive at the bookstore. I was mad at myself for being so stupid, but I had to think quickly. Using a combination of technology (iPod touch, MiFi, cell phone), I located the number of a local locksmith and quickly rang him up. "Uh, can you please come as soon as possible?" He agreed to be as fast as he could. 269/617 Much to my surprise, the locksmith pulled up in a van just three minutes later. Impressive, right? Then he got out his tools and approached the passenger door. In less than ten seconds, he had the door open, allowing me to retrieve my keys from the trunk and get on with my life. "How much do I owe you?" I asked. Perhaps it's because I don't own a car and the last time I paid a locksmith was ten years ago, or maybe I'm just cheap, but for whatever reason I expected him to ask for something like $20. Instead, he said, "That will be $50, please." I hadn't discussed the price with him before he came out and was in no position to negotiate, so I gave him the cash and thanked him.

But something was unsettling about the transaction, and I tried to figure out what it was. I was mad at myself for locking my keys in the car—it was obviously no one's fault but my own—but I also felt that 270/617 $50 was too much to pay for such a brief service. As I drove away, I realized that I secretly wanted him to take longer in getting to me, even though that would have delayed me further. I wanted him to struggle with unlocking my car as part of a major effort, even though that made no sense whatsoever. The locksmith met my need and provided a quick, comprehensive solution to my problem. I was unhappy about our exchange for no good reason. Mulling it over, I realized that the way we make purchasing decisions isn't always rational. I thought back to something that had happened in the early days of my business. I had produced a twenty-five-page report on booking discount airfare and sold it for $25. Many people bought it, but others complained: Twenty-five pages for $25? That's too expensive. 271/ 617 I knew I couldn't please everyone, but I didn't understand this specific objection. The point of the report was to help people save money on plane tickets, and many readers reported saving $300 or more after one quick read. "What does the length of the report have to do with the price?" I remember thinking about that one complaint. "If I gave you a treasure map, would you complain that it was only one page long?" It turned out the joke was on me. All of us place a subjective value on goods or services that may not relate to what they "should" be. Just as what we want and what we say we want aren't always the same thing, the way we place a value on something isn't always rational. You must learn to think about value the way your customers do, not necessarily the way you would like them to. A TRIP TO HOLLYWOOD FROM YOUR LIVING ROOM OR THE CORNER COFFEE SHOP. "Before beginning, prepare carefully." —MARCUS TULLIUS CICERO Let's take a trip to Hollywood, by way of our local cinema or movie theater. Every year, a number of blockbuster films come out that cost a huge amount of money to produce, often $100 million or more. Studio executives know they have only a limited window to ensure a big hit. If the opening weekend isn't huge, they may still have a good movie, but not the blockbuster they need to recoup their high costs. The executives also know that although some people don't decide which movie they want to see until they get to the theater, lots of other people go to see a particular movie. If they've been hearing about it in advance, building up their anticipation and getting excited, they're all the more eager to see the movie—and tell their friends about it too. 287/617 This is why Hollywood begins the "prelaunch" for a big film many months in advance, often a whole season or even an entire year in advance for the right film. During this time they are showing previews at the beginning of other movies, building buzz through an Internet campaign, and working the PR angles far in advance of the movie actually coming out. The pre-launch campaign is a success when people eagerly await the film, complaining about how long it takes to arrive, until the day—"finally"—it's ready to be screened for the public. Then, the studio hopes, hundreds of thousands of filmgoers will pay their money and stream into the theater. Without an active pre-launch campaign, the movie may be great but the odds of commercial success are far lower. The same principle holds true for microbusinesses. Whether a Hollywood movie or the debut of your new sock-knitting class, 288/617 launches are built primarily through a series of regular communications with prospects and existing customers. Just like the movie executives who release trailers over time (first a short one, then a longer one) and the press events that Apple built up over time with Steve Jobs at the helm (building anticipation for future products to a fever pitch), small businesses can reproduce this cycle in their own way.* Karol Gajda and Adam Baker, two friends with separate businesses in different parts of the country, decided to team up for a big project. Karol had completed an engineering degree from the University of Michigan, but never actually worked as an engineer. He first had the idea from reading a classic ninety-year-old marketing book called Scientific Advertising by Claude Hopkins. In the book, Hopkins discussed "fire sales"—the old-school, "everything must go" tactic used 289/617 by furniture stores for decades. Karol didn't have a furniture store, but he wondered ... What if we put together a modern-day fire sale, with an emphasis on giving away a ton of value for a low price, but only for a limited time? Karol and Adam were both in the information publishing business, and they quickly went to work, approaching other colleagues to participate. The pitch was intriguing: Contribute your products to the overall mix to be sold as a group for a low price and during a limited time. Oh, and if you help promote the offer to your own audience of customers and followers, you'll earn an 80 percent commission on everything you sell. It was a good pitch, and Karol and Adam had spent plenty of time building relationships and developing a strong reputation for their work. Out of twenty-five requests, twenty-three people said yes. 290/617 Packaging everything together, they ended up with a monster package valued at a retail price of $1,054. They would sell the package for $97, less than 10 percent of the overall value and a price to which they expected customers would respond well. The "hook" came from the fire-sale idea: The offer would be available for only seventy-two hours—no packages would ever be sold again after the limited time period. The big day came, and they put the offer online. For ten minutes nothing happened. Karol sat looking in anticipation at the stats in Austin while Adam was biting his nails in Indianapolis. Was something wrong? Fortunately not ... It turned out they were just ten minutes early. All of a sudden, a trickle of visitors became a stream, then a flood, as more and more people heard about the offer and came by to purchase. Wham! The server was hit hard, and Karol's Gmail account 291/617 reported "Notification of payment received" over and over. The flood continued for the rest of the day, slowed down a bit on the second day, and then picked back up at the end of the third and final day. When the smoke cleared, Karol and Adam added up the results. Total sales: $185,755 in three sleep-deprived days. Such was the power of a well-crafted product launch. It Was a Dark and Stormy Night Because a planned launch campaign can provide far better results than simply putting something out there and saying, "Hey, here you go," you'll want to think carefully about how to structure it. The campaign usually unfolds in a series of messages you send to 292/617 your audience, and you should keep the Hollywood analogy in mind: The worst thing you could do for a launch is to open your movie without letting anyone know. A much better thing is to tell a story. The story unfolds like this ... An early look at the future. In the first mention of your upcoming launch, you don't want to give all the details away; it's usually better to start with a simple heads-up. You want to say something like this: "Hey, I'm working on something interesting. It's going to be a big deal when it's finished, but for now I'm just letting you know that it's coming down the line." The goal is to slowly build anticipation for what eventually will be available for purchase. Why this project will matter. The most important early message about the launch (and one that has to be reinforced continually) is why your prospects and customers should care. In the blitz of communication 293/617 that we all process every day, why should anyone stop and pay attention to this project? The message you want to communicate is: "This is why this project will be a game changer, here's how people will benefit, and here's why you should care." The plan for the big debut. The previous two messages, as well as any others, have been about the project itself, not the actual launch. Here's where you roll out some of the details for the launch itself. When will it be? How will it work? Will there be some kind of bonus for early buyers? Most important, what do people need to know at this time? Whoa, we're almost ready! This communication happens right before the launch, sometimes as late as the day before. The message is: "This is the calm before the storm. We're coming down to the wire and are really excited about this." Any lastminute reminders or launch details are included here, and the goal is to convert 294/617 anticipation into an actual decision. (You want prospects to decide in advance that they want what you're putting together.) OMG, HERE IT IS! The message is: "It's finally here, everyone has been waiting, and now we're ready to go." This communication tends to be shorter than the others because if you've done your job right, many buyers are already prepared to purchase. Here's where you open the gates to the hordes ... or at least that's what you hope will happen. In this message you send them a link (or give them another way to purchase) and encourage them to take action. INTERLUDE Let's pause here for a moment. What happens immediately after this point is just as important as what has happened already. A good marketer doesn't rest on her laurels after a launch, because she knows she can probably increase the 295/617 results significantly with little effort. A launch often results in a response cycle like this: If the launch is a week long, you'll tend to see a strong response on the first and second days, followed by a significant downturn and then a big uptick right before the close. This further illustrates 296/617 why you need a launch cycle: If you have no closing, you won't see the uptick! If you just launch and move on, you'll have no opportunity for growth. Now back to the story ... Here's how it's going. Something always goes wrong in every launch. Here's a chance to address or correct it, along with updating everyone on how things are going. During this time, it's also important to share stories of happy customers who have purchased already. The message is, "Look at all these people who are already benefiting from our product." The clock's a-ticking. Right before the offer goes off the market, or before you remove the bonuses, or before the price goes up, here's where you make one final push. The message is, "It's almost over. Here's your last chance before you lose out." "I'd like to thank my mother for believing in me." Any good launch has a closing period 297/617 in which you bring the roller coaster to a stop, even if the offer will still be available in a different form. The message is, "It's all over now. Thanks, everyone. Here's what's coming next." Disaster and Recovery: "HORDE OF NEW CUSTOMERS" EDITION Like the problem of having too much money, having too many customers is usually a good problem to have—but it can still be a tough scramble if the customers all arrive at once and a key supplier isn't ready. Here's what David Wachtendonk, the founder of a party planning business in Chicago, learned when he received two thousand more customers than expected for a promotion. In June 2010 our company participated in a Groupon. We did some research, and it appeared this could be a good avenue for our company to get some exposure for a new concept we wanted to launch in Chicago. 298/617 After some discussion with the Groupon guys, we agreed it would be a match made in heaven. Our last remaining task was to find a venue that could support the deal. After some initial opportunities fell through, we found a new restaurant that agreed to work with us. The day the deal went live, we had no idea what was about to happen. Our Groupon rep estimated we would sell about 1,000 to 1,500 units … but 3,300 units later, the day ended. We thought we had systems in place to deal with growth, but unfortunately we became overwhelmed. The phone was off the hook and emails poured in, which we fielded to the best of our ability. Most of the customers were fairly understanding as we were a small business, but not everyone was nice about it. We found out after the deal had launched that the restaurant was in the middle of rebranding to a sports bar, which is not the 299/617 ideal situation for a dinner theater. Their clientele changed, the atmosphere was evolving, and the owner of the business did his best to accommodate us. Unfortunately, your best isn't always good enough, and our new customers let us know it. We worked tirelessly with their team to get them up to speed on how to handle large groups and even provided our own on-site hostess and manager for the majority of the shows with the hopes of improving the experience. Due to things out of our control, the quality didn't meet expectations at first—service became sloppy, and the overall experience was diluted. The first few shows were challenging, but over time the experience got better. Forty-seven shows later, we finally wrapped things up. Our company had done its research and what we thought was adequate due diligence for the deal, but our efforts fell short. We should have been more proactive and 300/617 done a better job communicating expectations to our customers. Thankfully, our team made it through the experience and can live to tell the story. The question people ask me all the time is, "Would you do another Groupon?" The honest answer is that I would. Along with the challenges the Groupon presented, it provided exposure that traditional marketing never would have achieved. As with everything else in life, it's important to keep your word with launches. If your offer ended at a set time and you had a big response, you'll invariably be contacted with requests for exceptions after it's over. It's tempting to take more money, but if you said it would end at a set time, you need to stick to your decision. In the long run, this works in your favor, because people will realize that you mean what you say. Karol and Adam received numerous requests for their bundled 301/617 package after the seventy-two-hour period had ended, but they politely declined each one. One more thing: If you admit to a flaw, weakness, or limitation in your product, this will probably help instead of harm you. This is because when we are evaluating a purchasing decision, we like to consider both the strengths and the weaknesses. If a product developer personally tells us it's not perfect—"and here's why"—we tend to trust him or her more. You can see this style of messaging in President Obama's 2012 reelection campaign. An early ad in favor of reelection contained the following statement from a supporter: "I don't agree with Obama on everything, but I respect and trust him." Meanwhile, an ad that launched the same week against reelection contained the following statement from someone who was 302/617 opposed: "I like Obama, but I just don't understand his policies." These are essentially the same statements, flipped around to place the emphasis on what each side wants voters to believe. Each message contains both an admission of uncertainty and an argument, thus making both pitches a good fit for independent voters who haven't made up their minds yet.† In all the messages you send (whether delivered via email or in another way), you'll want to be mindful of several qualities. The first and most important is what we've mentioned already: the need to tell a good story. On its own, however, a good story isn't always enough. You also need to think about "relatability" and timeliness. Relatability, which may or may not be a real word, refers to the need to ensure that the people who hear about the launch can relate to it. Do they see themselves in the characters in your 303/617 story, and can they clearly understand how it will help them? Do they get it? The final factor is timeliness, and it can be the critical difference between good results ("We did OK") and great results ("We killed it!"). Without timeliness, customers may evaluate the offer and agree that it's interesting, but fail to take action because there is no need for them to do so right away. You don't want to pressure people into buying if they're not ready, but you do want to instill a sense of urgency. That's why a good launch always factors in a concern for timeliness. It's Not (All) About the Sales The goal of a good launch is not just to convert as many prospects as possible; it's also to preserve your relationship with other prospects and increase your influence. The 304/617 reason this is important is because you don't want to hammer people too hard; it's better to build relationships over time. Some people will always complain whenever you sell anything at any price. There's nothing you can do about that attitude, so just accept it and don't cater to those people. But you do want to pay attention to your broader base. What are they saying about you? How do they perceive the value of your offer and the style of your messaging? A good launch should increase sales and influence at the same time. If you're getting positive feedback from people who don't buy your product but want to support you in other ways, you're on the right track. Storytelling and the Empire Building Kit Launch It was my most important launch to date: an online business course called the Empire Building Kit that eventually formed the basis 305/617 for this book. For months I conducted interviews and research, capturing lessons from unconventional entrepreneurs and extracting the secrets of their success. As I prepared to make it available, though, I felt stuck—something wasn't coming together, and I kept procrastinating on the launch date. While planning a trip to Europe and West Africa, I had a flight booked that eventually would take me to Chicago but no onward ticket to my home in Portland. On a whim I checked the Amtrak schedule, thinking there was no way I'd want to take a train halfway across the country but I might as well take a look. To my surprise, the name of the Amtrak train from Chicago to Portland was the Empire Builder. Hmmm. I began to get an idea, but initially thought it was too crazy to implement. That same evening, the doorbell rang and the UPS guy dropped off a package. When I opened the box, I 306/617 discovered a free messenger bag sent by some new friends at Tom Bihn's company (profiled in Chapter 13). The name of the bag was ... Empire Builder. I'm not sure if God, the universe, or Tom Bihn's company was sending me the message, but I decided to follow the idea where it led. I made plans to go to West Africa then fly home via Chicago and launch the Empire Building Kit on a single day, live from the Empire Builder train. Oh, and it also happened to be my birthday—so I made that part of the story as well. I asked my friend J. D. Roth to come along with me, so he and I met up in Chicago and prepared for the journey. Upon embarking on the train, we set up a "blogger's lounge" in the Amtrak viewing car complete with various Apple products—amusing the other passengers, many of whom were elderly sightseers. In the weeks before the big day, I had been telling my community about the plan 307/617 with a mixture of excitement and dread; I was excited to launch the new course but scared that I wouldn't be able to finish it in time. With so much riding on the story, there was no flexibility on the date and no backup plan if things didn't work out. Thankfully, everything worked as it should. I finished the final copyedits on my Lufthansa flight to Chicago. Two days later, we launched the Empire Building Kit to hundreds of eager buyers, many of whom had been waiting for it since the pre-launch campaign. The launch cleared over $100,000 in sales before I turned it off exactly twentyfour hours later as our train rolled through Washington State and down into Oregon. The message had a good story and built-in timeliness: Once we hit Portland, the deal was over. My favorite part was receiving emails from people who said they weren't interested in the course but had been enjoying the story of 308/617 the train ride. I don't always get it right, but this time everything fell into place. London Airport Launch, Eleven Hours to Brazil After finishing a university course, Andreas Kambanis struggled for six months, not wanting to get a real job and trying to build something for himself. The goal was to develop an iPhone app and online guide to London cycling routes, but the initial setbacks were significant. Among other things, Andreas used the name London Cyclist before realizing that there already was a publication with that name, triggering an angry letter and the threat of a lawsuit. Meanwhile, all of his friends had gone on to work for 309/617 companies, so they had money to go out at night while Andreas stayed home. Andreas stuck it out, planning for his first launch with a partner right before leaving on a personal trip to Brazil. A few weeks before departure, the partner dropped out. Andreas cut back on the expected deliverables but decided to keep going with both the launch and the trip. The big day came, and he launched the app from the Heathrow airport departure lounge literally thirty minutes before boarding the flight. Settling into economy class for the eleven-hour flight, he had plenty of time to think about his new business, but in the days before in-flight Internet was common, there wasn't anything he could do about it. As he explained later, going offline right after releasing the app probably wasn't the best decision, but without much of an audience, he didn't expect any real results to appear right away. After finally touching down in 310/617 São Paulo, Andreas couldn't resist activating the roaming feature of his iPhone for a quick check. Bleary-eyed and sitting in a cramped window seat, he pulled up the numbers and couldn't believe what he saw—a pile of orders was flooding in, just as Karol and Adam had experienced earlier. It wasn't a fortune, but in the time he had been flying across the Atlantic, the launch had paid for his plane ticket and the first week of lodging. Andreas continued on to a connecting flight to Rio, abandoning all hope of not using the roaming option on his phone, and kept watching the sales come through. I prefer to spend my launches at home with sixteen ounces of coffee in hand, dealing with the inevitable technical glitch while communicating with partners and buyers. But in this case, having the forced deadline of the upcoming flight—and then getting on the plane in Heathrow, ready or not—served 311/617 as a powerful motivation for Andreas. "It's hard to put into words why the physical deadline was such an important part of getting the project done," he told me. "I think it was so motivational because it seemed impossible to achieve, and it made me kill everything that didn't add to the project being finished."‡ A good launch strategy can help almost any business, online or offline. Let's take a look at how an independent publishing company used the same tactics that worked for Karol and Adam, but for a launch that was completely offline and local. Anastasia Valentine publishes children's books and used to work with "big companies who had gigantic marketing budgets." Naturally, she didn't have access to the same kind of resources for her own launch, but she knew enough to create anticipation over time for a specific event. 312/617 The first part was to start with the ask—to ask everyone she knew for help. "We weren't sure how to filter our requests," Anastasia said, "so instead of filtering, we just asked everyone for everything. We asked for newspaper coverage, TV appearances, endorsements, donations for a big party, and anything else we could think of." The requests paid off when she got a positive response to almost everything. When the big day arrived, the line went out the door, and Anastasia had made sure to create a good experience for the attendees. Since adults who buy children's books usually arrive with kids in tow, she added coloring spaces and a homemade pin-the-tooth-onthe-crocodile contest. Even though the launch was for an offline event, Web traffic increased by 267 percent and the mailing list doubled. Learning to ask was also instructive. "People we didn't think would have the slightest interest showed up ... with friends!" 313/617 she said. "Meanwhile, people who we thought were totally interested never even responded. The lesson was that you shouldn't assume someone isn't interested or won't attend or won't buy." If you're just getting started with your own launch planning, check out the Thirty-NineStep Product Launch Checklist below. This checklist has two uses: as a template for a new business planning its first launch and as an idea generator for an existing business. Thirty-Nine-

Step Product Launch Checklist Note: Every product launch is different. Use these steps as a guideline to your own. Often by adding one or two steps you would otherwise leave out, you'll get a significant increase in sales. THE BIG PICTURE 314/617 1. Ensure that your product or service has a clear value proposition.* What do customers receive when exchanging money for your offer? 2. Decide on bonuses, incentives, or rewards for early buyers. How will they be rewarded for taking action? 3. Have you made the launch fun somehow? (Remember to think about nonbuyers as well as buyers. If people don't want to buy, will they still enjoy hearing or reading about the launch?) 4. If your launch is online, have you recorded a video or audio message to complement the written copy? 5. Have you built anticipation into the launch? Are prospects excited? 6. Have you built urgency—not the false kind but a real reason for timeliness—into the launch? 7. Publish the time and date of the launch in advance (if it's online, some 315/617 people will be camped out on the site an hour before, hitting the refresh button every few minutes). 8. Proofread all sales materials multiple times ... and get someone else to review them as well. 9. Check all Web links in your shopping cart or payment processor, and then double-check them from a different computer with a different browser. *This is superimportant! USP means "unique selling proposition" and refers to the one thing that distinguishes your offering from all others. Why should people pay attention to what you are selling? You must answer this question well. NEXT STEPS 316/617 10. If this is an online product, is it properly set up in your shopping cart or with PayPal? 11. Test every step of the order process repeatedly. Whenever you change any variable (price, order components, text, etc.), test it again. 12. Have you registered all the domains associated with your product? (Domains are cheap; you might as well get the .com, .net, .org, and any very similar name if available.) 13. Are all files uploaded and in the right place? 14. Review the order page carefully for errors or easy-to-make improvements. Print it out and share it with several friends for review, including a couple of people who don't know anything about your business. 15. Read important communications (launch message, order page, sales 317/617 page) out loud. You'll probably notice a mistake or a poorly phrased sentence you missed while reading it in your head. 16. Have you or your designer created any custom graphics for the offer, including any needed ads for affiliates or partners? MONEY MATTERS 17. Set a clear monetary goal for the launch. How many sales do you want to see, and how much net income? (In other words, what will success look like?) 18.

Advise the merchant account or bank of incoming funds.* 19. Create a backup plan for incoming funds if necessary (get an additional 318/617 merchant account, plan to switch all payments to PayPal, etc.). 20. Can you add another payment option for anyone who has trouble placing an order? 21. For a high-priced product, can you offer a payment plan? (Note: It's common to offer a slight discount for customers paying in full. This serves as an incentive for customers who prefer to pay all at once while providing an alternative for those who need to pay over time.) *Merchant accounts are paranoid about large sums of money arriving in a short period of time. If you don't give them a headsup, you might run into problems. THE NIGHT BEFORE 319/617 22. Clear as much email as possible in addition to any other online tasks so you can focus on the big day tomorrow. 23. Write a strong launch message to your lists of readers, customers, and/or affiliates. 24. Prepare a blog post and any needed social media posts (if applicable). 25. Set two alarm clocks to ensure that you're wide awake and available at least one hour before the scheduled launch. THE BIG MORNING 26. Schedule your launch time to suit your audience, not you. All things being equal, it's usually best to launch early in the morning, East Coast time. 320/617 27. Soft launch at least ten minutes early to make sure everything is working. It's better for you to find the problems than to have your customers find them! 28. Write the first three to five buyers to say thanks and ask, "Did everything go OK in the order process?" (Side benefit: These buyers are probably your biggest fans anyway, so they'll appreciate the personal check-in.) 29. As long as it's possible, send a quick personal note to every buyer in addition to the automated thank-you that goes out. (If it's not possible every time, do it as often as you can.) PROMOTION (CAN BE DONE ON THE DAY OF LAUNCH OR BEFORE) 321/617 30. Most important: Ask for help spreading the word. Many readers, prospects, and acquaintances will help by telling their friends and followers, but you have to ask them. 31. Write to affiliates with a reminder about the new offering. 32. Write to journalists or media contacts, if appropriate. 33. Post on Twitter, Facebook, LinkedIn, and any other social networks you already participate in. (It's not usually a good idea to join a new network just to promote something.) FOLLOW-UP (DO THIS IN ADVANCE) 34. Write the general thank-you message that all buyers will receive when purchasing. 322/617 35. If applicable, write the first message for your email follow-up series that buyers will receive. 36. Outline additional content for future communication and plan to schedule it after you recover from the launch. GOING ABOVE AND BEYOND 37. How can you overdeliver and surprise your customers with this product? Can you include additional deliverables or some kind of unadvertised benefit? 38. Is there anything special you can do to thank your customers? (For a high-price launch, send postcards to each buyer; for something extra, call a few of your customers on the phone.) 323/617 THE SECOND TO LAST STEP 39. Don't forget to celebrate. It's a big day that you've worked up to for a long time. Go out to your favorite restaurant, have a glass of wine, buy something you've had your eye on for a while, or otherwise do something as a personal reward. You've earned it.After the launch, you may be tempted to take a break, and you probably should do something to celebrate or rest. But make it a short break, because what happens next is important. During the launch process, a lot of people were paying attention to you. You've captured additional attention and 325/617 trust in the form of new customers. Other prospects who considered the offer didn't find it compelling at this time, but perhaps you can serve them with something else later. Always return to the all-important value question: How can you help people more? After their big launch, Adam and Karol went back to their own businesses and active lives. Adam used part of his proceeds to buy an RV and tour the country with his family, and Karol began an unconventional pilgrimage to visit every roller coaster in America. At the same time, they kept thinking ahead, planning another big project that would result in more sales, more customers, and more impact. KEY POINTS A good launch is like a Hollywood movie: You first hear about it far in advance, then you hear more about it 326/617 before the debut, then you watch as crowds of people anxiously queue up for the opening. A good launch blends strategy with tactics. Strategy refers to "why" questions such as story, offer, and longterm plan. Tactics refers to "how" questions such as timing, price, and specific pitch. A series of regular communications with prospects before the launch will help you re-create the Hollywood experience with an audience of any size. Tell a good story and be sure to consider the question of timeliness: Why should people care about your offer now? Use the Thirty-Nine-Step Product Launch Checklist as a model. Not every step may apply to you, and you may want to add steps of your own. 327/617 *Any analysis of "launch marketing" should give credit to the classic book Influence by Robert Cialdini, who was one of the first to study how consumers decide to make purchasing decisions. Jeff Walker, an entrepreneur and educator, is also well known for his work on product launches. †In addition to admitting a flaw or weakness, popular launch tactics include giving away a free copy of the product (turning it into a contest in which the aspiring winners compete for it publicly) and showing off a "sneak preview" of the product.

ADVERTISING IS LIKE SEX: ONLY LOSERS PAY FOR IT. "Good things happen to those who hustle." —ANAÏS NIN One hundred and twenty miles from Boston in rural New Hampshire, hundreds of artists and art lovers gather twice a year for a communal experience. Before coming to the area, many of them connect online, arranging car-share services and planning meetups. After settling into lakeside cottages, they learn from professionals and spend time with one another, old friends and new friends alike. It all started five years ago when Elizabeth MacCrellish was feeling isolated from other artists and wanted to create more of a sense of community in her rural area. "I invited my friends to join me for a weekend gathering centered on the arts," she explained. She planned for a few dozen people, but 135 showed up—mostly from the West Coast, far from the small New England group she had expected. Thus was born Squam Art Workshops, named after a lake in central New 332/617 Hampshire. After that initial gathering, Elizabeth repeated the experience, first on an annual basis and then twice a year. The audience is one-third professional artists and two-thirds "regular people" with day jobs who enjoy arts and crafts as a hobby. Hundreds of people now come to each sold-out gathering. As the workshops grew, Elizabeth pulled back to regroup. She did no traditional advertising of any kind, but more people kept signing up, strictly through word of mouth. In the third year of Squam, Elizabeth added an extra session in a new location ... and ended up regretting it. She was tired and decided to spend the next year "dialing back and taking stock." (She was initially reluctant about speaking to me for this book, but warmed up after I promised to write about the importance of community and relationships in her work.) 333/ 617 To register for Squam, attendees have to mail in their payment and information. This old-school system is one way that Elizabeth maintains a close connection with her tribe. She also carefully assigns people to specific cottages to ensure that newcomers are welcomed and plays Whack-A-Mole in delicately preventing cliques from forming. Invitations to take the Squam show on the road have arrived from the United Kingdom, Australia, and a dozen cities in North America; she always declines. "I'm not a businessperson," she says. "I just do what feels right, and it keeps getting more interesting." Elizabeth isn't against capitalism, but she wants to be sure that the growth of her business happens in a way that is comfortable for her. Midway through one of our phone calls, she likened her business model to the Amish, talking about a time when she visited a New England farmer's market. Self-reliance is a core value in most 334/617 Amish communities, and nearly everyone participates in commerce one way or another. But there is very little actual salesmanship; the molasses cookies and apple strudel sell themselves. Even for high-ticket items, prices are nonnegotiable—take it or leave it. Elizabeth began the workshops as a personal project that grew into a sustainable business. "I never set out to build something more than a structured encounter with friends," she says. Five years later, managing Squam—and making sure it grows in the right way—is Elizabeth's full-time work. After the initial success, at least eight different workshops offering similar retreats sprang up elsewhere, many of which were founded by previous attendees who sought to replicate the event in their own way. It didn't matter, though—the original Squam was the experience you just had to have for yourself. 335/617 What Is Hustling? This chapter is all about hustling, or how to get the word out about a project. What does hustling mean? There are a few ways to look at it, but I like the approach in this poster by Joey Roth: The distinction between the three icons represents the difference (and the likely success or lack of success) of a person or business hoping to promote something for sale. A 336/617 charlatan is all talk, with nothing to back up their claims. A martyr is all action with plenty of good work to talk about, but remains unable or unwilling to do the talking. A hustler represents the ideal combination: work and talk fused together. Being willing to promote in an authentic, non-sleazy manner is a core attribute of microbusiness success. As Elizabeth's story illustrates, sometimes the best hustling lies in creating a great offer and getting people to talk about it. In other cases, you want to have as many of the right kind of customers as possible, so there's nothing wrong with putting yourself forward. In my work, the hustler image on the right is pretty much what I try to do every day as a writer and entrepreneur: lots of creating and lots of connecting. The connecting (i.e., the talk) isn't always directly related to the work at hand—sometimes I'm supporting other people with their hustling—but on a good 337/617 day, there's plenty of creating and plenty of connecting. Another way to look at it is Style without substance = flash (Also, no one respects these people.) Substance without style = unknown (Everyone who knows these people respects them, but not many people know them.) Style with substance = impact (This is the goal.) When you're first getting started with a project, how do you go from martyr to 338/617 hustler? It's simple. First things first:

Take the time to make something worth talking about—don't be a charlatan. But then start with everyone you know and ask for their help. Make a list of at least fifty people and divide them into categories (colleagues from a former job, college friends, acquaintances, etc.). As soon as the project is good to go, at least in beta form, touch base by sending them a quick note. Here's a sample message: Hi [name], I wanted to quickly let you know about a new project I'm working on. It's called [name of business or project], and the goal is to [main benefit]. We hope to [big goal, improvement, or idea]. Don't worry, I haven't added you to any lists and I won't be spamming you, but if you like the idea and would like to help out, here's what you can do: 339/617 [Action Point 1] [Action Point 2] Thanks again for your time. Note that you're not sending mass messages or sharing anyone's private info with the world; each message is personal, although the content is largely the same. You're also not "selling" anyone on the project; you're just letting people know what you're up to and inviting them to participate further if they'd like to. The action points can vary, but they should probably relate to joining a contact list (this way you have their permission to touch base with them further) and letting other people know about the project. The next step is to incorporate hustling into your ongoing regular work. 340/ 617 If You Build It, They Might Come ... It might happen by magic, but you'll probably have to tell them about it. Even with Elizabeth MacCrellish's low-key Amish selling model, she still began her summer workshops by recruiting friends and supporters. This is where hustling comes in. If half the work is building the house and the other half is selling it, here's how a few other people sold it: We spent no money on advertising for the first five months we were open. Instead, we decided to allocate more than half of our opening costs to have a thirty-by-fifty-foot mural of a bright and colorful tree painted on the side of the stand-alone brick building we're in. That speaks way louder than any ad we could 341/617 ever place. —Karen Starr, Hazel Tree Interiors When I launched my membership program, I decided to start with some beta testers. I invited a hundred of my top prospects to try it out for the first two months before I opened membership ... but I didn't send them an email invite. Instead, I sent a hostage letter in a brown paper bag—folded and taped. People really got a kick out of it, and it worked! The letter led to a sales page with a personal video invite from me. —Alyson Stanfield, Art Biz Coach We initially imagined a community of thousands for our triathlon and Ironman distance training programs. In reality, fewer members meant deeper roots and a much more powerful experience for everyone. Unlike most programs, which try to keep pushing the 342/617 price higher, we reward our members by decreasing the price the longer they remain in the program. This is because we recognize that the more experience they have, the more they can help other members ... and the more active they are in recruiting new members to join as well. —Patrick McCrann, Endurance Nation

Jonathan is an ex-lawyer turned serial entrepreneur and author. Several presenters were having a group discussion on building a tribe of followers, and someone in the room asked a question about writing a book: "What's the first step?" 343/617 One of the speakers gave a list of four or five ideas, and then at the end he said, "Oh, when you plan to write a book, you should also think about what you have to say." Jonathan and I looked at each other with the same thought: "Uh, isn't that the first step?" Getting the message out about your business is like writing a book: Before you do anything else, think about what you have to say. What's the message? Why is it important now, and why will people want to know about it? The Strategic Giving Marketing Plan 344/617 Freely give, freely receive: It works. The more you focus your business on providing a valuable service and helping people, the more your business will grow. A number of the subjects of our case studies discussed how giving (often described in different ways but with the same meaning) has been a core value of their business. One of the best descriptions came from Megan Hunt, the Omaha dressmaker we met in Chapters 1 and 3: My marketing plan could be called strategic giving. When I launch a new line of dresses each year, I contact two or three influential bloggers and create a custom dress for them, which always brings in tons of new customers when they write about it. But most importantly, I turn my attention toward my clients. Often, I upgrade someone's shipping to overnight for free, or double someone's order, or include a copy of my favorite 345/617 book with a handwritten note. I like to package my products for shipping like a gift to my best friend. This strategy has been a huge contributor to fast growth and popularity in my industry. John Morefield, an unemployed architect during a time when jobs were scarce, set up shop in a Seattle farmer's market with a sign that read "5-Cent Architecture Advice." In exchange for a nickel, he would give advice on any problem that homeowners, real estate agents, or anyone else brought to him. The 5-cent advice was effectively a lead-generation program that might lead to additional business, but John legitimately and genuinely offered professional advice without the expectation of more than a nickel. As news spread of the 5-cent architect, John got free advertising from CNN, NPR, the BBC, and numerous other media outlets. Because of the attention—and new clients who came in through the farmer's 346/617 market—John is now a successful self-employed architect, a key distinction from his peers who are still trying to get hired at firms. Another way to practice strategic giving is to deliberately not take advantage of every opportunity to increase income. As my own business grew and I received more public attention, I began to receive a lot of requests for consulting sessions. I never really saw myself as a consultant, but I figured, Why not? If this is what people want, maybe I can do it. I created a page on my website, received plenty of interest, and conducted a few sessions as a test. Long story short, the whole thing felt false and inauthentic to me. I had helped lots of people with specific problems before, but not on a pay-per-time basis. When I talked with people who had paid for access to me, I felt physically ill. I realized my discomfort was in doing it for money, so I stopped. 347/617 I still do some limited consulting whenever I can, but now I do it for free. With the right people and on my own terms, I enjoy it—especially without the pressure of knowing they are paying me to deliver. I'm not always able to offer helpful advice, but I know that when I can be helpful, that person will likely be there for me at some point in the future. It's not about keeping score or trading favors on a quid pro quo basis; it's about genuinely caring and trying to improve someone else's life whenever you can.* Like any kind of marketing, this practice can be manipulated or abused. Tourists landing at the international terminal at LAX are met outside by friendly people with official-looking clipboards who offer to help with directions to the city. "Hey, where are you headed today?" they ask. "Can I be of assistance?" After they provide directions or answer questions from unsuspecting tourists, there's a pitch: "I'm working today on 348/617 behalf of a great organization. Can you help us out with a donation?" The implied message is, I just helped you ... now it's your turn. This isn't the kind of strategic giving that serves your interests well in the long term. The intention of the airport solicitors isn't to be helpful; they are merely using helpfulness as a tool to gain the trust of unsuspecting tourists. Strategic giving is about being genuinely, truly helpful without the thought of a potential payback. Building Relationships Is a Strategy, Not a Tactic Getting to know people, helping them, and asking for help yourself can take you far. This is not a non-profit endeavor; it often pays off in real money (with interest!) over 349/617 time. But it is a long-term strategy, not a short-term tactic to copy for quick success. Originally from South Dakota, Scott Meyer was working as a professor of peace studies in the Arctic Circle in Tromsø, Norway. (It was a long way from home, but the winters were familiar, he explains.) Meanwhile, his brother John was a consultant for Accenture in Minneapolis. Scott and John's migration away from their roots was normal—back in South Dakota, there was a clear divide between "people who stayed" and "people who got out." After a few years away, both Scott and John began to think of returning home with a mission. South Dakota wasn't a bad place, and there was a growing community of entrepreneurs there, many of whom had a problem. Small businesses in the region tended to be run by people with fewer technical skills than those in Minneapolis or Chicago, the region's main hubs. "Around here," Scott 350/617 told me, "people tend to use an old-school phone book to contact someone, and many business owners struggle with using email effectively. We knew we could help them grow their business." Scott and John founded 9 Clouds, a consultancy designed to help local businesses reach more customers through improved communication while gently educating them along the way. They give clients the fish by helping them reach new customers. Their clients are smart but worry about wasting time with new technology. 9 Clouds shows them the benefits of learning new tools that have been proved to be useful. The firm works hard to drum up business, but it focuses first on drumming up value. "Every chance we get, we talk and share information with others and support them in their work," Scott says. "It may not be a sale or partnership, but building those relationships today always comes back around for 351/617 new opportunities tomorrow." The community is noticing: 9 Clouds won second place in the South Dakota Governor's Giant Vision contest, and John was recognized by BusinessWeek as an up-and-coming leader. 9 Clouds did $45,000 in net income during the first six months of operation, $180,000 the next year, and is now on track to becoming a mid-six-figure business. First Say Yes, Then Say "Hell Yeah" Other business books will tell you about saying no: how you should guard your time, "only do what you're good at," and turn down far more requests than you accept. As a business grows over time and options for growth become more selective, that may indeed be useful advice. But what if you took the opposite approach, especially at first? What if you deliberately said yes to every request unless you 352/617 had a good reason not to? The next time someone asks for something, try saying yes and see what it leads to. Whatever success I've had in my own work thus far has always come from saying yes, not from saying no. Derek Sivers, who founded a business he later sold for $22 million (he then donated the money to a charitable trust), offers an alternative strategy: As things get busy, evaluate your options according to the "hell yeah" test. When you're presented with an opportunity, don't just think about its merits or how busy you are. Instead, think about how it makes you feel. If you feel only so-so about it, turn it down and move on. But if the opportunity would be exciting and meaningful—so much so that you can say "hell yeah" when you think about it—find a way to say yes. 353/617 Give Something Away and Watch People Jump Are the crickets chirping in your business? There's nothing like a contest or giveaway to get people engaged. I regularly receive 1,000 comments or more on a single Facebook post giving away a $15 book. I used to wonder, "What is the last person thinking? 'Nine hundred ninety-nine people have entered, but maybe I'll be the lucky one'?" Over time I realized that it wasn't so much about winning as it was about social participation. If all your friends are putting their names down, why wouldn't you do the same thing?† The difference between a contest and a giveaway is fairly simple: A contest involves some kind of competition or judging, whereas a giveaway is a straight-up free offer provided to winners through random entries. There are pros and cons to each: A contest 354/617 usually requires more work for both the aspiring winners and the business hosting the contest, but it can generate more interest. A giveaway is quick and easy and can generate a large quantity of entries, but since there's usually nothing to do other than put your name down, the typical giveaway doesn't create much real engagement. For the best results, experiment over time with both methods. The $10,000, Ten-Hour Marketing and Sex Experiment "In the future, marketing will be like sex: Only the losers pay for it." 355/617 This widely circulated statement first appeared in a December 2010 article in Fast Company magazine. Guess what? The future is here. It may not be completely for losers, but the role of paid advertising in marketing has long since changed. The vast majority of case-study subjects I talked with built their customer base without any paid advertising at all; they did so largely through word of mouth. The One-Page Promotion Plan Goal: To actively and effectively recruit new prospects to your business without getting overwhelmed.

Do we have a clear winner? I think so, but with a couple of disclaimers. First, one could say that I had access to relationships that others don't have and those relationships were what determined the high hour-perhustle value. This may be partly true. However, the whole point of hustling is to put your relationships to good use, whatever they are. Not everyone may be able to earn 359/617 $756 per hustling hour. However, some situations could have produced an even higher hustling value. It is also true that hustling time is not unlimited. If I had $100,000 to spend instead of $10,000, the situation might indeed be different. Combining hustling with paid advertising (again, carefully selected) could be a viable option for some. The point is that hustling can take you far. When you're thinking about how to get the word out and build your business, think about hustling first and paid advertising later (if at all). One objection to the hustling and relationship-building strategies described in this chapter is that they take time. Well, of course they do—they're a big part of your work. But if you're worried about spending all day on a social networking site, you can avoid doing that by sticking to a series of quick check-ins. I maintain a text file of 360/617 information and links to share, and a couple of times a day I go online and post something. At the same time, I scan all the messages that have come through for me and respond to as many as possible. Although I sometimes spend more time out of habit or interest, the whole process doesn't have to take any longer than ten to fifteen minutes a day. The point is to do what makes sense to you. Get up in the morning and get to work. Make something worth talking about and then talk about it. Who do you know? How can they help? And of course, the answer lies in being incredibly helpful yourself. KEY POINTS If you're not sure where to spend your business development time, spend 50 percent on creating and 50 percent on connecting. The most powerful 361/617 channel for getting the word out usually starts with people you already know. If you build it, they might come ... but you'll probably need to let them know what you've built and how to get there. When you're first getting started, say yes to every reasonable request. Become more selective (consider the "hell yeah" test) as you become more established. Use the One-Page Promotion Plan to maintain a regular schedule of connecting with people as you also spend time building other parts of your business. *I use this example to illustrate that having a good opportunity doesn't mean you 362/617 should pursue it. I'm not opposed to consulting in general. It just wasn't a good fit for me. †I thought 1,000 entries for a basic giveaway was pretty good until Jaden Hair from Steamy Kitchen told me she receives as many as 50,000 entries for her giveaways, all for a prize as simple as a set of cookbooks. 363/617 365/617 UNCONVENTIONAL FUNDRAISING FROM KICKSTARTER TO

UNLIKELY CAR LOANS. "Money is better than poverty, if only for financial reasons." —WOODY ALLEN Naomi Dunford was a teenage mother and a high-school dropout. By the time she was pregnant with her second child, she was living in a homeless shelter. After making it out of the shelter by working odd jobs, Naomi was determined to improve her circumstances however she could. Despite the obvious disadvantages—being a mom at age seventeen, leaving high school—she also had a few things going for her. Her dad had built several businesses from scratch, imparting knowledge and experience along the way. Her mom was a marketer. And back in the day, her grandfather was in advertising. In other words, marketing was in Naomi's blood, so it wasn't a huge stretch for her to imagine herself in a different life. 367/617 Without sharing her background with potential customers at first, Naomi opened a consulting company called IttyBiz. Tag line: "Marketing for businesses without marketing departments." Later she would add products, courses, and referrals to other professionals, but Naomi started with a single consulting service: the service of brainstorming. Over the course of an hour and for an initial fee of $250, she would evaluate marketing ideas and provide feedback on ways to improve them. Nothing more, nothing less. You might wonder how many people pay for this service (answer: a lot), and whether it's worth it (answer: keep reading). Naomi is originally from London, Ontario, but I met her in London, England, where she was living near her mother. While riding the tube around the city and wandering through an outdoor clothing market, I asked for her advice on a situation in my business. She listened for two minutes and asked a few 368/617 clarifying questions. Then, without much of a pause, she said, "Here's what you should do," and gave me a list of specific actions and ideas while I frantically wrote them down. I took her advice and spent a few hours applying it in my next project. As a result, I made at least $15,000 more over the next year because of her action list. (I didn't pay Naomi's fee of $250, but I hope she appreciates this extended testimonial.) As she sharpened her message and connected with more people, the business grew. At the end of her first full year, Naomi published a short video explaining how she had earned almost $200,000 so far. This came as a big surprise to the online world, because Naomi wasn't known very well—she wasn't an Internet celebrity, she didn't have a million followers—and in fact, a lot of people who stumbled upon her website were immediately turned off by the coarse language and her distinct "call it like I see it" style. Article 369/ 617 titles included "What to Do When You're Scared Shitless" and "Moral of the Story: Topless Edition (with Photos)." But Naomi's audience wasn't put off at all. One of the things Naomi does well is continuously remind her clients about the need for actually making money. This may sound simple, but busy entrepreneurs can easily become overwhelmed with all kinds of projects and tasks that have nothing to do with making money. Putting the focus on income and cash flow—measuring everything else against those standards—ensures that a business remains healthy. Here's how Naomi explains it: Remember that the goal of business is profit. It's not being liked, or having a huge social media presence, or having amazing products that nobody buys. It is not having a beautiful website, or perfectly crafted email newsletters, or an incredibly popular blog. In larger 370/617 businesses, this is called accountability to shareholders. Business is not a popularity contest. The CEO doesn't get away with saying, "But look at all these people who like us on Facebook!" Shareholders will not accept that. You are the majority shareholder in your business, and you have to protect your investment. You have to make sure that your recurring activities are as directly tied to making money as possible. There's nothing wrong with having a hobby, but if you want to call it a business, you have to make money. Naomi is right: On any given day, there are all kinds of things you can do that have nothing to do with making money—but you should be careful about those distractions, because without the money, there is no business. Many aspiring business owners make two common, related mistakes: thinking too much about where to get money to start their 371/617 project and thinking too little about where the business income will come from. Fixing these problems (or avoiding them in the first place) requires a simple solution: Spend as little money as possible and make as much money as you can. Part I: Hang On to Your Wallet Inspired by her second child, Heather Allard invented two wearable baby blankets that became a worldwide sensation. The blankets were featured on Access Hollywood and sold in more than 200 stores, and it was all she could do to keep up. After the birth of her third child in 2006, Heather sold the products to a larger company in order to spend more time with the family. Success! She wasn't done with entrepreneurship, 372/617 though; the next step was to help other women, especially mothers, learn to do what she had accomplished. She started her next business, The Mogul Mom, with the goal of mentoring busy women who wanted to create more independence through a small business. The baby blanket business was highly successful, but it also became a high-spending operation as the product took off. On reflection, Heather realized that she would need to run her second act differently: I had gotten into a ton of start-up debt with my product company and spent thousands on things that I absolutely did not need (big advertising campaigns, a custom e-commerce website, a publicist, etc.), and I definitely did not want to do that with The Mogul Mom. Therefore, when I spend money on The Mogul Mom, it's for things that will continue to build my brand and boost my sales while allowing me ample time with my 373/617 family—things like Web design, payments to a small group of contributors, or a new computer. The distinction Heather points out at the end is important: She's not reluctant to spend money on things that will (1) build her brand and (2) boost her sales. This kind of spending can grow a business. If you can spend $100 and create $200 in value from it, why wouldn't you? It's the other kind of spending—the unproven ad campaigns and unneeded custom websites—that Heather learned to stay away from. Lesson: Spend only on things that have a direct relationship to sales. The stories from Naomi and Heather illustrate two important principles, both related to money. The first principle is that a business should always focus on profit. (Always remember, no money, no business.) The second principle is that borrowing money or 374/617 investing a lot of money to start a business is completely optional. This doesn't mean that there are no examples of businesses that have done well through traditional methods; it just means that borrowing is no longer essential. Don't think of it as a necessary evil; think of it as an undesirable option to be pursued only if you have a way to limit risk or are sure you know what you're doing. If you don't know what you're doing when you're starting out, that's OK, you're in good company. Almost every entrepreneur pursues projects with a much-trial-and-mucherror system. But since it's easy to try things without losing your shirt, why seek investment and go into debt for something that may or may not work? It's completely possible to start on a very low budget without hindering the odds of success. Consider the reports of many in our study group: 375/617 • Chelly Vitry started a business as a tour guide for Denver food lovers, connecting them to restaurants and food producers. Startup costs: $28. Recent annual income: $60,000. • Michael Trainer started a media production company for $2,500, the cost of a nice camera, which he later sold to recoup the cost in full. He then went on to work with two Nobel Prize winners: the Acumen fund and the Carter Center. • Tara Gentile started her small publishing business for $80, hoping to earn enough money to be able to stay home with her daughter. One year later, she earned enough money ($75,000) that her husband could stay home as well. • Chris Dunphy and Cherie Ve Ard started Technomadia, a software consultancy for health-care providers, for $125. The business now produces net 376/617 income of more than $75,000 as Chris and Cherie travel the world. • A former store designer for Starbucks, Charlie Pabst needed a $3,500 computer for his Seattle design business. But after he had the powerful machine and a $100 business license, he was good to go. Annual income: just under $100,000. These stories are not outliers. When I began the research for this book, I received more than 1,500 nominations, with similar stories from all over the world. You can see the range of startup costs from our study group in the graph below. The average cost of the initial investment was $610.60.* 377/617 You might expect that certain types of businesses are easier to start with limited funds, and that is correct. It's also the whole point: Since it's so much easier to start a microbusiness, why do something different unless or until you know what you're doing? Small is beautiful, and all things considered, small is often better. 378/617 Unconventional Fundraising from Kickstarter to Car Loans What if you've thought it through and you do need to raise money somehow? Whenever possible, the best option is your own savings. You'll be highly invested in the success of the project, and you won't be in debt to anyone else. But if this isn't possible, you can also consider "crowdraising" funds for your project through a service such as Kickstarter.com. Shannon Okey did this with a project to boost her craft publishing business. She asked for $5,000 and received $12,480 in twenty days thanks to a nice video and well-written copy. Before going to the masses, Shannon went to her bank for a small loan. Her business was profitable and promising, with several new publications coming out over the next year. This wasn't just any bank. It was a community bank in Ohio where she had an excellent personal and business relationship. 379/617 Shannon was a meticulous bookkeeper with a conservative attitude toward finances; she brought along detailed sales figures and a clear plan to repay the money. Unfortunately, when she mentioned "craft publishing," she was dead in the water. "They looked at me like I was a silly, silly woman who couldn't possibly know anything about running a business," she said. The rejection turned into an opportunity. Taking the project on Kickstarter generated both funds and widespread interest in the project. Nearly three hundred backers came through with donations ranging from $10 to $500, leaving the project fully funded with capital to spare. Oh, and Shannon was not one for going quietly. After she reached the $10,000 level in her Kickstarter campaign, she printed out the front page of the site, wrapped the page around a lollipop, and sent it off to the bank's underwriters. "I think they got the message," she says. 380/617 As I collected stories for the book, I was mostly interested in people who avoided debt completely. But I did hear two fun stories about borrowing money that I thought were worth sharing. On a flight from Hong Kong to London, Emma Reynolds and her future business partner Bruce Morton had an idea for a consultancy that would work with big companies to improve their staffing and resourcing. They calculated that they would need at least $17,000 to start the new firm. There was just one problem ... or actually, two: Emma was twenty-three and unlikely to get a business loan, and Bruce was going through a divorce and would also be a poor candidate for a business loan. Somewhere during the twelve-hour flight, one of them realized that although they couldn't get a business loan, they could probably get a car loan. Bruce proceeded to do just that, borrowing $17,000 for a car and then investing the 381/617 funds in the business with Emma instead. They paid back the car loan within ten months, and the bank never found out that there was no actual car. Now the firm employs twenty people, is highly profitable, and has multiple offices in four countries.† Finally, here's a fun story from Kristin McNamara, who started a California gym specializing in climbing: To fund the latest incarnation of the gym, we called upon the community to "invest" in us, much like a three-year CD. We offered 3 percent above prime, which is more than you could get then or now, and people I've never even seen at the facility came up with the cash to get it started. My partner and I, the founders, are the only paid full-time staff, and we just hired someone to manage the volunteers for us for a small 382/617 stipend. Our community fundraising project brought in $80,000. As these lessons in improvisation show, if you need to raise money, there's more than one way to do it.

Make More Money (Three Key Principles to Focus on Profit) As we've seen, it's usually much more important to focus your efforts on making money as soon as possible than on borrowing startup capital. In different ways, many of our case studies focused on three key principles that helped them become profitable (either profitable in the first place or more profitable as the business grew). I've noticed that the same thing holds true in my businesses. The more I focus on these things, the better off I am. In short, they are as follows: 1. Price your product or service in relation to the benefit it provides, not the cost of producing it. 2. Offer customers a limited range of prices. 3. Get paid more than once for the same thing. We'll look at each of them below. Principle 1: Base Prices on Benefits, Not Costs .

we looked at benefits versus features. Remember that a feature is descriptive ("These clothes fit well and look nice") and a benefit is the value someone receives from the item in question ("These clothes make you feel healthy and attractive"). We tend to default to talking about features, but since most purchases are emotional decisions, it's much more persuasive to talk about benefits. 385/617 Just as you should usually place more emphasis on the benefits of your offering than on the features, you should think about basing the price of your offer on the benefit—not the actual cost or the amount of time it takes to create, manufacture, or fulfill what you are selling. In fact, the wrong way to decide on pricing is to think about how much time it took to make it or how much your time is "worth." How much your time is worth is a completely subjective matter. Bill Clinton makes as much as $200,000 for a single one-hour speech. You might not want to pay Clinton (or any president) $200,000 to speak at your next family pizza night, but for whatever reason, some companies are willing to invest that much. When you base your pricing on the benefits you provide, be prepared to stand your ground, because some people will always complain about the price being too high no matter what it is. Almost none of the people I 386/617 met with talked about thriving in their new businesses because they always offered the lowest price. What works for Walmart probably won't work for you or me. Very few businesses will succeed on the basis of such a cutthroat strategy; that's why competing on value is so much better.‡ Gary Leff, the frequent flyer guy who helps busy people book their vacations, charges a flat rate for the service ($250 at press time). Sometimes it takes him a fair amount of work to research and book the trip, but other times he gets lucky and it can take as little as two minutes of research and a ten-minute phone call. Gary knows that the people he's booking the trip for don't care whether it takes ten minutes or two hours; they are paying for his expertise in getting the flights they want. Time cost: variable, but averages thirty minutes per booking 387/ 617 Benefit: first-class and business-class tickets for worldwide vacations Cost: $250 (key point: does not vary based on time) Tsilli Pines, who makes contemporary Judaic stationery, created a Haggadah (a booklet used at the Passover meal) that most frequently is sold in bulk. Single copies are available, but far more people choose a bundle of five or ten. Materials cost: $3 each Benefit: nicely designed memento for families to use when observing Passover Cost to buyers: $14 each (key point: not directly related to the materials cost) We could trace this theme throughout almost every story in the book. Some examples are even more extreme, especially in information publishing. Every day, people purchase $1,000+ courses that cost virtually nothing 388/617 to distribute; all the costs are in development and initial marketing. When you think about the price of a new project, ask yourself: "How will this idea improve my customers' lives, and what is that improvement worth to them?" Then set your price accordingly, while still being clear that the offer is a great value. Principle 2: Offer a (Limited) Range of Prices Choosing an initial price for your service that is based on the benefit provided to customers is the most important principle to ensure profitability. But to create optimum profitability or at least to build more cushion into your business model, you'll next want to present more than one price for your offer. This practice typically makes a huge difference to the bottom line, because it allows you to increase income without increasing your customer base. 389/617 Look at Apple, which famously produces very few products and doesn't bother to compete on price. Even though there are few products, there is always a range of prices and options. You can buy the latest iGadget or computer at the entry level (which, knowing Apple, isn't cheap), one or more midlevels, or one "superuser" high-end level. The leadership team at Apple—and anyone using a similar model—knows that this kind of pricing allows the company to earn much more money than it otherwise would. This is the case partly because some people will always choose the biggest and best, even if the biggest and best is much more expensive than the regular version. These kinds of sales will increase the overall selling price. Also, having a high-end version creates an "anchor price." When we see a superhigh price, we tend to consider the lower price as much more reasonable ... thus creating a fair bargain in our minds. The internal thinking 390/617 goes like this: "Wow, $2 million for the latest MacBook is a lot, but hey, the $240,000 model is almost as good." Let's look at an example of two pricing options: one offered at a set price and one on a tiered structure. Keep in mind that you can substitute any prices here to apply this to another business. Option 1: The World's Greatest Widget Price: $87 Option 1 is simple and presents the choice as follows: Do you want to buy this widget or not? Here's an alternative that is almost always better: Option 2: The World's Greatest Widget Choose Your Preferred Widget Option Below 1. Greatest Widget Ever, Budget Version. Price: $87 391/617 2. Greatest Widget Ever, Even Better Version. Price: $129 3.

Greatest Widget Ever, Exclusive Premium Version. Price: $199 Option 2 presents the choice as follows: Which widget package would you like to buy? Chances are, some consumers will choose the Exclusive Premium Version, others will choose the Budget Version, but most will opt for the Even Better Version. You don't want to go too crazy, but you can experiment with this model to add yet another tier in the form of a "really premium version" at the top or a "freemium" version at the bottom that lets customers try part of the service without paying anything.

The key to this strategy is to offer a limited range of prices: not so many as to create confusion but enough to provide buyers with a legitimate choice. Notice the important distinction that naturally happens when you offer a choice: Instead of asking them whether they'd like to buy your widget, you're asking which widget they would like to buy. 393/617 Options for creating a price range include: Super-Amazing Version (Gold, First Class, Premium), Product + Setup Help (the same thing sold with special help), and any kind of exclusivity or limited-quantity selection. You can literally sell the same product at different prices with no other change. As long as you don't imply that there are added features in the higher-price version, it's not unethical. Big companies do it all the time; it's how cell phone carriers, hotels, and airlines make money. To reduce confusion, though, it's better if you can add something with real value to each higher-level version of the offer. Principle 3: Get Paid More Than Once The final strategy for making sure your business gets off to a good start is to ensure that your payday doesn't come along only once—you'd much rather have repeated paydays, from the same customers, over and 394/617 over on a reliable basis. You may have heard of the terms continuity program, membership site, and subscriptions. They all mean roughly the same thing: getting paid over and over by the same customers, usually for ongoing access to a service or regular delivery of a product. Back when people read newspapers (actual paper ones), they would subscribe to have them delivered to their doorstep or office. These days, iTunes and Netflix offer subscriptions to your favorite TV show or a regular series of movies. The utility company has a recurring billing program; every month you pay it for the ability to turn the lights on and heat your water. For decades, the Book of the Month Club (in various forms) has delivered new books to its members on a recurring basis. Almost any business can create a continuity program. Speaking of book clubs, there is also a Pickle of the Month Club, an Olive Oil 395/617 of the Month Club, and a Dog Treat of the Month Club. In Portland, my friend Jessie operates a Cupcake of the Month club. If you like bonsai plants but aren't able to keep them alive very long, the Bonsai of the Month Club is for you, but you'll have to choose among four competing companies that offer different versions.§ Why is getting paid over and over such a big deal? First, because it can bring in a lot of money, and second, because it's reliable income that isn't dependent on external factors. Let's run some quick numbers, assuming you offer a subscription service for $20 a month: 100 subscribers at $20 = monthly revenue of $2,000 or yearly revenue of $24,000 1,000 subscribers at $20 = monthly revenue of $20,000 or yearly revenue of $240,000 396/ 617 You can tweak either the number of subscribers or the price of the recurring service to see dramatic improvements. For example, adding 50 more subscribers generates $1,000 more per month, or $12,000 more per year. Raising the price to $25 a month with a subscriber base of 1,000 generates $5,000 more per month, or $60,000 more per year. Adjusting both options—attracting more subscribers and raising the price—generates an even greater increase. (Note: Don't get too hung up on the exact numbers here. The point is that in almost every case, a recurring billing model will produce much more income over time than will a single-sale model.) Even better, after you attract customers to a recurring model (and ensure that you keep them very happy), they are much more likely to purchase other things from you. Brian Clark is an expert at continuity programs, 397/617 having created a true empire from the art of moving customers from one-time purchases into recurring subscriptions. Here's what he has to say about this process: Our general model is to offer a varied line of complementary products and services. Some are one-time purchases that begin the customer's relationship with us, and others are software and hosting services that involve recurring monthly or quarterly billing. While we strive to build all our product lines, the general strategy is to move as many one-time purchase customers as possible to a more lucrative recurring service. For example, our StudioPress division sells WordPress themes (designs) to online publishers and has over 50,000 customers. These are one-time purchases, although many people end up coming back to purchase additional design 398/617 options. We also provide ongoing support to all of these customers. Over time, we offer our Scribe SEO service or our new WordPress hosting service to our StudioPress customers, which transfers the nature of the relationship into one that is much more economically beneficial for us. But the secret ingredient to this migration is the trust we've developed with those customers from the initial one-time purchase. We treat people well, period. This means before an initial sale is made with our free content, and even better once they become a customer, no matter the size of the purchase. The key to this model is not market share. It's share of the customer. And to gain more of each customer's budget, you first have to zealously treat every customer as a "best" customer, no 399/ 617 matter which ones actually end up becoming the proverbial "customer for life." The most important thing Brian says here is in the last paragraph: "It's not market share; it's share of the customer." Like many of the people in this book, Brian doesn't spend much time worrying about what other people are doing—he worries about improving his customers' lives through helpful services. As a result, he gets paid over and over again. Getting paid more than once is great, but be aware of a couple of concerns. First, many consumers are wary of subscriptions, because they worry that they'll keep getting billed for the service after they stop using it or that it will be a big hassle to cancel. (To deal with the second problem, I created a "no pain in the ass" cancellation button for my site.) To encourage broad waves of initial 400/617 sign-ups, many programs offer free or lowcost trials to get new prospects in the door. This works, but there is often a huge dropout rate after the trial ends. Just be aware of this, and make sure you continue to provide value as long as people are paying. The $35,000 Experiment One day I received an intriguing message from one of my customers, who successfully built a new business over the past year and is now making an average of $4,000 to $5,000 a month from his industry. In the email he told me about the results from an interesting experiment. I asked if I could share the results with other customers (and eventually put it in this book), but he was concerned about his competition learning how easy it was to increase profits. He finally said I could share this information as long as I didn't unmask him. Here's his follow-up note to me with the details: 401/ 617 As mentioned yesterday, I wanted to check something in my product. I set up an experiment that only tested a single variable: price. On one sales page I had $49, and on another $89. Nothing was different at all—same copywriting, same order process, same fulfillment. To be honest, I thought that $49 was a better price, but I had set that price somewhat arbitrarily. Guess what? Conversion went down ... slightly. But overall income actually increased! This is what really surprised me. I discovered that I could sell less but actually make more money due to the higher price. I then decided to test it at $99. Why not, right? But from $89 to $99 I saw a bit more of a drop-off, and I got worried. I'm now back at $89, and even with the lower conversion factored in, I worked out that I've given myself a $24 raise on every product that sells. These days we 402/617 are selling at least four copies a day. If everything else remains consistent, I'll make $35,040 more this year ... all from one test. I've decided to do some more tests. :) Isn't that interesting? Here's how the numbers break down in this example: Note that if the conversion rate dropped further, say, to 1 percent instead of 1.5 percent, the price change would not be a good idea. But in some cases, the news is actually better than it is in this example: When you raise the price, you don't always see a drop in 403/617 the conversion rate. If you successfully raise prices without lowering the conversion rate, it's time to order the champagne. The point is that experimenting with price is one of the easiest ways to create higher profits (and sustainability) in a business. If you're not sure what price to use for something, try a higher one without changing anything else and see what happens. You might find yourself with an extra $24 per sale—maybe more. You Have More Than You Think After I met Naomi Dunford in England, I saw her again a year later in Austin, Texas, where we were both in town for the South by 404/617 Southwest (SXSW) Interactive Festival. Earlier that day, she had run into a money problem. The problem wasn't a lack of money; her business was doing extremely well, on the way to breaking the $1 million a year barrier. The problem was access to money. Because Naomi is Canadian but has lived in the United States, the United Kingdom, and elsewhere, she often has issues with her PayPal account being closed as she travels the world, leaving her with plenty of funds in the account but no way to access them. In this case, she needed $900 to register for a conference that had just been announced ... and would sell out quickly. What to do? Naomi realized that although she didn't have $900 with her, she probably knew someone in Austin willing to loan her the use of a credit card so she could register. Asking around, she found three volunteers in the 405/617 first two minutes who all said, "Sure, no problem. Here's my card." As we talked about it further, we realized that most of us have access to all kinds of financial and social capital that we don't usually think about but could call upon easily if necessary. If one guy hadn't lent her his credit card, someone else would have. The trick was that she had to be willing to think creatively. If she had just said, "Oh, I guess I can't register now," she would have missed out. Being able to think of different means to achieve her goal led Naomi out of the homeless shelter a decade ago and to the highly successful IttyBiz. "Right before starting," she said, "I was taking the bus to work, making 55 percent of a $30,000 income. My phone was cut off from lack of payment. Now I employ six people and help hundreds of others become self-employed." We all have more than we think. Let's put it to good use.

TWEAKING YOUR WAY TO THE BANK: HOW SMALL ACTIONS CREATE BIG INCREASES IN INCOME. "Remind people that profit is the difference between revenue and expense. This makes you look smart." —SCOTT ADAMS Over and over, the subjects of our case studies discussed how growing the business wasn't nearly as hard as starting the business. "It took a while to find something that worked," a common statement began, "but once we were rolling, we gained traction and quickly took off." As we saw with Nick's story in Chapter 6—the guy who was thrilled about selling his first $50 print—sometimes the first sale is the hardest but also the most rewarding. Several others said much the same thing: "The day I got my first sale was when I knew the business was going to work out. Everything that came afterward was reinforcement of the initial success." 414/617 I call it "the first $1.26 is the hardest" principle, because one day many years ago I made my first $1.26 with a new project while on a layover in Brussels. I couldn't afford a single Belgian waffle on the day's take, but I had a good feeling about the future. In this chapter, we'll look at ways to move on up by increasing income in an existing business. How does this happen? No doubt there are a few different factors. Momentum is important, as is the ongoing attention of the business owner. The longer a microbusiness is around, with customers and onlookers saying good things about it, the more the word will spread. In addition to these natural factors, a series of small, regular actions is all it takes for many businesses to go from zero to hero in a short period of time. These actions are called tweaks. Nev Lapwood was a classic ski bum. He lived in Whistler, British Columbia, and worked 415/617 "off and on" in restaurants at night while snowboarding during the day. Life was basic but good ... until the limited employment ended when Nev was laid off. Needing to make ends meet, he began offering snowboard lessons, a part-time gig that was highly valued by his students. Teaching students in person on the Whistler slopes was fun and rewarding, but it also had a number of built-in unavoidable limitations: lots of competition, relatively few clients, and limited times of year when he could work. Nev knew that people all over the world wanted to learn about snowboarding—what if he could teach them all virtually, without needing to be in the same place? Getting his act together, Nev worked with a couple of close friends to create Snowboard Addiction, a worldwide series of snowboarding tutorials. It was an instant hit, drawing customers from twenty countries and making $30,000 416/617 in year one—not bad for a ski bum. (Since Nev had never been that focused on making money, that was the highest annual income he had ever had at that point.) The next year, he put more thought into the business, scaling up with affiliates and a broader range of products. The result: just under $100,000 in net income. Nev was still on the slopes during the day but worked closely with his new partners during the downtimes to scale the business even further. The next plan was foreign language translation: Snowboard Addiction went out around the world in nine languages, with more versions scheduled to roll out based on customer demand. Naturally, the growing business had its challenges. An untrained and accidental entrepreneur, Nev had to learn a lot about strategy, accounting, and marketing. Stickers that were ordered from China arrived months late and in an unusable condition. Just two years in, however, the business was 417/617 on track to earn at least $300,000. As we've heard over and over in other stories, Nev speaks proudly of his new independence. "Frankly, starting this business after being laid off has been the best decision of my life," he says. "The greatest benefit has been the freedom and ability to do what I like. My plan is to travel for six months of every year and run the business for the other six months of each year." And of course, while he's running the business, he still finds plenty of time to hit the slopes. Tweaking Your Way to the Bank: The Big Picture The not-so-secret to improving income in an existing business is through tweaks: small changes that create a big impact. If a product typically has a 1.5 percent conversion rate 418/617 and you increase the rate to 1.75 percent, the difference adds up to a lot of money as time goes on. If a business normally attracts four new customers a day and begins attracting five, the impact is tremendous. Not only is the business now earning 25 percent more income, it has diversified its customer base.* If you grow your traffic a little and also increase your conversion rate a little while also increasing the average sales price a little ... your business grows a lot. These are the most important areas on which to focus your tweak efforts, so let's look at them closely. INCREASE TRAFFIC. Whether you have a website or a storefront, without people who regularly drop by to see your offer, you have no business. Traffic means attention. How much attention is your business getting? I heard from a new business owner who was disappointed in the results of her first 419/617 product launch because only four people had purchased. "How many prospects were on your list?" I asked. "I'm not entirely sure," she said. "Maybe one hundred?" I said I was impressed, because 4 percent is a great conversion rate for many businesses. The problem wasn't getting more of her limited audience to purchase. It was getting more of an audience in the first place. The best thing to do in this situation is to focus on increasing traffic, thereby bringing in more potential customers.† INCREASE CONVERSION. Once you have a stable base of attention (whether measured in site traffic or another way), you'll want to look closely at the conversion rate: the percentage of prospects who become customers. The classic way to increase the conversion rate is through testing by measuring one copywriting attempt (or offer, or headline, or 420/617 something else) against another and going with the winner. Traffic ? A/B test ? compare results After you have a winner, you move on to another test, always challenging the "champion" against another idea. (Google Optimizer allows you to do this for free.) This can indeed be a good strategy. One tip, however: It may be more important to pay close attention to where customers come from than to what you can do to convert them once they arrive. "Testing is important, but it pales in comparison to the traffic source," author and entrepreneur Ramit Sethi told me. "People love to spend time split-testing headlines, copy, graphics, even tiny boxes. They can usually achieve greater returns by focusing on the source." 421/617 INCREASE AVERAGE SALES PRICE. If you can increase the average sales price per order, this will increase your bottom line, just as increasing traffic or conversion will. You can do this most easily through upsells, crosssells, and sales after the sale. If you shop on Amazon.com, you've probably seen its "related items" and "customers who bought this item also bought these items" features. These features are highlighted (and widely replicated elsewhere) for a simple reason: They work extremely well. The difference between upsells, cross-sells, and sales after the sale is illustrated below: 422/617 (A good shopping cart and payment processor will allow you to add these items easily. If yours doesn't, it's time to change services.) SELL MORE TO EXISTING CUSTOMERS. Your existing customers are likely to respond to sales, promotions, or additional offers of any kind. By reaching out to them more frequently, you'll almost certainly bring in additional income. You'll want to be careful about not pushing them too much, but the key is balance: Your customers want to hear from you. They have given you money in exchange for something they value. Make it easy for them to do so again and again. 423/617 Tweaking Your Way to the Bank: All the Details When I talked with business owners about the kind of tweaks they worked on, many said things such as "The most important thing is to keep taking action." Others mentioned setting aside half an hour every morning to work strictly on business improvements before diving in to the actual running of the business. All of this sounds good, but it also begs the question: If you decide to take action, what does action look like? How do you spend your daily half hour on business improvements? Here are some common examples of action-based tweaking. CREATE A HALL OF FAME. Shine a spotlight on your best customers; let them tell their 424/617 own stories about how they've been helped through your business. It helps to provide a variety of stories, as people will relate to different perspectives and backgrounds. This provides "social proof" that your product or service works for all kinds of people. INSTITUTE A NEW UPSELL. Adding a good upsell offer—or several—is probably the easiest and most powerful strategy you can use to ramp up your average order size. Some business owners are initially apprehensive about upsells, not wanting to apply a highpressure or "sleazy" technique. But a good upsell isn't sleazy at all; it's contextually appropriate and inspires appreciation from customers. "Wow, thanks for the offer!" is a common response. Think about going to a restaurant where you hadn't planned on eating dessert, but the waiter's recommendation of the chocolate bread pudding is so compelling that you have to try it ... and it's 425/617 delicious. You were successfully upsold, and you were happy about it. The confirmation page that appears after an online purchase is one of the best and most underused places for an upsell offer. Right after a customer has purchased, they are highly inclined to purchase something else. Make a strong offer here, and your conversion rate can be 30 percent or higher. ENCOURAGE REFERRALS. Most people know that word of mouth is the greatest source of new business, but instead of waiting for something to happen, you can encourage your customers to spread the word.‡ When asking for referrals, it helps to be specific: "Can you send our offer to three of your friends?" or "Can you 'like' our page on Facebook?" might be a good fit. Again, the confirmation page after a purchase is a good place to do this, in addition to a mailing sent a few days later. 426/617 HOLD A CONTEST. As mentioned in Chapter 9, some people become extremely motivated about contests and giveaways. Find a way to give away a prize and invite people to compete. The bigger the prize or the more unique the contest, the better. You may not make a ton of sales from a contest, but it will bring you more attention and a greater audience for future sales.

INTRODUCE THE MOST POWERFUL GUARANTEE YOU CAN THINK OF. Most businesses have boring guarantees: If you don't like this, you'll get your money back. But when we buy something, our money isn't all we're concerned with. We're also concerned about time and validation. If I have to return something, will it be a pain in the ass? Make it the opposite of a pain in the ass—some businesses provide a guarantee of 110 percent, ensuring that the burden is on the business to deliver. Zappos famously created free 427/617 shipping both ways to take away the hesitation about buying shoes without trying them on. A host of competitors had to follow suit.§ ALTERNATIVELY, MAKE A BIG DEAL ABOUT OFFERING NO GUARANTEE. Instead of providing an incredible guarantee, provide no guarantee—and make a big deal about this fact. Note that this strategy usually works better for high-end products. It will likely decrease overall sales but increase the commitment level from those who do purchase. Ironically, people who pay for high-end products tend to be better customers all around. "Low-paying buyers are the worst," one business owner who sold a broad range of products at different prices told me. "We have far more complaints from people who pay $10 and expect the world than from those who pay $1,000." I've noticed a similar effect in my own business, with people buying the lower-priced version of something 428/ 617 generating a much higher rate of customer service issues than those who buy the higherpriced version. The key lesson in all these ideas is to always be experimenting. Try new things and see what happens. Product to Service, Service to Product Another easy thing many existing businesses can do to add a new revenue source quickly is to create a service from a product-based business or create a product from a servicebased business. Remember the story about the restaurant in Chapter 2? Most people go to a restaurant so they can relax and let the staff serve them. But others really are interested in how the cooking works, so restaurants sometimes offer cooking classes to show 429/617 off their favorite recipes and create more loyalty among frequent diners. The key is that the lessons are held on Saturday or Sunday afternoons, times when the restaurant is closed or not very busy. Saturday night is reserved for the main event of regular dining. If you have a product business, ask yourself this question: "My product is x ... how can I teach customers about y?" Then create a new version of your offering that includes consulting, coaching, a "jump-start" session, premium technical support, or something else. Make it clear that customers don't need the service; they can get by on their own with just the product. But for those who are interested in some extra hand-holding, the service is available and waiting for them. Perry Marshall, a Chicago-based business consultant, made the switch from product to service by offering an educational course based on knowledge he usually shared through a one-time product. Perry had 430/617 written a popular report that sold multiple copies every day for $50 each. He was also busy offering one-on-one personal consulting, but one day someone gave him an idea: "Everyone who buys this report loves it, but they don't always know how to implement what you teach. They also don't need your high-end one-on-one consulting, so why not offer a series of jump-start workshops that people could take as a group?" Perry wasn't sure at first but decided to give it a try. When the idea generated more than a million dollars for his small firm, he was astounded. Alternatively, if you operate a servicebased business, consider how you can introduce a "productized" version of the service. My designer, Reese Spykerman, does work that is so great that when word got out, a lot of people began noticing and asking her for quotes. It didn't take long for Reese to have far more inquiries than she could handle. Reese's husband, Jason, manages the 431/ 617 inquiries that come in every day, and he noticed that they fit into three categories. Category 1: Prospects with significant money to spend who would likely be good clients. In these cases, Jason consulted with Reese, agreed to accept the clients if they still wished to proceed, and issued them a quote for the requested work. Category 2: Prospects who didn't have any money to spend (designers receive a lot of these queries, unfortunately) or people who just weren't the right fit for Reese's work. In this case, Jason politely declined the request and encouraged them to look elsewhere. These two categories were fairly straightforward, and as hundreds of inquires came in over the course of an average year, Jason became astute in telling right away which 432/617 group someone was in. But there was another, third category that was more complicated. Category 3: Prospects who had some money to spend, were nice people with interesting projects, and didn't need a completely custom solution. The third category was complicated because Reese and Jason didn't want to send them away, but they also didn't want to take on an excessive number of projects, thus limiting Reese's design time for key clients. They did some careful subcontracting, but they didn't want to become a low-end provider or farm out much of the work to others. After considering different options, Reese and Jason decided to create a series of "themes" and website headers that customers could purchase for a flat rate. These options weren't the same as a genuinely 433/

617 custom-crafted site design, but they were a lot better than everything else on the market. Providing both a product and a service helps with your marketing as well. You can say to prospects, "Hey, my service costs a lot of money because everything is customized. But if you just need a general solution, you can get this version for much less." Some customers will still want the customized solution, but this way you don't shut the door on others who like the idea but can't afford the high-end work. What Sets Happy Knits Apart: AN EXAMINATION OF A THRIVING RETAIL PRACTICE How does a retail establishment thrive when those around it struggle? Welcome to Happy Knits, a yarn store and Internet retailer based in the trendy Southeast area of Portland, Oregon. Here are five ways Happy Knits stands out. 434/617 A welcoming space. Knitters are welcome to stay for hours, whether shopping or knitting. Guests who happen to be accompanying knitters—usually husbands or children—are also welcome to hang out, sit in comfy chairs, and use the free WiFi while the knitter of the family looks around. (Most, though not all, knitters are women.) A clear online strategy. Most retail stores have a website, but few combine a physical location with an online shopping experience as well as Happy Knits does. "Online is limitless," says store owner Sarah Young. Even with a large retail space, online sales from around the world constitute more than half the sales. She works the system by maintaining close ties with Ravelry, a social network specifically for knitters, and providing frequent email updates and offers to previous customers. 435/617 Great displays (in store) and great photos (online). Display, color, and placement are important, so Happy Knits includes a staging area for professional photos in a back room of the store. I asked Sarah why she doesn't just use the photos provided by the manufacturer the way other stores do. "Because they're not good enough," she told me. "We try to do everything here with a focus on quality." Exclusive deals. By working with yarn companies as partners, Happy Knits creates exclusivity that is hard to emulate. You might think this is an unfair advantage, but the companies offered these deals to Sarah because her customers said such good things about the store and because she is careful to pay vendors on time. (Lesson: To get an unfair advantage, provide remarkable service.) Love for customers. Every order sent by mail includes a personalized thank-you note 436/617 from an employee, encouraging customers to call if they need help with a pattern, plus free samples of other products. If an item is back ordered because of a computer glitch, an employee will call the customer proactively to

apologize and ask if she would like a substitution. "Be nice to people and provide a great service" may not sound like much of a differentiation, but all these things add up. Whether you have a retail store or not, you could learn something from Happy Knits. Note to Service Providers: Raise Prices Regularly 437/617 You might expect that a price increase has a tendency to filter some customers away from the business while making up for the loss with higher overall income. Sometimes this is indeed the case, but many of the service providers I talked with were surprised that almost no one left after an increase. Several said that when they told their customers or clients about the increase, the response was, "It's about time! You're worth more than you've been charging." (When your clients complain about the price being too low, you should listen.) Andy Dunn is a developer in Belfast, Northern Ireland. He left his day job after pitching a Web application to a CEO. Crucially, Andy didn't just pitch an idea—he had the idea and then acted on it by creating the entire app and sending it over to the CEO, requesting approval. Impressed, the CEO called him up to say thanks, and even agreed 438/617 to underwrite the expenses for some additional features. Out on his own, Andy had no problem attracting new business, but he did have a big problem with pricing. Wanting to appear attractive to prospective clients, he priced his services so low that they were unprofitable. In one case he ended up several thousand euros in debt by bidding too low and then outsourcing part of the work. After that experience, he knew he'd have to make a change. The change came in the form of a 25 percent raise, something he was initially afraid to do, but he was greatly relieved after it was done. "The simple act of raising my rates by 25 percent allowed me to either work seven hours less a week or make a significant increase in my monthly income," he told me on a Skype call from Belfast. "The other, unexpected benefit was that it gave me much more confidence. Until I upped the rates, I 439/617 didn't make the connection that I was worth more than I had been charging." Andy's story was repeated in various forms by other service providers and a few productbased businesses too. In 2010 I conducted a separate study of fourteen freelancers who had raised their rates successfully. I asked them how they did it, what they expected to happen, and what actually happened. These freelancers were working in completely different fields, including a veterinarian, a voice coach, a sign language interpreter, and the more typical crowd of consultants, writers, and designers. They were also located throughout the English-speaking world, including Canada, Australia,

New Zealand, South Africa, the United Kingdom, and the United States. Despite the diverse backgrounds and regions, I heard the same story over and over: "Before my price increase, I was worried that no one would hire me again. After the price 440/617 increase, I realized how easy it was, and I wish I had done it sooner." In most cases, the change was anticlimactic. Clients said, "OK, sure," and moved on. I also asked about suggestions for other service providers who are thinking about raising their rates. The most common advice was to maintain a practice of regular rate increases so that it becomes normal and expected. One freelancer likened it to going to the grocery store: No one expects the price of milk to be the same from year to year. We all know that over time it's going to go up, and the same should be true for the prices we charge clients. Another suggested an annual date for changing prices, either January 1 or the beginning of your calendar year if it's different. Others said that they offered an ongoing discount for current clients, among whom the work is more familiar and a strong relationship already exists. 441/617 Lastly, remember to price on the basis of value, not time. One designer sent us a good example of what not to do: "I have a colleague who moderates her rate according to how busy the day was and how long her lunch break was. Crazy!" Our correspondent is right: Customers pay for what you deliver, not how long you spend at lunch. The Best Social Media Strategy: Talk About Yourself You may have heard that the way to build a following on Twitter or other social networks is to promote other people's work. People don't want to hear you talk about yourself all the time, right? This advice is well-meaning and sounds good on the surface. Unfortunately, it's also wrong. Promoting other people's work and sharing links to interesting articles is fine, but don't expect that merely doing that will help you gain followers or attention. People 442/617 follow you (or your business) because that's what they're interested in—you. I follow Shaquille O'Neal's tweets and posts because I'm interested in what he has to say. If he spent all his time talking about other people and mentioning his other fans, I wouldn't be as interested. What should you talk about online? It's simple: Talk about yourself and your business. Really. If people don't like what you do or say, they can unfollow you, but chances are that you'll gain far more followers than you lose. Finally, remember that online social networks are merely reflections of what's happening elsewhere. Want more Twitter followers? Then do something interesting ... away from Twitter. 443/617 A Cautionary Note There's no point pursuing growth for growth's sake; you should scale a business only if you really want to. Many of the subjects of our case studies said they had turned down growth opportunities in a deliberate plan to remain small: "I just didn't want the hassle of managing people." The decision on going big versus staying small is unique to each person (we'll look at it much more in the next two chapters), but in this section we want to focus on things you can do to increase income without hiring additional employees or bringing in outside investors. All the tweaks mentioned above can be done by a solopreneur. Some might be easier with assistants, contractors, or employees, but none require a team. Before we close it out, let's look at a key distinction between two different kinds of growth. 444/617 You can grow a business one of two ways: horizontally, by going wide and creating different products to apply to different people, or vertically, by going deep and creating more levels of engagement with customers. The flowchart on this page shows how this works. Different businesses will find that one solution suits them better than the other, and it's also possible to pursue limited growth in both areas. Mostly, though, you can keep moving on up, tweaking your way to the bank and growing your business. The first $1.26—or the first sale—may be the hardest, but after that, your most difficult choice may be deciding between many good options for growth.

INSTRUCTIONS ON CLONING YOURSELF FOR FUN AND PROFIT. "I'm not a businessman; I'm a business, man." —JAY-Z As business models go, buying a franchise that is based on someone else's company is usually a bad idea. The basic buy-our-franchise pitch runs like this: Raise a quarter of a million dollars by withdrawing your life savings, borrowing from family members, and maxing out your credit cards. Pay most of that money up front to a company that will generously allow you to work for it. Operate the business precisely the way they tell you, with no exceptions allowed. Every decision, from whom you hire to what services you offer to where you locate your store, is made by the company. They'll even tell you what color shirt you are required to wear in "your own business." If the business succeeds, you'll make an average of $47,000 a year after scraping by for three years on the same fifty-hour workweeks you could spend at someone else's company with a lot less stress. In this winning scenario, your ultimate success won't be 452/617 that you started a business: You'll have bought yourself a job. If the business fails, which happens more often than most franchise companies want to admit, the company will take back the store from you and resell it to someone else. When they do this, they won't count your failure as a store closure in their statistics. Thus, when you hear statistics that suggest a high percentage of franchise locations remain open, you have no idea who is operating them and who owes $250,000 that they have no way to repay. How does that proposal sound to you? Probably not so great—which is why buying into someone else's operation isn't usually the opportunity it may seem from the outside. Thankfully, there's an alternative: building a real business of your own, something that you have ownership of and control over. Buying into someone else's franchise isn't usually a good idea, but 453/617 figuring out how to leverage your own efforts is almost always worth careful consideration. You're Only One Person ... or Maybe Two Who says you can't be in more than one place at one time? In fact, there are several ways to grow a business through the use of leverage. Franchising yourself isn't just doing more; it's about taking your skills, activities, and passions to a higher level to create better returns. The difference between franchising yourself and just doing more is that you take the time to be strategic. Let's look at a couple of examples. Nathalie Lussier was an up-and-coming software engineer. Originally from Quebec, she had interned in Silicon Valley and now had the chance to take a big job on Wall 454/617 Street. Her family said it was the job of her dreams ... but as Nathalie thought more about it, she realized it was the job of someone else's dreams. Turning down the offer, she returned to Canada and decided to pursue a different idea. Nathalie had a personal success story of dramatically improving her health after switching to a raw foods diet. Eating only fruits, vegetables, and nuts sounded crazy at first, but the results spoke for themselves: In the first month, she lost more than ten pounds and suddenly had energy throughout the day. As she talked with her friends, Nathalie was a natural evangelist—not pushy or judgmental, but offering tips and strategies that people could use to make real improvements even if they weren't ready to jump into a completely raw diet as Nathalie had done. After relocating to Toronto, the idea was to build a small business helping other people make the adjustment to raw foods. Being a 455/617 software engineer (and a self-described geek like Brett Kelly in Chapter 4), Nathalie programmed a database, set up an app, and built her own website. The first incarnation was Raw Food Switch, which correctly represented the concept but seemed a bit boring. One day Nathalie noticed that the same letters—and therefore the same website—could be rendered as Raw Foods Witch, leading to a new theme. Dressing in character with a pointed black hat for photo shoots, she rebranded the whole business around herself. Nathalie created programs, one-time products, and individual consultation sessions in the same way we've seen others do throughout the book. Raw Foods Witch grew into a $60,000 business after the first year. What's not to love? Just one thing: "From the outside," she told me at a vegetarian restaurant in Toronto, "it looked like all I talked about was raw foods. No one realized I had 456/617 done all the programming and really enjoyed the intersection of business and technology." The second business came about unexpectedly after Nathalie began getting tech inquiries from her raw foods clients who were also creating businesses. She decided to create a separate brand for tech consulting, operating under her own name instead of the moniker she used in the other business. Raw Foods Witch is still a powerful brand—friends and clients report that other shoppers have mentioned her in the grocery store when they see a cart full of avocados—but she restructured the business to run on 80 percent autopilot. It still brings in a good income, but now Nathalie spends her time building the second business. Instead of doing one or the other, Nathalie effectively franchised herself. After Nathalie set up the tech consultancy, she had to go back to the raw foods business and make some changes. The business had 457/617 always been dependent on new products and launches, and since her focus was now elsewhere, she had to reduce that dependency while ensuring that it would produce income on a more regular basis. Across the border and a few states away, Brooke Thomas founded New Haven Rolfing, a holistic health practice. The clinic attracts a clearly defined group of clients: people who want to address chronic pain and mobility problems. (No one comes to see Brooke when they're feeling great.) By the time they arrive at New Haven Rolfing, many have gone through a long list of other treatments that haven't helped. Brooke is a testimony to the treatment she provides—she became pain-free through Rolfing after twenty-three years, having lived her whole life to that point with problems related to a birth injury. Before she moved to Connecticut, Brooke operated similar businesses in California and 458/617 New York. With each move she learned a little more about what to do and what to avoid. Opening the same kind of business in different cities was insightful. After moving to New Haven, she had filled her client list within four weeks, and then she took on a partner to manage additional appointments. A single mother with a young child, Brooke works part-time but still earns more than $70,000 a year from the practice. Repeated success in different cities involved getting to know other care providers, and Brooke noticed that some were more business-savvy than others. By using her real-world experience, Brooke created Practice Abundance, a training program for other wellness providers. Offering a series of support modules and a community forum, Practice Abundance was a business course that focused strictly on ways to improve a practice. Other resources took a very traditional approach. In Brooke's words, "they 459/617 assume that everyone wants to get an MBA, when the reality is that most of them just want to run their practice better." Brooke had diversified to two groups of people: those she served through individual care, and her fellow caregivers who could benefit from non-MBA business advice. Both Nathalie and Brooke found a way to reach two different audiences: a core group and a related group. As a business grows and the business owner begins itching for new projects, he or she essentially has two options for self-made franchising: Option 1: Reach more people with the same message. Option 2: Reach different people with a new message. 460/617 Either option is valid, and both can be rewarding. For the first option, it may be helpful to think of the "hub-and-spoke" model when building a brand, especially online. In this model, the hub is your main website: often an e-commerce site where something is sold, but it could also be a blog, a community forum, or something else. The hub is a home base with all the content curated by you or your team and ultimately where you hope to drive new visitors, prospects, and customers. The spokes, also known as outposts, are all the other places where you spend your time.* These places could include social networking sites, the comments section of your blog or other blogs, actual meetings or networking events, or something else. You can see how this works in the image below: 461/617 The goal for each of the outposts is to support the work of the home base, not usually the outpost itself. It can be a trap to spend too much time with any of the outposts, because things change, some outposts become less popular over time. You also own the content and work you create in the home base, 462/617 whereas most of what happens in an outpost is "owned" by another company. Disaster and Recovery: "STUCK IN MALI AGAIN" EDITION As a full-time freelance photographer based in Accra, Ghana, Nyani Quarmyne is no stranger to adventure. In West Africa, there are few laws that are widely followed, especially when it comes to copyright and intellectual property. Most of the time, everything works out—but not always. Here's how Nyani tells the story: When I was just starting out, I shot a couple of small jobs for a Ghanaian creative agency. Shortly thereafter I got a call from them asking if I could do an urgent shoot for a new client, necessitating travel to a couple of countries in the region. The deadline was really tight; it was a get-the-call-today463/617 and-leave-in-the-morning kind of thing, and even the details of exactly where we would be going remained in flux until the last minute. Having shot for the agency before, they had seen and signed my contracts previously, and I made the mistake of thinking they understood how I work and the basis on which I was undertaking this job. So in the rush I omitted to get the paperwork squared away, and off we went. The shoot went really well, and I produced what I consider to be some very strong work. All was well until we were on a rural road far from any city or airport. While we were driving along, the client demanded copyright of the images—not part of the deal as far as I was concerned—and threatened to have me detained at a remote border in a politically unstable nation unless I handed them over. Not wanting to sample the hospitality of the local gendarmes, I conceded and lost some of the 464/617 strongest images I had shot to date. I learned my lesson, though: Next time, be sure to get the paperwork done first. Partnership: How 1 + 1 = 3 One path to franchising yourself is to team up with a trusted partner. This doesn't mean you completely merge your business with that person; in fact, the easiest and most common way to partner with someone is to create a joint venture. In this arrangement, two or more people join forces to collaborate on a single new project. (Karol and Adam's "fire sale" project, described in Chapter 8, is a joint venture.) In other arrangements, an all-new business is created that is jointly owned by the 465/617 partners. That's what Patrick McCrann and Rich Strauss did. They were both high-end performance coaches for athletes and decided to team up to create Endurance Nation, a training program and community for triathletes. They divide responsibilities on the basis of what they're each good at. Patrick calls all the new members on the phone to welcome them, and Rich crafts an online training plan for them.† However it's structured, the goal of a partnership is to grow beyond what each person can create on his or her own. Ralf Hildebrandt operates an international professional services firm based in Stuttgart, Germany. Here's how he explains why 1 + 1 can equal 3: "My rule of thumb is that a successful partnership (or any type of collaboration) should create a combined business which is at least 33 percent larger than the sum of what the two individuals could achieve on their own. 466/617 "People are often inclined to think that distributing work to a few others is what partnership is about," Ralf continued. "But that is just subcontracting. True partnership must create more than just a divided list of tasks." Courtesy of Pamela Slim, a coach, author, and expert on partnerships, here's an abbreviated list of decisions you should make at the beginning of any joint venture: • How will the money be divided? (Common splits include an even 50-50, 60-40 with the higher share going to the partner who does more work, and 45-45 with 10 percent reserved for administrative costs.) • What are the responsibilities of each partner? • What kind of information is shared between partners? • How will the project be jointly marketed? 467/617 • How long will our agreement be in place? • How often will we touch base to discuss the partnership? Check out the One-Page Partnership Agreement for a simple way to spell out basic agreements between two parties. One-Page Partnership Agreement Keep it simple. Remember that the relationship is the most important part; choosing to keep it strong and trusting is more important than having the right clauses and legal language. Many of our subjects report doing business for large amounts of money on a long-term basis without any contracts at all. Here's a starting point. You should consult a qualified third party if you'd like to define your obligations more clearly or if you're concerned about something. 468/617 Partners: [Partner 1] and [Partner 2]. These partners agree to collaborate in good faith on a mutually beneficial project known as [project name]. Overview: [summary of project, including outcomes and expected results] Revenue Sharing: Net income for the project will be split on the basis of [percentage] percent to [Partner 1] and [percentage] percent to [Partner 2]. All minor costs associated with the project will be deducted prior to calculating net income. If any particular cost exceeds [amount], both partners must approve the decision. Life of Revenue-Sharing Agreement: The revenue-sharing agreement will last for [period of time], at the end of which the partners will decide if it should be continued, discontinued, or revised. 469/617 Publication and Sale: The project will be offered for sale on [websites and any other sources]. Customer Support: [Partner 1] will be responsible for [duties]. [Partner 2] will be responsible for [duties]. Project feedback from customers will be shared between both parties. Marketing: Both parties will actively market the project to ensure its success. This will include promotion on [websites], through each partner's online community and offline networks, and each party requesting coverage of the project from other influential websites. Time Line: The partners agree to complete all aspects of the project to prepare for launch on [date]. 470/617 The Battle of Outsourcing Jamila Tazewell followed a common path after graduating from art school: She waited tables in New York City while dreaming of something else. Fortunately, waiting on tables was the only waiting she did—she also took action to start a business.

She started by making "outlandish handbags" and unique wallets. "I was convinced I would magically become an accessories star overnight," she says, initially assuming that a fashion house would see her products and offer to distribute them. "Then I saw I could actually sell my handbags and wallets myself. That's when I decided to pursue the opportunity further." Jamila headed west to Los Angeles to sell her accessories full-time without relying on a waitress job to pay the bills this time. It worked, but only just barely: She did 471/617 everything herself, and the business struggled to find its feet. She was glad she no longer waited tables, but as with buying someone else's franchise, Jamila felt like she bought herself a job. Three years in, Jamila was ready to make a change. She hired a local seamstress to make the product under her supervision, a move she describes as "challenging but necessary." After that, she brought in someone to do the printing and shipping as well. This was a big step that required "a brutal process of trial and error, but getting the product out of my home office was incredibly liberating. It felt like my child was finally old enough to go off to boarding school or something." Interestingly, this perspective is not universally accepted. Several other topics covered in the study resulted in a wave of similar responses. Many members of our group spoke of bootstrapping and limited business plans in the same way, and the 472/ 617 connection between freedom and value was a key theme for almost everyone. But there was one topic that resulted in a wave of divergent opinions. That topic was employing contractors or "virtual assistants," also known as outsourcing. On this topic, input ranged from "love it" to "hate it" to "it's complicated."

BECOME AS BIG AS YOU WANT TO BE (AND NO BIGGER). "Nothing will work unless you do." —MAYA ANGELOU Among the people we've met in our story thus far, a few are active risk takers, charging ahead to storm the castle, career or finances be damned if they fail. But far more common are those who carefully take the time to build a business step by step. It's a myth that all those who choose to go it alone are Type A motorcycle riders, betting it all on the success or failure of one project. Entrepreneurs are not necessarily risk takers; it's just that they define risk and security differently from the way other people do. Tsilli Pines, an Israeli-American designer who now lives in my hometown of Portland, Oregon, exemplifies the group of cautious entrepreneurs. Over the course of eight years, she crafted a business making ketubot, custom-designed Jewish wedding contracts. During most of that time, the business was a night-and-weekend project she worked on after coming home from the design studio where she was employed. With a regular paycheck from the day job, Tsilli felt safe experimenting with the business and learning 506/617 as she went along. She also noticed an important side benefit to working this way: With limited hours to spend on the business, she had to make them count. Thanks to referrals from happy couples, the business grew slowly but steadily, with more orders each year. Each ketubah was a labor of love, priced at $495. As 2009 drew to a close, Tsilli felt prepared to make the leap. She gave notice to her boss and colleagues and prepared to go full-time. This was it! She had jumped! Except ... the view on the other side wasn't all she had expected. The first week of freedom felt great; the second week she began to wonder, What do I do all day? "I underestimated the value of having some work that was collaborative and not self-directed," she said. Over the next few months, the business earned less than expected. Orders were still coming in and the situation was far from desperate, but Tsilli felt trapped, drained of 507/617 the creativity she had thrived on while starting up. "The all-or-nothing paradigm was too much pressure," she continued. "I'm running a creative business, but it's a creativity killer for me to define my whole income on the need to continuously deploy my creativity." It was a hard decision to make, but six months after leaving the design firm, she approached the owners with a proposal: How about coming back part-time? They said yes and were happy to have her. Moving back to the studio three days a week was the right fit. When she had left six months earlier, she had a lot of responsibility as the lead designer; there was no way she could stick around in a lesser role without first leaving for a while. Coming back in under the radar gave her the security of having a certain amount of fixed income while retaining the freedom of working half-time on her other projects. Also, Tsilli now worked as 508/617 a contractor instead of an employee, and that gave her an unexpected but important sense of still earning all her income "on her own," with roughly half coming from the studio and half from her business. It was right for her to leave, and it was right to go back. The business is still profitable, but without the pressure of needing to rely on it exclusively. Tsilli summarizes it like this: "The feeling I have is that I'm still laying brick after brick. The different pieces interlock, and over time they may build to critical mass. But right now I'm in a good place." The Choice Tsilli's story illustrates the real challenge that befalls almost everyone with the opportunity to make a major career change and go 509/617 it alone: finding a way to build systemization into the business, and deciding what role the business will play in the rest of their lives. Sooner or later, every successful business owner—accidental or otherwise—faces a choice: Where are we going with this thing? As described throughout the book, many of the members of our group made a deliberate decision to stay small, creating a "freedom business" for the purpose of having the freedom. Others chose to grow by carefully recruiting employees and going all in. Here's how three people faced this critical choice, resolving it in different ways. Option 1: Stay Small No one is truly a born entrepreneur, but Cherie Ve Ard probably comes close. Working on her own since she was twenty, she's now thirty-eight and has never looked back. Her father was also an entrepreneur, starting the family software business that Cherie 510/ 617 eventually took over. The company develops custom software solutions for health-care providers. In 2007 she hit the road with Chris Dunphy, her partner, and they traveled by RV across America. Being on the road while running a software company led to an obvious expansion: Cherie and Chris started a side business making mobile apps. Business is good, but Cherie has purposely declined to pursue a number of expansion ideas. Here's how she puts it: "Without a doubt, the smartest decision I made was to set a specific intention to not grow the business. Growing up as the daughter of an entrepreneur, I watched my father's creativity and inventor mind-set get sapped as the business grew from just him to over fifty employees. The stress wore him down and diminished his quality of life." When I last spoke to Cherie, she was on the island of Saint John, where she and Chris had settled in for a stay of a few months 511/617 ("maybe longer, or as long as we feel like it"). Cherie earns a good income of at least $50,000 a year but is insistent that the money isn't the point. "My feeling of being a successful business owner is based on the quality of life I lead, not the amount of money I earn," she says. "I own my business. The business doesn't own me." Option 2: Go Medium In the SoDo area of downtown Seattle, a factory hums with the sound of sewing machines. Chinese-American women, many of whom have worked at the factory for years, diligently apply patches to backpacks and laptop bags. I tour the factory with Tom Bihn, the owner, and his business partner, Darcy Gray. With more than twenty employees and his own factory, Tom isn't afraid of growth. But he turned his back on the biggest growth opportunity of all: distributing his popular bags 512/ 617 through big-name retailers, many of which have asked repeatedly for partnerships. I was curious about this decision, so I sent Tom and Darcy an email later to ask for more input. Here's what they said: We chose to be our own manufacturer and direct retailer initially because it's more interesting. We get to march to our own drummer, so to speak. If the goal is simply to make money, well, that's just boring. We wanted to make a cool business, with cool products, cool customers, and cool employees; we wanted to build a brand and a long-term place in the world. To sell to mass-market retailers may or may not be lucrative, but it does little for brand identity. It can also tie your fortune to a company over which you have no control: If they go down, you may go too. Our future is tied to what we do, decisions we make, and that's wicked good fun. 513/617 Marching to your own drummer is certainly interesting, and as Tom pointed out in another conversation, it may be a better business model as well. Cash flow for their business comes from many individual customers, so they never have to worry about one big store dropping their inventory (or defaulting on their debt). Because there's only one source, Tom Bihn bags are well positioned against being perceived as a commodity. Tom and Darcy are able to charge a good price for the bags and ensure that they can continue to support all the employees. When asked about any bad days or negative experiences in the business, Tom said something I've been thinking about ever since: "All the bad days have two things in common: You know the right thing to do, but you let somebody talk you out of doing it." At least in this case, Tom never let himself get talked out of what was clearly the right thing for him. 514/617 Option 3: Split the Difference Sometimes the choice between small and big has more than two answers. A creative individual can learn her lessons about the wrong kind of growth and then apply them to the right kind. Meet Jessica Reagan Salzman, owner of a one-person bookkeeping shop in Attleboro, Massachusetts. I knew Jessica was a numbers person when she provided estimated income for the next year of exactly $110,899. Many entrepreneurs are lost in the bigger picture and aren't certain about their finances. They tended to answer my questions about income projections with statements like "Uh, about one hundred, maybe one-fifty or so." With Jessica, there was no need for follow-up. Ironically, Jessica started the business after an unsettling experience at a new job she had just taken for a CPA. As she was settling into the job, she kept tallying figures and wondering why something wasn't 515/617 balancing properly. She finally figured it out: Not only was the firm in trouble, it wouldn't have enough to pay her when the very first bookkeeping cycle came around. Oops. Jessica quit and decided to go it alone. Right from the beginning, the business was profitable at a decent part-time level, and

Jessica was focused on raising a family without worrying about making a ton of money. But one day, her husband, Michael, called and said he was coming home early. "That's nice," she said. "Any special occasion?" There was a pause before he told her the rest of the news: He had been laid off, effective immediately. Jessica's business had been successful as a side project, but it didn't make nearly enough money to support a family, with their second child just three weeks old at that point. After the shock wore off, they talked about options, and Jessica decided to take the business to a higher level. Her husband 516/617 became the primary caregiver at home, and Jessica went to work. The business quickly grew and all was well under the new arrangement, but then it started growing too fast. "We had made major progress in the direction of growing revenues," she said, "but we had also experienced soaring costs, and our bottom line clearly reflected the necessity for a major change. "I just assumed that's what you were supposed to do," she continued. "As the business improves, you hire people. Right?" Unfortunately, although hiring people can sometimes help a business grow, it always creates much higher costs and fixed obligations. Jessica made more changes, switching her business to a sole proprietorship and returning to a one-woman shop.* 517/617 Don't Be a Firefighter: Work on Your Business Regardless of which path you take, as your project grows in scope, you can find yourself spending all your time responding to things and little time actually creating anything. The solution to this common problem is to focus on working on your business as opposed to in it. When you're operating the business, you spend time putting out fires and keeping everything running as it should. Working on the business requires a higherlevel approach. Every morning, set aside forty-five minutes without Internet access. Devote this time exclusively to activities that improve your business—nothing that merely maintains the business. Think forward motion ... What can you do to keep things moving ahead? Consider these areas: 518/617 BUSINESS DEVELOPMENT. This is work that grows the business. What new products or services are in the works? Are there any partnerships or joint ventures you're pursuing? OFFER DEVELOPMENT. This kind of work involves using existing resources in a new way. Can you create a sale, launch event, or new offer to generate attention and income? FIXING LONG-STANDING PROBLEMS. In every business, there are problems that creep up that you learn to work around instead of addressing directly. Instead of perpetually ignoring these issues, use your non-firefighting time to deal with the root of the problem. Health Insurance In the United States, it's the big question facing many prospective entrepreneurs: "How 519/617 can I insure my family when I'm self-employed?" (Canadians and others can skip this section and breathe easy.) Unfortunately, universal health care is still a long way off before we catch up with the rest of the developed world. To get some options, I surveyed our group of case studies (those from the U.S.) and also conducted several online conversations with large groups on Twitter and Facebook. The answers varied considerably. Someone wrote, "Get screwed and pay a lot of money for coverage that doesn't help you." Alas, in some cases, that statement may not be much of a stretch. But in other cases you have choices. Here are some of the most common ones. Buy a high-deductible policy and pay cash for visits to the doctor. Perhaps the most common solution among the self-employed is to shop around and purchase a 520/617 high-deductible policy to cover serious illness or accident. Then set aside a savings fund—either self-managed or with a health savings account (HSA)—to cover doctor's visits and preventive care. It's best to compare quotes from an independent broker, and in some cases a local or national group may offer a discounted policy. Several people mentioned the Freelancers Union, for example.† Join a concierge program. A concierge program is the opposite of a high-deductible policy that covers only serious problems. For a monthly fee ($150 to 300 on average), you can visit the same doctor for most primary and preventive needs. You'll also get the doctor's email address and "call anytime" cell phone number, and the doctor will act as an advocate and referrer if you need more serious care. Some people combine a concierge program with another policy to ensure that 521/617 both short-term and disaster prevention needs are met. Get insured through your partner. A number of business owners wrote to tell me that they relied on their spouse or partner's job to cover both of them while they worked full-time or part-time in the business. Courtney Carver was diagnosed with multiple sclerosis in 2006, and her medical bills would be $8,000 a month without insurance. "I feel fortunate that my husband works for a company that has group insurance," she says. "For now, starting a business together with him leaving his job is not an option because of my medical condition. We are looking at other out-of-state options for the future but are tied to his job for the insurance for now." Of course, this option isn't available to you if you're single or if your partner doesn't have a job that provides insurance benefits, 522/617 but if you do have the option, it may very well be the best one. Stay on COBRA as long as possible. If you have lost your job, COBRA allows you to continue receiving the same health-care coverage for a certain length of time at the same price your former employer paid. You have to pay for it, but because it originally was based on a group rate, the cost is often lower (and coverage may be better) than that of any plan you could purchase yourself. Several people spoke of extending COBRA coverage for up to three years as they built their businesses. Self-insure or use an HSA. "My healthcare plan involves prayer, vitamins, and avoiding sharp objects," Amy Oscar told me on Twitter. Others explained that they were just being pragmatic about the poor options 523/617 available to them, weighing the costs and what they perceived as limited benefits of an expensive plan they weren't likely to use. If you have a family or health-care issues, you may not be comfortable with this option. PRICING REVIEW. As discussed in Chapter 11, you should review your prices regularly to determine whether a price increase is in order. In addition, consider adding appropriate upsells, cross-sells, or other income-generating tools to your arsenal. CUSTOMER COMMUNICATION. This involves not just dealing with emails or general inquiries, but initiating communication through newsletters and updates. A key rule for all these activities is to initiate, not respond. Doing this for just forty524/617 five minutes a day can bring huge rewards even when everything else is crazy and you spend the rest of the day putting out fires. Onward! Monitoring Your Business Regardless of your growth strategy, you'll want to pay attention to the health of your business. The best way to do this is with a two-pronged strategy: Step 1: Select one or two metrics and be aware of them at any given time, focusing on sales, cash flow, or incoming leads. Step 2: Leave everything else for a biweekly or monthly review where you delve into the overall business more carefully. 525/ 617 Some members of our group were much more diligent about tracking metrics than others, with a number of people talking about being obsessive over data and others saying they had "no idea" about what was happening in the business. (My opinion on this approach: Personalities and skill sets vary, but be wary of delegating all financial knowledge to someone else. Having no idea about money stuff is usually a bad sign.) The metrics you want to track will vary with the kind of business. Here are a few of the most common examples. Sales per day: How much money is coming in? Visitors or leads per day: How many people are stopping by to take a look or signing up for more information? Average order price: How much are people spending when they order? 526/617 Sales conversion rate: What percentage of visitors or leads become customers? Net promoter score:

What percentage of customers would refer your business to someone else? Some businesses choose more specific metrics. Brandy Agerbeck, the graphic facilitator we met in Chapter 7, earns her living through corporate and non-profit bookings. Every year she needs a certain amount of bookings, so she keeps a set of index cards to track this number. When the index cards fill up, she knows she's good for a while and can focus on other things. Once or twice a month it's good to take a deeper look at the business and record some metrics that should be improving over time. The kinds of things you'll probably be interested in are more detailed sales figures, site traffic and social media, and the growth of the business. You can get a free spreadsheet 527/617 to help with this process in the online resources for this book at 100startup.com. Built to Sell: Going Really Long John Warrillow built and sold four companies before "retiring" to write, speak, and invest. After learning his lessons through those four experiences, he now advocates a specific model for owners of small companies who wish to sell their business one day. Most of John's recommendations relate to the need to create an actual company or organization that can thrive outside the business owners' specific skills. In other words, the built-to-sell model is different from the model we've looked at in this book. Many of our case studies involve people who went into business for 528/617 themselves because it was fun, not because they wanted to build something and then cash out. However, John's recommendations are solid for owners who want to pass a business on, and some of them can be adapted to improve a business even if you want to stick around. You can see how the two models compare in the table below. BUILT TO SELL—$100 STARTUP COMPARISON In trying to decide which path to pursue, the simple question to answer is: "What kind of freedom do you want?" John's model is all about creating an entity apart from yourself and then selling it for a big payday. The $100 Startup model is more about transitioning to 529/ 617 a business or independent career that is based on something you love to do—in other words, something intrinsically related to the owner's skill or passion. Neither model is better; it just depends on your goals. If you'd like to have the option of selling your business one day, John's point is that you have to plan for it by taking specific steps. The most important step in creating an independent identity for the business is to create a product or service with the potential to scale. This is an important distinction from many of the businesses we've described thus far, so let's take a look at how John explains it. 530/617 A scalable business is built on something that is both teachable and valuable. A CPA provides a highly valuable service, but it isn't easily teachable (she can't just bring someone into her practice and hand it over to him). On the other hand, you can teach someone how to bus tables at a restaurant in a few minutes, but that isn't a valuable service (lots of people can bus tables). Therefore, a business that has the potential to be 531/617 sold easily for a high profit offers something at the intersection of teachable and valuable. John built a subscription service that conducted financial research and provided a series of informative reports. This was highly valuable to his clients but also teachable to other employees. Another time he built a firm that produced consumer focus groups for big companies—again, a highly valuable service, but also replicable under new ownership. The solutions found by Tsilli, Cherie, Tom, Jessica, and John varied considerably. In implementing their solutions, each of them said yes to something while saying no to something else. Tom declined to accept the deals from big-box retailers, but he wasn't afraid to hire employees and grow on his own terms. Cherie preferred to keep things small and intimate. Tsilli found security by 532/617 growing her business and working as a contractor for her former employer. What united these different experiences was a sense of controlling their own destiny and finding freedom in nurturing a meaningful project. As your own project grows, you'll also need to make decisions based on your preferences and specific vision. Just remember that these are good decisions to make and a good position to be in. KEY POINTS There's more than one road to freedom, and some people find it through a combination of different working arrangements. "Going long" by pursuing growth and deciding to stay small are both acceptable options, and you can split the difference by "going medium." It all depends on what kind of freedom you'd like to achieve. 533/617 Work "on" your business by devoting time every day to activities specifically related to improvement, not just by responding to everything else that is happening. Regularly monitor one or two key metrics that are the lifeblood of your business. Check up on the others monthly or bimonthly. A business that is scalable is both teachable and valuable. If you ever want to sell your business, you'll need to build teams and reduce owner dependency. *Jessica's business is called Heart Based Bookkeeping, and she likes to call herself a soul proprietor: someone who is emotionally and spiritually invested in her work.

"Your time is limited, so don't waste it living someone else's life." —STEVE JOBS Almost everyone we've met in the book so far has some kind of failure-to-success story. In many cases, the story is about a product launch that fell flat, a partnership gone wrong, or the loss of motivation for the wrong project. "I tried something and it didn't work out ... but then I moved on to something else" is a common refrain. All these stories are valid and interesting, but I've never heard a rise-from-the-ashes story quite as compelling as that of John T. Unger, a sculpture artist from a small town in Michigan. John's story is a tour de force of failure and fear that turned into resilience and success. As John tells it, the third best thing that ever happened to him was having the roof of his studio collapse from under him while he was standing on it, frantically trying to shovel snow. The building was completely destroyed, and John spent the rest of the Michigan winter alternating between 539/617 shivering while he worked and warming himself with an illegal unvented kerosene heater. It was a nightmare scenario, but then a funny thing happened: The bank came out to assess the damage and gave him a $10,000 commission. John used the commission as a down payment on two buildings he had been trying to purchase for a while. "I don't think the bank would have gone for the deal without the disaster," he says. "It forced them to take a real look at my business instead of them just thinking of me as another broke artist." The second best thing that ever happened to John was losing his last day job as a graphic designer during the dot-com crash of 2000. The loss of the job led to the loss of everything else—his income, his girlfriend, his apartment, and even a piece of his thumb in an accident incurred while he was moving out of the apartment. While he was working the day job (seven days a week in 1999, seven 540/617 days total in 2000), he also was working as much as ten hours a day on his art business. After both of these experiences—losing the building and losing the day job—John was depressed and thought hard about what to do next. His friends advised him to suck it up and find work wherever he could, but in rural Michigan those days, John knew that there wasn't much work to be found. It was now or never, so he stuck with his goal and continued making progress. The best thing that ever happened to John, as he tells the story, was a late-night disagreement with a crazed cab driver, who pulled him into the back room of a diner and held a gun to his head for a full ten minutes, screaming and threatening to pull the trigger. John finally escaped and walked out into another cold Michigan night, sweating, trembling, and glad to be alive. "I get it!" John yelled at the sky as he hobbled away. "I'm just so lucky!" 541/617 "You don't really worry about the small things after that," John says now. "Everything takes on a whole other level of meaning." Unwanted Advice and Unneeded Permission Much of this book contains various forms of advice, but don't confuse advice for permission. You don't need anyone to give you permission to pursue a dream. If you've been waiting to begin your own $100 startup (or anything else), stop waiting and begin. Charlie Pabst, a Seattle-based designer who left the corporate world to go it alone, said that the best thing he did was learn to ignore advice, even from friends who meant well. "My business and the life I lead now would never have happened had I not been 542/617 obnoxiously stubborn to my own will," he said. "The fact is that the majority of people don't own their own businesses. And a certain percentage of that majority will not be happy or supportive about your exiting the nine-to-five world." While usually well-meaning, unsolicited advice from people who think they know better can be unnecessary and distracting. Here's how Chelly Vitry, the founder of a Denver food tour business, puts it: The biggest lesson I learned was to trust my own judgment. When I started my tour business, I got all sorts of advice from people around me, ranging from why it wouldn't work at all to how things should be run on a day-to-day basis. I had researched it and knew it was a viable idea, so I decided to keep my own counsel and quit asking people what they thought. 543/617 People who know less about the business than me do not get to make decisions about it. I value input, but now I seek it out from people who have unique perspectives about how I can improve. Sometimes the best advice is none at all. If you know what you need to do, the next step is simply to do it. Stop waiting. Start taking action. What Are We Afraid Of? Toward the end of many follow-up discussions with most of the business owners profiled in the book, I asked about their biggest fears, worries, or concerns. All these people had been successful, earning at least $50,000 a year from their projects (many were earning much more), but what were 544/617 they worried about? What kept them up at night? Their concerns fit into two broad areas: external and internal. External concerns tended to relate to money and a changing marketplace. For example, a few businesses had been created to exploit imbalances in technology. These projects can be very profitable for a time, but when the music stops playing, the ride is over. A business that grows primarily from strong Google rankings or good placement in the iTunes store ("favored by the gods of Apple," as one person put it) is in danger of losing it all if fortunes change. Scott McMurren, who published the Alaska coupon books, said he was closely watching the online coupon craze, considering ways to update the business to be more digitalfriendly. The role of competition was mentioned frequently, although in very different ways. Several people said they weren't worried 545/617 about what other businesses were doing, because they found it more productive to keep moving forward with their own original work. Others did worry, especially about building something unique only to see it copied or "stolen" by a more established company. Marianne Cascone, who makes children's clothing in a small partnership she runs with her cousin, illustrated this concern well: Our biggest fear, since the beginning, is that our products will be "knocked off" and our prices will be undercut. We are covered by patents and trademarks, but it still happens from time to time. However, I am a firm believer that if I focus 100 percent on creating a quality product, we will rise to the top every time. We do not get sidetracked on other projects; we focus on keeping our customers extremely satisfied. There is still a chance that I will walk into Target and 546/617 see my design on their shelf under another company's name. We are just hoping to have a place in that market so they are truly competing with us and not stealing from us. Those who had expanded by hiring employees tended to worry about making sure they had enough cash flow and recurring income to keep the payroll going. If you own a solo shop and business tightens up, you may be able to tighten up along with it. But if you owe people a fixed amount of money on a fixed schedule, you can't do that. One business produced more than $2 million in annual revenue but earned only $60,000 in net income for the owner, in large part because of the high overhead of employing people and investing in infrastructure. Holly Minch mentioned the Goldilocks principle: the idea that success is found within certain margins and not at the extremes. "I want the clients to get real value out of 547/617 what we deliver," she said, "but not at the expense of our bottom line. And I want the team to have enough work to live well but not so much work that we're not living." Others worried about "faking it" or needed to keep the wheels rolling after the initial passion faded away. "My biggest fear is that my consulting and writing becomes mediocre," said Alyson Stanfield in Colorado. "Success seems to be the ability to keep going, to keep the doors open," said Lee Williams-Demming in Costa Rica. "Be careful of letting clients take your business in a direction that makes you hate your job," said Britta Alexander, one half of the husband-and-wife team running a marketing company in Hastings-on-Hudson, New York. "The further you go down that road, the harder it will be to correct course. And it's really hard to quit your job when it's your own company." 548/617 Digging deeper, the fears and worries were more closely related to issues of identity. "I love my work," someone said, "but what if I love only the work, or what if the thing I love is no longer fun because now it's all work?" Statements like these usually were followed by clarifying ones such as "Starting this business, no matter the eventual outcome, has been worth the energy, effort, and sacrifices it has taken thus far to get it off the ground." One of our case studies, a Canadian manufacturer, said: "I used to be afraid to fail. I wanted concrete numbers telling me that we weren't going to lose before I took the leap. But if nobody was going to die, even in the absolute worst-case scenario, then what the hell was I so afraid of? I've never looked back." A European designer was even more dramatic: "Do you want to know the honest truth? In the early days, I almost expected my business to be a failure. I believed that it 549/ 617 had to be that way because it is the first business I have ever run, and I know the biggest successes have the biggest failures behind them. It sounds perverse but I almost wanted it to fail so I could look back and say, 'Yep, that one failed, but I learned from it!' " (Fortunately or not, his business is doing just fine.) The Moment They Knew As I reviewed thousands of pages of survey data and made countless follow-up calls, I learned to ask people if the decision to start their business had been worth it. You might think that such a question is simplistic; wouldn't most responses be "yes"? Well, perhaps … but one of the best parts of the study was hearing exactly how a group of diverse people answered this question. There was 550/617 usually a story behind the affirmative answer, and the story often related to a particular day, event, or moment when they knew their business was going to work. As we come to the end of this journey, I thought you should hear from a few of them directly.

The story about freedom and value doesn't end in the Western world; these themes are just as important in helping people create opportunities for themselves wherever they are. In many parts of Africa and Asia, more people work as buyers and sellers in the informal economy than work as employees for someone else. They may not all be professional bloggers or mobile application developers (yet), but they earn their living through the principles outlined in this book. In Phnom Penh, Cambodia, I met a tuktuk driver named Rhett. Tuk-tuks are the open-air taxis of Southeast Asia in which you can ride anywhere in the city for a dollar or two. Some tuk-tuk drivers, just like some cab drivers in other places around the world, are unreliable and dishonest. Rhett, however, is both reliable and honest, always arriving early to pick up a passenger and sometimes delivering regular customers to their destinations at no charge. Most tuk-tuk drivers in Cambodia make just $2 to $5 a day, but Rhett earns up to $50 a day. He does this through a combination of hard work and careful strategy. The hard work comes by not sleeping or gambling the afternoon away as many of his colleagues do. The strategy lies in understanding that he is better off by serving regular clients instead of constantly roaming the streets looking for one-time fares. While I was in town visiting a friend, Rhett made it clear that he was at my service, giving me his 569/617 mobile number and telling me to call him "day and night." After his core business model of serving regulars was established, Rhett created "multiple streams of income" by adding a sign for a popular bakery on the back of his tuk-tuk. The bakery pays him a fixed amount each month, plus a small commission for any business he brings in. He also regularly asks his customers for referrals and testimonials to increase his client base. If a customer needs help getting to a destination outside of Phnom Penh, Rhett will find a taxi or bus driver available for hire, making sure he is honest and then following up with the customer after the trip to confirm that all went well. He does all of this while speaking only limited English ("I practice every day, but my tongue becomes tired," he told me) and without any formal education at all. Some of the extra money he earns goes to a savings 570/617 fund, a safety net almost no other tuk-tuk driver has. His daughter is now in college, the first in their family to finish high school. As you work to improve your own circumstances, with freedom as the goal and value as the currency that gets you there, consider how these principles apply elsewhere. I like Rhett's story because it shows that creativity and initiative will get you far, regardless of the starting point. In many parts of the world, however, the starting point is much farther away than it is for most readers of this book. Starting a business in the developing world is often a difficult, highly bureaucratic endeavor—which is why so many people like Rhett operate in the informal sector. In some of these places, millions of people still lack access to clean water and other basic needs. In my own business and writing career, I invest at least 10 percent of all revenue with organizations that make better 571/617 improvements around the world than I could make on my own. (This includes the royalties for this book, so if you've purchased it, thanks for the help.) I don't consider this investment a charitable act; I consider it a natural response to the fact that I've been more fortunate than others.

CHAPTER TWO

REWORK

The new reality This is a different kind of business book for different kinds of people--from those who have never dreamed of starting a business to those who already have a successful company up and running. It's for hard-core entrepreneurs, the Type A go-getters of the business world. People who feel like they were born to start, lead, and conquer. It's also for less intense small-business owners. People who may not be Type A but still have their business at the center of their lives. People who are looking for an edge that'll help them do more, work smarter, and kick ass. It's even for people stuck in day jobs who have always dreamed about doing their own thing. Maybe they like what they do, but they don't like their boss. Or maybe they're just bored. They want to do something they love and get paid for it. Finally, it's for all those people who've never considered going out on their own and starting a business. Maybe they don't think they're cut out for it. Maybe they don't think they have the time, money, or conviction to see it through. Maybe they're just afraid of putting themselves on the line. Or maybe they just think business is a dirty word. Whatever the reason, this book is for them, too. There's a new reality. Today anyone can be in business. Tools that used to be out of reach are now easily accessible. Technology that cost thousands is now just a few bucks or even free. One person can do the job of two or three or, in some cases, an entire department. Stuff that was impossible just a few years ago is simple today. You don't have to work miserable 60/80/100-hour weeks to make it work. 10-40 hours a week is plenty. You don't have to deplete your life savings or take on a boatload of risk. Starting a business on the side while keeping your day job can provide all the cash flow you need. You don't even need an office. Today you can work from home or collaborate with people you've never met who live thousands of miles away. It's time to rework work. Let's get started.Ignore the real world "That would never work in the real world."

You hear it all the time when you tell people about a fresh idea. This real world sounds like an awfully depressing place to live. It's a place where new ideas, unfamiliar approaches, and foreign concepts always lose. The only things that win are what people already know and do, even if those things are flawed and inefficient. Scratch the surface and you'll find these "real world" inhabitants are filled with pessimism and despair. They expect fresh concepts to fail. They assume society isn't ready for or capable of change. Even worse, they want to drag others down into their tomb. If you're hopeful and ambitious, they'll try to convince you your ideas are impossible. They'll say you're wasting your time. Don't believe them. That world may be real for them, but it doesn't mean you have to live in it. We know because our company fails the real-world test in all kinds of ways. In the real world, you can't have more than a dozen employees spread out in eight different cities on two continents. In the real world, you can't attract millions of customers without any salespeople or advertising. In the real world, you can't reveal your formula for success to the rest of the world. But we've done all those things and prospered. The real world isn't a place, it's an excuse. It's a justification for not trying. It has nothing to do with you.Learning from mistakes is overrated In the business world, failure has become an expected rite of passage. You hear all the time how nine out of ten new businesses fail. You hear that your business's chances are slim to none. You hear that failure builds character. People advise, "Fail early and fail often." With so much failure in the air, you can't help but breathe it in. Don't inhale. Don't get fooled by the stats. Other people's failures are just that: other people's failures. If other people can't market their product, it has nothing to do with you. If other people can't build a team, it has nothing to do with you. If other people can't price their services properly, it has nothing to do with you. If other people can't earn more than they spend ... well, you get it. Another common misconception: You need to learn from your mistakes. What do you really learn from mistakes? You might learn what not to do again, but how valuable is that? You still don't know what you should do next. Contrast that with learning from your successes. Success gives you real ammunition. When something succeeds, you know what worked--and you can do it again. And the next time, you'll probably do it even better. Failure is not a prerequisite for success. A Harvard Business School study found already-successful entrepreneurs are far more likely to succeed again (the success rate for their future companies is 34 percent). But entrepreneurs whose companies failed the first time had almost the same follow-on success rate as people starting a company for the first time: just 23 percent. People who failed before have the same amount of success as people who have never tried at all.* Success is the experience that actually counts. That shouldn't be a surprise: It's exactly how nature works. Evolution doesn't linger on past failures, it's always building upon what worked. So should you. Planning is guessing Unless you're a fortune-teller, long-term business planning is a fantasy. There are just too many factors that are out of your hands: market conditions, competitors, customers, the economy, etc. Writing a plan makes you feel in control of things you can't actually control. Why don't we just call plans what they really are: guesses. Start referring to your business plans as business guesses, your financial plans as financial guesses, and your strategic plans as strategic guesses. Now you can stop worrying about them as much. They just aren't worth the stress. When you turn guesses into plans, you enter a danger zone. Plans let the past drive the future. They put blinders on you. "This is where we're going because, well, that's where we said we were going." And that's the problem: Plans are inconsistent with improvisation. And you have to be able to improvise. You have to be able to pick up opportunities that come along. Sometimes you need to say, "We're going in a new direction because that's what makes sense today." The timing of long-range plans is screwed up too. You have the most information when you're doing something, not before you've done it. Yet when do you write a plan? Usually it's before you've even begun. That's the worst time to make a big decision. Now this isn't to say you shouldn't think about the future or contemplate how you might attack upcoming obstacles. That's a worthwhile exercise. Just don't feel you need to write it down or obsess about it. If you write a big plan, you'll most likely never look at it anyway. Plans more than a few pages long just wind up as fossils in your file cabinet. Give up on the guesswork. Decide what you're going to do this week, not this year. Figure out the next most important thing and do that. Make decisions right before you do something, not far in advance. It's OK to wing it. Just get on the plane and go. You can pick up a nicer shirt, shaving cream, and a toothbrush once you get there. Working without a plan may seem scary. But blindly following a plan that has no relationship with reality is even scarier.Why grow? People ask, "How big is your company?" It's small talk, but they're not looking for a small answer. The bigger the number, the more impressive, professional, and powerful you sound. "Wow, nice!" they'll say if you have a hundred-plus employees. If you're small, you'll get an "Oh ... that's nice." The former is meant as a compliment; the latter is said just to be polite. Why is that? What is it about growth and business? Why is expansion always the goal? What's the attraction of big besides ego? (You'll need a better answer than "economies of scale.") What's wrong with finding the right size and staying there? Do we look at Harvard or Oxford and say, "If they'd only expand and branch out and hire thousands more professors and go global and open other campuses all over the world ... then they'd be great schools." Of course not. That's not how we measure the value of these institutions. So why is it the way we measure businesses? Maybe the right size for your company is five people. Maybe it's forty. Maybe it's two hundred. Or maybe it's just you and a laptop. Don't make assumptions about how big you should be ahead of time. Grow slow and see what feels right--premature hiring is the death of many companies. And avoid huge growth spurts too--they can cause you to skip right over your appropriate size. Small is not just a stepping-stone. Small is a great destination in itself. Have you ever noticed that while small businesses wish they were bigger, big businesses dream about being more agile and flexible? And remember, once you get big, it's really hard to shrink without firing people, damaging morale, and changing the entire way you do business. Ramping up doesn't have to be your goal. And we're not talking just about the number of employees you have either. It's also true for expenses, rent, IT infrastructure, furniture, etc. These things don't just happen to you. You decide whether or not to take them on. And if you do take them on, you'll be taking on new headaches, too. Lock in lots of expenses and you force yourself into building a complex businesss--one that's a lot more difficult and stressful to run. Don't be insecure about aiming to be a small business. Anyone who runs a business that's sustainable and profitable, whether it's big or small, should be proud. Workaholism Our culture celebrates the idea of the workaholic. We hear about people burning the midnight oil. They pull all-nighters and sleep at the office. It's considered a badge of honor to kill yourself over a project. No amount of work is too much work. Not only is this workaholism unnecessary, it's stupid. Working more doesn't mean you care more or get more done. It just means you work more. Workaholics wind up creating more problems than they solve. First off, working like that just isn't sustainable over time. When the burnout crash comes--and it will--it'll hit that much harder. Workaholics miss the point, too. They try to fix problems by throwing sheer hours at them. They try to make up for intellectual laziness with brute force. This results in inelegant solutions. They even create crises. They don't look for ways to be more efficient because they actually like working overtime. They enjoy feeling like heroes. They create problems (often unwittingly) just so they can get off on working more. Workaholics make the people who don't stay late feel inadequate for "merely" working reasonable hours. That leads to guilt and poor morale all around. Plus, it leads to an ass-in-seat mentality--people stay late out of obligation, even if they aren't really being productive. If all you do is work, you're unlikely to have sound judgments. Your values and decision making wind up skewed. You stop being able to decide what's worth extra effort and what's not. And you wind up just plain tired. No one makes sharp decisions when tired. In the end, workaholics don't actually accomplish more than nonworkaholics. They may claim to be perfectionists, but that just means they're wasting time fixating on inconsequential details instead of moving on to the next task. Workaholics aren't heroes. They don't save the day, they just use it up. The real hero is already home because she figured out a faster way to get things done. Enough with "entrepreneurs" Let's retire the term entrepreneur. It's outdated and loaded with baggage. It smells like a members-only club. Everyone should be encouraged to start his own business, not just some rare breed that self-identifies as entrepreneurs. There's a new group of people out there starting businesses. They're turning profits yet never think of themselves as entrepreneurs. A lot of them don't even think of themselves as business owners. They are just doing what they love on their own terms and getting paid for it. So let's replace the fancy-sounding word with something a bit more down-toearth. Instead of entrepreneurs, let's just call them starters. Anyone who creates a new business is a starter. You don't need an MBA, a certificate, a fancy suit, a briefcase, or an above-average tolerance for risk.

Make a dent in the universe To do great work, you need to feel that you're making a difference. That you're putting a meaningful dent in the universe. That you're part of something important. This doesn't mean you need to find the cure for cancer. It's just that your efforts need to feel valuable. You want your customers to say, "This makes my life better." You want to feel that if you stopped doing what you do, people would notice. You should feel an urgency about this too. You don't have forever. This is your life's work. Do you want to build just another me-too product or do you want to shake things up? What you do is your legacy. Don't sit around and wait for someone else to make the change you want to see. And don't think it takes a huge team to make that difference either. Look at Craigslist, which demolished the traditional classified-ad business. With just a few dozen employees, the company generates tens of millions in revenue, has one of the most popular sites on the Internet, and disrupted the entire newspaper business. The Drudge Report, run by Matt Drudge, is just one simple page on the Web run by one guy. Yet it's had a huge impact on the news industry--television producers, radio talk show hosts and newspaper reporters routinely view it as the go-to place for new stories.* If you're going to do something, do something that matters. These little guys came out of nowhere and destroyed old models that had been around for decades. You can do the same in your industry. Scratch your own itch The easiest, most straightforward way to create a great product or service is to make something you want to use. That lets you design what you know--and you'll figure out immediately whether or not what you're making is any good. At 37signals, we build products we need to run our own business. For example, we wanted a way to keep track of whom we talked to, what we said, and when we need to follow up next. So we created Highrise, our contact-management software. There was no need for focus groups, market studies, or middlemen. We had the itch, so we scratched it. When you build a product or service, you make the call on hundreds of tiny decisions each day. If you're solving someone else's problem, you're constantly stabbing in the dark. When you solve your own problem, the light comes on. You know exactly what the right answer is. Inventor James Dyson scratched his own itch. While vacuuming his home, he realized his bag vacuum cleaner was constantly losing suction power--dust kept clogging the pores in the bag and blocking the airflow. It wasn't someone else's imaginary problem; it was a real one that he experienced firsthand. So he decided to solve the problem and came up with the world's first cyclonic, bagless vacuum cleaner. * Vic Firth came up with the idea of making a better drumstick while playing timpani for the Boston Symphony Orchestra. The sticks he could buy commercially didn't measure up to the job, so he began making and selling drumsticks from his basement at home. Then one day he dropped a bunch of sticks on the floor and heard all the different pitches. That's when he began to match up sticks by moisture content, weight, density, and pitch so they were identical pairs. The result became his product's tag line: "the perfect pair." Today, Vic Firth's factory turns out more than 85,000 drumsticks a day and has a 62 percent share in the drumstick market.+ Track coach Bill Bowerman decided that his team needed better, lighter running shoes. So he went out to his workshop and poured rubber into the family waffle iron. That's how Nike's famous waffle sole was born.++ These people scratched their own itch and exposed a huge market of people who needed exactly what they needed. That's how you should do it too. When you build what you need, you can also assess the quality of what you make quickly and directly, instead of by proxy. Mary Kay Wagner, founder of Mary Kay Cosmetics, knew her skin-care products were great because she used them herself. She got them from a local cosmetologist who sold homemade formulas to patients, relatives, and friends. When the cosmetologist passed away, Wagner bought the formulas from the family. She didn't need focus groups or studies to know the products were good. She just had to look at her own skin.* Best of all, this "solve your own problem" approach lets you fall in love with what you're making. You know the problem and the value of its solution intimately. There's no substitute for that. After all, you'll (hopefully) be working on this for years to come. Maybe even the rest of your life. It better be something you really care about. Start making something We all have that one friend who says, "I had the idea for eBay. If only I had acted on it, I'd be a billionaire!" That logic is pathetic and delusional. Having the idea for eBay has nothing to do with actually creating eBay. What you do is what matters, not what you think or say or plan. Think your idea's that valuable? Then go try to sell it and see what you get for it. Not much is probably the answer. Until you actually start making something, your brilliant idea is just that, an idea. And everyone's got one of those. Stanley Kubrick gave this advice to aspiring filmmakers: "Get hold of a camera and some film and make a movie of any kind at all."* Kubrick knew that when you're new at something, you need to start creating. The most important thing is to begin. So get a camera, hit Record, and start shooting. Ideas are cheap and plentiful. The original pitch idea is such a small part of a business that it's almost negligible. The real question is how well you execute. No time is no excuse The most common excuse people give: "There's not enough time." They claim they'd love to start a company, learn an instrument, market an invention, write a book, or whatever, but there just aren't enough hours in the day. Come on. There's always enough time if you spend it right. And don't think you have to quit your day job, either. Hang onto it and start work on your project at night. Instead of watching TV or playing World of Warcraft, work on your idea. Instead of going to bed at ten, go to bed at eleven. We're not talking about all-nighters or sixteenhour days--we're talking about squeezing out a few extra hours a week. That's enough time to get something going. Once you do that, you'll learn whether your excitement and interest is real or just a passing phase. If it doesn't pan out, you just keep going to work every day like you've been doing all along. You didn't risk or lose anything, other than a bit of time, so it's no big deal. When you want something bad enough, you make the time--regardless of your other obligations. The truth is most people just don't want it bad enough. Then they protect their ego with the excuse of time. Don't let yourself off the hook with excuses. It's entirely your responsibility to make your dreams come true. Besides, the perfect time never arrives. You're always too young or old or busy or broke or something else. If you constantly fret about timing things perfectly, they'll never happen. Draw a line in the sand As you get going, keep in mind why you're doing what you're doing. Great businesses have a point of view, not just a product or service. You have to believe in something. You need to have a backbone. You need to know what you're willing to fight for. And then you need to show the world. A strong stand is how you attract superfans. They point to you and defend you. And they spread the word further, wider, and more passionately than any advertising could. Strong opinions aren't free. You'll turn some people off. They'll accuse you of being arrogant and aloof. That's life. For everyone who loves you, there will be others who hate you. If no one's upset by what you're saying, you're probably not pushing hard enough. (And you're probably boring, too.) Lots of people hate us because our products do less than the competition's. They're insulted when we refuse to include their pet feature. But we're just as proud of what our products don't do as we are of what they do. We design them to be simple because we believe most software is too complex: too many features, too many buttons, too much confusion. So we build software that's the opposite of that. If what we make isn't right for everyone, that's OK. We're willing to lose some customers if it means that others love our products intensely. That's our line in the sand. When you don't know what you believe, everything becomes an argument. Everything is debatable. But when you stand for something, decisions are obvious. For example, Whole Foods stands for selling the highest quality natural and organic products available. They don't waste time deciding over and over again what's appropriate. No one asks, "Should we sell this product that has artificial flavors?" There's no debate. The answer is clear. That's why you can't buy a Coke or a Snickers there. This belief means the food is more expensive at Whole Foods. Some haters even call it Whole Paycheck and make fun of those who shop there. But so what? Whole Foods is doing pretty damn well. Another example is Vinnie's Sub Shop, just down the street from our office in Chicago. They put this homemade basil oil on subs that's just perfect. You better show up on time, though. Ask when they close and the woman behind the counter will respond, "We close when the bread runs out." Really? "Yeah. We get our bread from the bakery down the street early in the morning, when it's the freshest. Once we run out (usually around two or three p.m.), we close up shop. We could get more bread later in the day, but it's not as good as the freshbaked bread in the morning. There's no point in selling a few more sandwiches if the bread isn't good. A few bucks isn't going to make up for selling food we can't be proud of." Wouldn't you rather eat at a place like that instead of some generic sandwich chain? Mission statement impossible There's a world of difference between truly standing for something and having a mission statement that says you stand for something. You know, those "providing the best service" signs that are created just to be posted on a wall. The ones that sound phony and disconnected from reality. Imagine you're standing in a rental-car office. The room's cold. The carpet is dirty. There's no one at the counter. And then you see a tattered piece of paper with some clip art at the top of it pinned to a bulletin board. It's a mission statement:Our mission is to fulfill the automotive and commercial truck rental, leasing, car sales and related needs of our customers and, in doing so, exceed their expectations for service, quality and value.We will strive to earn our customers' long-term loyalty by working to deliver more than promised, being honest and fair and "going the extra mile" to provide exceptional personalized service that creates a pleasing business experience.We must motivate our employees to provide exceptional service to our customers by supporting their development, providing opportunities for personal growth and fairly compensating them for their successes and achievements ... * And it drones on. And you're sitting there reading this crap and wondering, "What kind of idiot do they take me for?" The words on the paper are clearly disconnected from the reality of the experience. It's like when you're on hold and a recorded voice comes on telling you how much the company values you as a customer. Really? Then maybe you should hire some more support people so I don't have to wait thirty minutes to get help. Or just say nothing. But don't give me an automated voice that's telling me how much you care about me. It's a robot. I know the difference between genuine affection and a robot that's programmed to say nice things. Standing for something isn't just about writing it down. It's about believing it and living it. Outside money is Plan Z One of the first questions you'll probably ask: Where's the seed money going to come from? Far too often, people think the answer is to raise money from outsiders. If you're building something like a factory or restaurant, then you may indeed need that outside cash. But a lot of companies don't need expensive infrastructure--especially these days. We're in a service economy now. Service businesses (e.g., consultants, software companies, wedding planners, graphic designers, and hundreds of others) don't require much to get going. If you're running a business like that, avoid outside funding. In fact, no matter what kind of business you're starting, take on as little outside cash as you can. Spending other people's money may sound great, but there's a noose attached. Here's why: You give up control. When you turn to outsiders for funding, you have to answer to them too. That's fine at first, when everyone agrees. But what happens down the road? Are you starting your own business to take orders from someone else? Raise money and that's what you'll wind up doing. "Cashing out" begins to trump building a quality business. Investors want their money back--and quickly (usually three to five years). Long-term sustainability goes out the window when those involved only want to cash out as soon as they can. Spending other people's money is addictive. There's nothing easier than spending other people's money. But then you run out and need to go back for more. And every time you go back, they take more of your company. It's usually a bad deal. When you're just beginning, you have no leverage. That's a terrible time to enter into any financial transaction. Customers move down the totem pole. You wind up building what investors want instead of what customers want. Raising money is incredibly distracting. Seeking funding is difficult and draining. It takes months of pitch meetings, legal maneuvering, contracts, etc. That's an enormous distraction when you should really be focused on building something great. It's just not worth it. We hear over and over from business owners who have gone down this road and regret it. They usually give a variation on the investment-hangover story: First, you get that quick investment buzz. But then you start having meetings with your investors and/or board of directors, and you're like, "Oh man, what have I gotten myself into?" Now someone else is calling the shots. Before you stick your head in that noose, look for another way. You need less than you think Do you really need ten people or will two or three do for now? Do you really need $500,000 or is $50,000 (or $5,000) enough for now? Do you really need six months or can you make something in two? Do you really need a big office or can you share office space (or work from home) for a while? Do you really need a warehouse or can you rent a small storage space (or use your garage or basement) or outsource it completely? Do you really need to buy advertising and hire a PR firm or are there other ways to get noticed? Do you really need to build a factory or can you hire someone else to manufacture your products? Do you really need an accountant or can you use Quicken and do it yourself? Do you really need an IT department or can you outsource it? Do you really need a full-time support person or can you handle inquiries on your own? Do you really need to open a retail store or can you sell your product online? Do you really need fancy business cards, letterhead, and brochures or can you forego that stuff? You get the point. Maybe eventually you'll need to go the bigger, more expensive route, but not right now. There's nothing wrong with being frugal. When we launched our first product, we did it on the cheap. We didn't get our own office; we shared space with another company. We didn't get a bank of servers; we had only one. We didn't advertise; we promoted by sharing our experiences online. We didn't hire someone to answer customer e-mails; the company founder answered them himself. And everything worked out just fine. Great companies start in garages all the time. Yours can too.Start a business, not a startup Ah, the startup. It's a special breed of company that gets a lot of attention (especially in the tech world). The start up is a magical place. It's a place where expenses are someone else's problem. It's a place where that pesky thing called revenue is never an issue. It's a place where you can spend other people's money until you figure out a way to make your own. It's a place where the laws of business physics don't apply. The problem with this magical place is it's a fairy tale. The truth is every business, new or old, is governed by the same set of market forces and economic rules. Revenue in, expenses out. Turn a profit or wind up gone. Startups try to ignore this reality. They are run by people trying to postpone the inevitable, i.e., that moment when their business has to grow up, turn a profit, and be a real, sustainable business. Anyone who takes a "we'll figure out how to profit in the future" attitude to business is being ridiculous. That's like building a rocket ship but starting off by saying, "Let's pretend gravity doesn't exist." A business without a path to profit isn't a business, it's a hobby. So don't use the idea of a startup as a crutch. Instead, start an actual business. Actual businesses have to deal with actual things like bills and payroll. Actual businesses worry about profit from day one. Actual businesses don't mask deep problems by saying, "It's OK, we're a startup." Act like an actual business and you'll have a much better shot at succeeding. Building to flip is building to flop Another thing you hear a lot: "What's your exit strategy?" You hear it even when you're just beginning. What is it with people who can't even start building something without knowing how they're going to leave it? What's the hurry? Your priorities are out of whack if you're thinking about getting out before you even dive in. Would you go into a relationship planning the breakup? Would you write the prenup on a first date? Would you meet with a divorce lawyer the morning of your wedding? That would be ridiculous, right? You need a commitment strategy, not an exit strategy. You should be thinking about how to make your project grow and succeed, not how you're going to jump ship. If your whole strategy is based on leaving, chances are you won't get far in the first place. You see so many aspiring businesspeople pinning their hopes on selling out. But the odds of getting acquired are so tiny. There's only a slim chance that some big suitor will come along and make it all worthwhile. Maybe 1 in 1,000? Or 1 in 10,000? Plus, when you build a company with the intention of being acquired, you emphasize the wrong things. Instead of focusing on getting customers to love you, you worry about who's going to buy you. That's the wrong thing to obsess over. And let's say you ignore this advice and do pull off a flip. You build your business, sell it, and get a nice payday. Then what? Move to an island and sip pina coladas all day? Will that really satisfy you? Will money alone truly make you happy? Are you sure you'll like that more than running a business you actually enjoy and believe in? That's why you often hear about business owners who sell out, retire for six months, and then get back in the game. They miss the thing they gave away. And usually, they're back with a business that isn't nearly as good as their first. Don't be that guy. If you do manage to get a good thing going, keep it going. Good things don't come around that often. Don't let your business be the one that got away. Less mass Embrace the idea of having less mass. Right now, you're the smallest, the leanest, and the fastest you'll ever be. From here on out, you'll start accumulating mass. And the more massive an object, the more energy required to change its direction. It's as true in the business world as it is in the physical world. Mass is increased by ... Long-term contracts Excess staff Permanent decisions Meetings Thick process Inventory (physical or mental) Hardware, software, and technology lock-ins Long-term road maps Office politics Avoid these things whenever you can. That way, you'll be able to change direction easily. The more expensive it is to make a change, the less likely you are to make it. Huge organizations can take years to pivot.

They talk instead of act. They meet instead of do. But if you keep your mass low, you can quickly change anything: your entire business model, product, feature set, and/or marketing message. You can make mistakes and fix them quickly. You can change your priorities, product mix, or focus. And most important, you can change your mind.*Jim Rutenberg, "Clinton Finds Way to Play Along with Drudge," New York Times, Oct. 22, 2007. *"Fascinating Facts About James Dyson, Inventor of the Dyson Vacuum Cleaner in 1978," www.ideafinder.com/history/inventors/dyson.htm+Russ Mitchell, "The Beat Goes On," CBS News, Sunday Morning, Mar. 29, 2009, www.tinyurl.com/cd8gjq++Eric Ransdell, "The Nike Story? Just Tell It!" Fast Company, Dec. 19, 2007, www.fastcompany.com/magazine/31/nike.html*"Mary Kay Ash: Mary Kay Cosmetics," Journal of Business Leadership 1, no. 1 (Spring 1988); American National Business Hall of Fame, www.anbhf.org/laureates/mkash.html*"Stanley Kubrick--Biography," IMDB, www.imdb.com/name/nm00004o/bio*Mission, Enterprise Rent-a-Car, http://aboutus.enterprise.com/who_we_are/mission.html CHAPTER PROGRESS Embrace constraints "I don't have enough time/money/people/experience." Stop whining. Less is a good thing. Constraints are advantages in disguise. Limited resources force you to make do with what you've got. There's no room for waste. And that forces you to be creative. Ever seen the weapons prisoners make out of soap or a spoon? They make do with what they've got. Now we're not saying you should go out and shank somebody--but get creative and you'll be amazed at what you can make with just a little. Writers use constraints to force creativity all the time. Shakespeare reveled in the limitations of sonnets (fourteen-line lyric poems in iambic pentameter with a specific rhyme scheme). Haiku and limericks also have strict rules that lead to creative results. Writers like Ernest Hemingway and Raymond Carver found that forcing themselves to use simple, clear language helped them deliver maximum impact. The Price Is Right, the longest-running game show in history, is also a great example of creativity born from embracing constraints. The show has more than a hundred games, and each one is based on the question "How much does this item cost?" That simple formula has attracted fans for more than thirty years. Southwest--unlike most other airlines, which fly multiple aircraft models--flies only Boeing 737s. As a result, every Southwest pilot, flight attendant, and ground-crew member can work any flight. Plus, all of Southwest's parts fit all of its planes. All that means lower costs and a business that's easier to run. They made it easy on themselves. When we were building Basecamp, we had plenty of limitations. We had a design firm to run with existing client work, a seven-hour time difference between principals (David was doing the programming in Denmark, the rest of us were in the States), a small team, and no outside funding. These constraints forced us to keep the product simple. These days, we have more resources and people, but we still force constraints. We make sure to have only one or two people working on a product at a time. And we always keep features to a minimum. Boxing ourselves in this way prevents us from creating bloated products. So before you sing the "not enough" blues, see how far you can get with what you have. Build half a product, not a half-assed product You can turn a bunch of great ideas into a crappy product real fast by trying to do them all at once. You just can't do everything you want to do and do it well. You have limited time, resources, ability, and focus. It's hard enough to do one thing right. Trying to do ten things well at the same time? Forget about it. So sacrifice some of your darlings for the greater good. Cut your ambition in half. You're better off with a kick-ass half than a half-assed whole. Most of your great ideas won't seem all that great once you get some perspective, anyway. And if they truly are that fantastic, you can always do them later. Lots of things get better as they get shorter. Directors cut good scenes to make a great movie. Musicians drop good tracks to make a great album. Writers eliminate good pages to make a great book. We cut this book in half between the next-to-last and final drafts. From 57,000 words to about 27,000 words. Trust us, it's better for it. So start chopping. Getting to great starts by cutting out stuff that's merely good. Start at the epicenter When you start anything new, there are forces pulling you in a variety of directions. There's the stuff you could do, the stuff you want to do, and the stuff you have to do. The stuff you have to do is where you should begin. Start at the epicenter. For example, if you're opening a hot dog stand, you could worry about the condiments, the cart, the name, the decoration. But the first thing you should worry about is the hot dog. The hot dogs are the epicenter. Everything else is secondary. The way to find the epicenter is to ask yourself this question: "If I took this away, would what I'm selling still exist?" A hot dog stand isn't a hot dog stand without the hot dogs. You can take away the onions, the relish, the mustard, etc. Some people may not like your toppings-less dogs, but you'd still have a hot dog stand. But you simply cannot have a hot dog stand without any hot dogs. So figure out your epicenter. Which part of your equation can't be removed? If you can continue to get by without this thing or that thing, then those things aren't the epicenter. When you find it, you'll know. Then focus all your energy on making it the best it can be. Everything else you do depends on that foundation. Ignore the details early on Architects don't worry about which tiles go in the shower or which brand of dishwasher to install in the kitchen until after the floor plan is finalized. They know it's better to decide these details later. You need to approach your idea the same way. Details make the difference. But getting infatuated with details too early leads to disagreement, meetings, and delays. You get lost in things that don't really matter. You waste time on decisions that are going to change anyway. So ignore the details--for a while. Nail the basics first and worry about the specifics later. When we start designing something, we sketch out ideas with a big, thick Sharpie marker, instead of a ballpoint pen. Why? Pen points are too fine. They're too highresolution. They encourage you to worry about things that you shouldn't worry about yet, like perfecting the shading or whether to use a dotted or dashed line. You end up focusing on things that should still be out of focus. A Sharpie makes it impossible to drill down that deep. You can only draw shapes, lines, and boxes. That's good. The big picture is all you should be worrying about in the beginning. Walt Stanchfield, famed drawing instructor for Walt Disney Studios, used to encourage animators to "forget the detail" at first. The reason: Detail just doesn't buy you anything in the early stages.* Besides, you often can't recognize the details that matter most until after you start building. That's when you see what needs more attention. You feel what's missing. And that's when you need to pay attention, not sooner. Making the call is making progress When you put off decisions, they pile up. And piles end up ignored, dealt with in haste, or thrown out. As a result, the individual problems in those piles stay unresolved. Whenever you can, swap "Let's think about it" for "Let's decide on it." Commit to making decisions. Don't wait for the perfect solution. Decide and move forward. You want to get into the rhythm of making choices. When you get in that flow of making decision after decision, you build momentum and boost morale. Decisions are progress. Each one you make is a brick in your foundation. You can't build on top of "We'll decide later," but you can build on top of "Done." The problem comes when you postpone decisions in the hope that a perfect answer will come to you later. It won't. You're as likely to make a great call today as you are tomorrow. An example from our world: For a long time, we avoided creating an affiliate program for our products because the "perfect" solution seemed way too complicated: We'd have to automate payments, mail out checks, figure out foreign tax laws for overseas affiliates, etc. The breakthrough came when we asked, "What can we easily do right now that's good enough?" The answer: Pay affiliates in credit instead of cash. So that's what we did. We stuck with that approach for a while and then eventually implemented a system that pays cash. And that's a big part of this: You don't have to live with a decision forever. If you make a mistake, you can correct it later. It doesn't matter how much you plan, you'll still get some stuff wrong anyway. Don't make things worse by overanalyzing and delaying before you even get going. Long projects zap morale. The longer it takes to develop, the less likely it is to launch. Make the call, make progress, and get something out now-- while you've got the motivation and momentum to do so. Be a curator You don't make a great museum by putting all the art in the world into a single room. That's a warehouse. What makes a museum great is the stuff that's not on the walls. Someone says no. A curator is involved, making conscious decisions about what should stay and what should go. There's an editing process. There's a lot more stuff off the walls than on the walls. The best is a sub-sub-subset of all the possibilities. It's the stuff you leave out that matters. So constantly look for things to remove, simplify, and streamline. Be a curator. Stick to what's truly essential. Pare things down until you're left with only the most important stuff. Then do it again. You can always add stuff back in later if you need to. Zingerman's is one of America's best-known delis. And it got that way because its owners think of themselves as curators. They're not just filling their shelves. They're curating them. There's a reason for every olive oil the team at Zingerman's sells: They believe each one is great. Usually, they've known the supplier for years. They've visited and picked olives with them. That's why they can vouch for each oil's authentic, full-bodied flavor. For example, look how the owner of Zingerman's describes Pasolivo Olive Oil on the company Web site:I tasted this oil for the first time years ago, on a random recommendation and sample. There are plenty of oils that come in nice bottles with very endearing stories to tell--this was no exception--but most simply aren't that great. By contrast Pasolivo got my attention as soon as I tasted it. It's powerful, full and fruity. Everything I like in an oil, without any drawbacks. It still stands as one of America's best oils, on par with the great rustic oils of Tuscany. Strongly recommended.* The owner actually tried the oil and chooses to carry it based on its taste. It's not about packaging, marketing, or price. It's about quality. He tried it and knew his store had to carry it. That's the approach you should take too. Throw less at the problem Watch chef Gordon Ramsay's Kitchen Nightmares and you'll see a pattern. The menus at failing restaurants offer too many dishes. The owners think making every dish under the sun will broaden the appeal of the restaurant. Instead it makes for crappy food (and creates inventory headaches). That's why Ramsay's first step is nearly always to trim the menu, usually from thirty-plus dishes to around ten. Think about that. Improving the current menu doesn't come first. Trimming it down comes first. Then he polishes what's left. When things aren't working, the natural inclination is to throw more at the problem. More people, time, and money. All that ends up doing is making the problem bigger. The right way to go is the opposite direction: Cut back. So do less. Your project won't suffer nearly as much as you fear. In fact, there's a good chance it'll end up even better. You'll be forced to make tough calls and sort out what truly matters. If you start pushing back deadlines and increasing your budget, you'll never stop. Focus on what won't change A lot of companies focus on the next big thing. They latch on to what's hot and new. They follow the latest trends and technology. That's a fool's path. You start focusing on fashion instead of substance. You start paying attention to things that are constantly changing instead of things that last. The core of your business should be built around things that won't change. Things that people are going to want today and ten years from now. Those are the things you should invest in. Amazon.com focuses on fast (or free) shipping, great selection, friendly return policies, and affordable prices. These things will always be in high demand. Japanese automakers also focus on core principles that don't change: reliability, affordability, and practicality. People wanted those things thirty years ago, they want them today, and they'll want them thirty years from now. For 37signals, things like speed, simplicity, ease of use, and clarity are our focus. Those are timeless desires. People aren't going to wake up in ten years and say, "Man, I wish software was harder to use." They won't say, "I wish this application was slower." Remember, fashion fades away. When you focus on permanent features, you're in bed with things that never go out of style. Tone is in your fingers Guitar gurus say, "Tone is in your fingers." You can buy the same guitar, effects pedals, and amplifier that Eddie Van Halen uses. But when you play that rig, it's still going to sound like you. Likewise, Eddie could plug into a crappy Strat/Pignose setup at a pawn shop, and you'd still be able to recognize that it's Eddie Van Halen playing. Fancy gear can help, but the truth is your tone comes from you. It's tempting for people to obsess over tools instead of what they're going to do with those tools. You know the type: Designers who use an avalanche of funky typefaces and fancy Photoshop filters but don't have anything to say. Amateur photographers who want to debate film versus digital endlessly instead of focusing on what actually makes a photograph great. Many amateur golfers think they need expensive clubs. But it's the swing that matters, not the club. Give Tiger Woods a set of cheap clubs and he'll still destroy you. People use equipment as a crutch. They don't want to put in the hours on the driving range so they spend a ton in the pro shop. They're looking for a shortcut. But you just don't need the best gear in the world to be good. And you definitely don't need it to get started. In business, too many people obsess over tools, software tricks, scaling issues, fancy office space, lavish furniture, and other frivolities instead of what really matters. And what really matters is how to actually get customers and make money. You also see it in people who want to blog, podcast, or shoot videos for their business but get hung up on which tools to use. The content is what matters. You can spend tons on fancy equipment, but if you've got nothing to say ... well, you've got nothing to say. Use whatever you've got already or can afford cheaply. Then go. It's not the gear that matters. It's playing what you've got as well as you can. Your tone is in your fingers. Sell your by-products When you make something, you always make something else. You can't make just one thing. Everything has a by-product. Observant and creative business minds spot these by-products and see opportunities. The lumber industry sells what used to be waste--sawdust, chips, and shredded wood--for a pretty profit. You'll find these by-products in synthetic fireplace logs, concrete, ice strengtheners, mulch, particleboard, fuel, and more. But you're probably not manufacturing anything. That can make it tough to spot your by-products. People at a lumber company see their waste. They can't ignore sawdust. But you don't see yours. Maybe you don't even think you produce any byproducts. But that's myopic. Our last book, Getting Real, was a by-product. We wrote that book without even knowing it. The experience that came from building a company and building software was the waste from actually doing the work. We swept up that knowledge first into blog posts, then into a workshop series, then into a .pdf, and then into a paperback. That byproduct has made 37signals more than $1 million directly and probably more than another $1 million indirectly. The book you're reading right now is a by-product too. The rock band Wilco found a valuable by-product in its recording process. The band filmed the creation of an album and released it as a documentary called I Am Trying to Break Your Heart. It offered an uncensored and fascinating look at the group's creative process and infighting. The band made money off the movie and also used it as a stepping-stone toward reaching a wider audience. Henry Ford learned of a process for turning wood scraps from the production of Model T's into charcoal briquets. He built a charcoal plant and Ford Charcoal was created (later renamed Kingsford Charcoal). Today, Kingsford is still the leading manufacturer of charcoal in America.* Software companies don't usually think about writing books. Bands don't usually think about filming the recording process. Car manufacturers don't usually think about selling charcoal. There's probably something you haven't thought about that you could sell too. Launch now When is your product or service finished? When should you put it out on the market? When is it safe to let people have it? Probably a lot sooner than you're comfortable with. Once your product does what it needs to do, get it out there. Just because you've still got a list of things to do doesn't mean it's not done. Don't hold everything else up because of a few leftovers. You can do them later. And doing them later may mean doing them better, too. Think about it this way: If you had to launch your business in two weeks, what would you cut out? Funny how a question like that forces you to focus. You suddenly realize there's a lot of stuff you don't need. And what you do need seems obvious. When you impose a deadline, you gain clarity. It's the best way to get to that gut instinct that tells you, "We don't need this." Put off anything you don't need for launch. Build the necessities now, worry about the luxuries later. If you really think about it, there's a whole lot you don't need on day one. When we launched Basecamp, we didn't even have the ability to bill customers! Because the product billed in monthly cycles, we knew we had a thirty-day gap to figure it out. So we used the time before launch to solve more urgent problems that actually mattered on day one. Day 30 could wait. Camper, a brand of shoes, opened a store in San Francisco before construction was even finished and called it a Walk in Progress. Customers could draw on the walls of the empty store. Camper displayed shoes on cheap plywood laid over dozens of shoe boxes. The most popular message written by customers on the walls: "Keep the store just the way it is."* Likewise, the founders of Crate and Barrel didn't wait to build fancy displays when they opened their first store. They turned over the crates and barrels that the merchandise came in and stacked products on top of them.+ Don't mistake this approach for skimping on quality, either. You still want to make something great. This approach just recognizes that the best way to get there is through iterations. Stop imagining what's going to work. Find out for real.*Walt Stanchfield, Drawn to Life: 20 Golden Years of Disney Master Classes, vol. 1, The Walt Stanchfield Lectures, Oxford, UK: Focal Press, 2009. *Pasolivo Olive Oil, Zingerman's, www.zingermans.com/product.aspx?productid=o-psl*"About Kingsford: Simply a Matter of Taste," Kingsford, www.kingsford.com/about/index.htm*Fara Warner, "Walk in Progress," Fast Company, Dec. 19, 2007, www.fastcompany.com/magazine/58/lookfeel.html+Matt Valley, "The Crate and Barrel Story," Retail Traffic, June 1, 2001, retailtrafficmag.com/mag/retail_crate_barrel_story CHAPTER PRODUCTIVITY Illusions of agreement The business world is littered with dead documents that do nothing but waste people's time. Reports no one reads, diagrams no one looks at, and specs that never resemble the finished product. These things take forever to make but only seconds to forget. If you need to explain something, try getting real with it. Instead of describing what something looks like, draw it. Instead of explaining what something sounds like, hum it. Do everything you can to remove layers of abstraction. The problem with abstractions (like reports and documents) is that they create illusions of agreement. A hundred people can read the same words, but in their heads, they're imagining a hundred different things. That's why you want to get to something real right away. That's when you get true understanding. It's like when we read about characters in a book--we each picture them differently in our heads. But when we actually see people, we all know exactly what they look like. When the team at Alaska Airlines wanted to build a new Airport of the Future, they didn't rely on blueprints and sketches. They got a warehouse and built mock-ups using cardboard boxes for podiums, kiosks, and belts. The team then built a small prototype in Anchorage to test systems with real passengers and employees. The design that resulted from this getting-real process has significantly reduced wait times and increased agent productivity.* Widely admired furniture craftsman Sam Maloof felt it was impossible to make a working drawing to show all the intricate and fine details that go into a chair or stool. "Many times I do not know how a certain area is to be done until I start working with a chisel, rasp, or whatever tool is needed for that particular job," he said.+ That's the path we all should take. Get the chisel out and start making something real. Anything else is just a distraction. Reasons to quit It's easy to put your head down and just work on what you think needs to be done. It's a lot harder to pull your head up and ask why. Here are some important questions to ask yourself to ensure you're doing work that matters: Why are you doing this? Ever find yourself working on something without knowing exactly why? Someone just told you to do it. It's pretty common, actually. That's why it's important to ask why you're working on_______. What is this for? Who benefits? What's the motivation behind it? Knowing the answers to these questions will help you better understand the work itself. What problem are you solving? What's the problem? Are customers confused? Are you confused? Is something not clear enough? Was something not possible before that should be possible now? Sometimes when you ask these questions, you'll find you're solving an imaginary problem. That's when it's time to stop and reevaluate what the hell you're doing. Is this actually useful? Are you making something useful or just making something? It's easy to confuse enthusiasm with usefulness. Sometimes it's fine to play a bit and build something cool. But eventually you've got to stop and ask yourself if it's useful, too. Cool wears off. Useful never does. Are you adding value? Adding something is easy; adding value is hard. Is this thing you're working on actually making your product more valuable for customers? Can they get more out of it than they did before? Sometimes things you think are adding value actually subtract from it. Too much ketchup can ruin the fries. Value is about balance. Will this change behavior? Is what you're working on really going to change anything? Don't add something unless it has a real impact on how people use your product. Is there an easier way? Whenever you're working on something, ask, "Is there an easier way?" You'll often find this easy way is more than good enough for now. Problems are usually pretty simple. We just imagine that they require hard solutions. What could you be doing instead? What can't you do because you're doing this? This is especially important for small teams with constrained resources. That's when prioritization is even more important. If you work on A, can you still do B and C before April? If not, would you rather have B and C instead of A? If you're stuck on something for a long period of time, that means there are other things you're not getting done. Is it really worth it? Is what you're doing really worth it? Is this meeting worth pulling six people off their work for an hour? Is it worth pulling an allnighter tonight, or could you just finish it up tomorrow? Is it worth getting all stressed out over a press release from a competitor? Is it worth spending your money on advertising? Determine the real value of what you're about to do before taking the plunge. Keep asking yourself (and others) the questions listed above. You don't need to make it a formal process, but don't let it slide, either. Also, don't be timid about your conclusions. Sometimes abandoning what you're working on is the right move, even if you've already put in a lot of effort. Don't throw good time after bad work. Interruption is the enemy of productivity If you're constantly staying late and working weekends, it's not because there's too much work to be done. It's because you're not getting enough done at work. And the reason is interruptions. Think about it: When do you get most of your work done? If you're like most people, it's at night or early in the morning. It's no coincidence that these are the times when nobody else is around. At 2 p.m., people are usually in a meeting or answering e-mail or chatting with colleagues. Those taps on the shoulder and little impromptu get-togethers may seem harmless, but they're actually corrosive to productivity. Interruption is not collaboration, it's just interruption. And when you're interrupted, you're not getting work done. Interruptions break your workday into a series of work moments. Forty-five minutes and then you have a call. Fifteen minutes and then you have lunch. An hour later, you have an afternoon meeting. Before you know it, it's five o'clock, and you've only had a couple uninterrupted hours to get your work done. You can't get meaningful things done when you're constantly going start, stop, start, stop. Instead, you should get in the alone zone. Long stretches of alone time are when you're most productive. When you don't have to mind-shift between various tasks, you get a boatload done. (Ever notice how much work you get done on a plane since you're offline and there are zero outside distractions?) Getting into that zone takes time and requires avoiding interruptions. It's like REM sleep: You don't just go directly into REM sleep. You go to sleep first and then make your way to REM. Any interruptions force you to start over. And just as REM is when the real sleep magic happens, the alone zone is where the real productivity magic happens. Your alone zone doesn't have to be in the wee hours, though. You can set up a rule at work that half the day is set aside for alone time. Decree that from 10 a.m. to 2 p.m., people can't talk to each other (except during lunch). Or make the first or last half of the day your alone-time period. Or instead of casual Fridays, try no-talk Thursdays. Just make sure this period is unbroken in order to avoid productivity-zapping interruptions. And go all the way with it. A successful alone-time period means letting go of communication addiction. During alone time, give up instant messages, phone calls, email, and meetings. Just shut up and get to work. You'll be surprised how much more you get done.

Also, when you do collaborate, try to use passive communication tools, like email, that don't require an instant reply, instead of interruptive ones, like phone calls and face-to-face meetings. That way people can respond when it's convenient for them, instead of being forced to drop everything right away. Your day is under siege by interruptions. It's on you to fight back. Meetings are toxic The worst interruptions of all are meetings. Here's why: They're usually about words and abstract concepts, not real things. They usually convey an abysmally small amount of information per minute. They drift off-subject easier than a Chicago cab in a snowstorm. They require thorough preparation that most people don't have time for. They frequently have agendas so vague that nobody is really sure of the goal. They often include at least one moron who inevitably gets his turn to waste everyone's time with nonsense. Meetings procreate. One meeting leads to another meeting leads to another ... It's also unfortunate that meetings are typically scheduled like TV shows. You set aside thirty minutes or an hour because that's how scheduling software works (you'll never see anyone schedule a seven-minute meeting with Outlook). Too bad. If it only takes seven minutes to accomplish a meeting's goal, then that's all the time you should spend. Don't stretch seven into thirty. When you think about it, the true cost of meetings is staggering. Let's say you're going to schedule a meeting that lasts one hour, and you invite ten people to attend. That's actually a ten-hour meeting, not a one-hour meeting. You're trading ten hours of productivity for one hour of meeting time. And it's probably more like fifteen hours, because there are mental switching costs that come with stopping what you're doing, going somewhere else to meet, and then resuming what you were doing beforehand. Is it ever OK to trade ten or fifteen hours of productivity for one hour of meeting? Sometimes, maybe. But that's a pretty hefty price to pay. Judged on a pure cost basis, meetings of this size quickly become liabilities, not assets. Think about the time you're actually losing and ask yourself if it's really worth it. If you decide you absolutely must get together, try to make your meeting a productive one by sticking to these simple rules: Set a timer. When it rings, meeting's over. Period. Invite as few people as possible. Always have a clear agenda. Begin with a specific problem. Meet at the site of the problem instead of a conference room. Point to real things and suggest real changes. End with a solution and make someone responsible for implementing it. Good enough is fine A lot of people get off on solving problems with complicated solutions. Flexing your intellectual muscles can be intoxicating.

Then you start looking for another big challenge that gives you that same rush, regardless of whether it's a good idea or not. A better idea: Find a judo solution, one that delivers maximum efficiency with minimum effort. Judo solutions are all about getting the most out of doing the least. Whenever you face an obstacle, look for a way to judo it. Part of this is recognizing that problems are negotiable. Let's say your challenge is to get a bird's-eye view. One way to do it is to climb Mount Everest. That's the ambitious solution. But then again, you could take an elevator to the top of a tall building. That's a judo solution. Problems can usually be solved with simple, mundane solutions. That means there's no glamorous work. You don't get to show off your amazing skills. You just build something that gets the job done and then move on. This approach may not earn you oohs and aahs, but it lets you get on with it. Look at political campaign ads. A big issue pops up, and politicians have an ad about it on the air the next day. The production quality is low. They use photos instead of live footage. They have static, plain-text headlines instead of fancy animated graphics. The only audio is a voice-over done by an unseen narrator. Despite all that, the ad is still good enough. If they waited weeks to perfect it, it would come out too late. It's a situation where timeliness is more important than polish or even quality. When good enough gets the job done, go for it. It's way better than wasting resources or, even worse, doing nothing because you can't afford the complex solution. And remember, you can usually turn good enough into great later. Quick wins Momentum fuels motivation. It keeps you going. It drives you. Without it, you can't go anywhere. If you aren't motivated by what you're working on, it won't be very good. The way you build momentum is by getting something done and then moving on to the next thing. No one likes to be stuck on an endless project with no finish line in sight. Being in the trenches for nine months and not having anything to show for it is a real buzzkill. Eventually it just burns you out. To keep your momentum and motivation up, get in the habit of accomplishing small victories along the way. Even a tiny improvement can give you a good jolt of momentum. The longer something takes, the less likely it is that you're going to finish it. Excitement comes from doing something and then letting customers have at it. Planning a menu for a year is boring. Getting the new menu out, serving the food, and getting feedback is exciting. So don't wait too long--you'll smother your sparks if you do. If you absolutely have to work on long-term projects, try to dedicate one day a week (or every two weeks) to small victories that generate enthusiasm. Small victories let you celebrate and release good news. And you want a steady stream of good news. When there's something new to announce every two weeks, you energize your team and give your customers something to be excited about. So ask yourself, "What can we do in two weeks?" And then do it. Get it out there and let people use it, taste it, play it, or whatever. The quicker it's in the hands of customers, the better off you'll be. Don't be a hero A lot of times it's better to be a quitter than a hero. For example, let's say you think a task can be done in two hours. But four hours into it, you're still only a quarter of the way done. The natural instinct is to think, "But I can't give up now, I've already spent four hours on this!" So you go into hero mode. You're determined to make it work (and slightly embarrassed that it isn't already working). You grab your cape and shut yourself off from the world. And sometimes that kind of sheer effort overload works. But is it worth it? Probably not. The task was worth it when you thought it would cost two hours, not sixteen. In those sixteen hours, you could have gotten a bunch of other things done. Plus, you cut yourself off from feedback, which can lead you even further down the wrong path. Even heroes need a fresh pair of eyes sometimes--someone else to give them a reality check. We've experienced this problem firsthand. So we decided that if anything takes one of us longer than two weeks, we've got to bring other people in to take a look. They might not do any work on the task, but at least they can review it quickly and give their two cents. Sometimes an obvious solution is staring you right in the face, but you can't even see it. Keep in mind that the obvious solution might very well be quitting. People automatically associate quitting with failure, but sometimes that's exactly what you should do. If you already spent too much time on something that wasn't worth it, walk away. You can't get that time back. The worst thing you can do now is waste even more time. Go to sleep Forgoing sleep is a bad idea. Sure, you get those extra hours right now, but you pay in spades later: You destroy your creativity, morale, and attitude. Once in a while, you can pull an all-nighter if you fully understand the consequences. Just don't make it a habit. If it becomes a constant, the costs start to mount:Stubbornness: When you're really tired, it always seems easier to plow down whatever bad path you happen to be on instead of reconsidering the route. The finish line is a constant mirage and you wind up walking in the desert way too long. Lack of creativity: Creativity is one of the first things to go when you lose sleep. What distinguishes people who are ten times more effective than the norm is not that they work ten times as hard; it's that they use their creativity to come up with solutions that require one-tenth of the effort. Without sleep, you stop coming up with those one-tenth solutions. Diminished morale: When your brain isn't firing on all cylinders, it loves to feed on less demanding tasks. Like reading yet another article about stuff that doesn't matter. When you're tired, you lose motivation to attack the big problems. Irritability: Your ability to remain patient and tolerant is severely reduced when you're tired. If you encounter someone who's acting like a fool, there's a good chance that person is suffering from sleep deprivation. These are just some of the costs you incur when not getting enough sleep. Yet some people still develop a masochistic sense of honor about sleep deprivation. They even brag about how tired they are. Don't be impressed. It'll come back to bite them in the ass. Your estimates suck We're all terrible estimators. We think we can guess how long something will take, when we really have no idea. We see everything going according to a best-case scenario, without the delays that inevitably pop up. Reality never sticks to best-case scenarios. That's why estimates that stretch weeks, months, and years into the future are fantasies. The truth is you just don't know what's going to happen that far in advance. How often do you think a quick trip to the grocery store will take only a few minutes and then it winds up taking an hour? And remember when cleaning out the attic took you all day instead of just the couple of hours you thought it would? Or sometimes it's the opposite, like that time you planned on spending four hours raking the yard only to have it take just thirty-five minutes. We humans are just plain bad at estimating. Even with these simple tasks, our estimates are often off by a factor of two or more. If we can't be accurate when estimating a few hours, how can we expect to accurately predict the length of a "six-month project"? Plus, we're not just a little bit wrong when we guess how long something will take--we're a lot wrong. That means if you're guessing six months, you might be way off: We're not talking seven months instead of six, we're talking one year instead of six months. That's why Boston's "Big Dig" highway project finished five years late and billions over budget. Or the Denver International Airport opened sixteen months late, at a cost overrun of $2 billion. The solution: Break the big thing into smaller things. The smaller it is, the easier it is to estimate. You're probably still going to get it wrong, but you'll be a lot less wrong than if you estimated a big project. If something takes twice as long as you expected, better to have it be a small project that's a couple weeks over rather than a long one that's a couple months over. Keep breaking your time frames down into smaller chunks. Instead of one twelveweek project, structure it as twelve one-week projects. Instead of guesstimating at tasks that take thirty hours or more, break them down into more realistic six-to-ten-hour chunks. Then go one step at a time. Long lists don't get done Start making smaller to-do lists too. Long lists collect dust. When's the last time you finished a long list of things? You might have knocked off the first few, but chances are you eventually abandoned it (or blindly checked off items that weren't really done properly). Long lists are guilt trips. The longer the list of unfinished items, the worse you feel about it. And at a certain point, you just stop looking at it because it makes you feel bad. Then you stress out and the whole thing turns into a big mess. There's a better way. Break that long list down into a bunch of smaller lists. For example, break a single list of a hundred items into ten lists of ten items. That means when you finish an item on a list, you've completed 10 percent of that list, instead of 1 percent. Yes, you still have the same amount of stuff left to do. But now you can look at the small picture and find satisfaction, motivation, and progress. That's a lot better than staring at the huge picture and being terrified and demoralized. Whenever you can, divide problems into smaller and smaller pieces until you're able to deal with them completely and quickly. Simply rearranging your tasks this way can have an amazing impact on your productivity and motivation. And a quick suggestion about prioritization: Don't prioritize with numbers or labels. Avoid saying, "This is high priority, this is low priority." Likewise, don't say, "This is a three, this is a two, this is a one, this is a three," etc. Do that and you'll almost always end up with a ton of really high-priority things. That's not really prioritizing. Instead, prioritize visually. Put the most important thing at the top. When you're done with that, the next thing on the list becomes the next most important thing. That way you'll only have a single next most important thing to do at a time. And that's enough. Make tiny decisions Big decisions are hard to make and hard to change. And once you make one, the tendency is to continue believing you made the right decision, even if you didn't. You stop being objective. Once ego and pride are on the line, you can't change your mind without looking bad. The desire to save face trumps the desire to make the right call. And then there's inertia too: The more steam you put into going in one direction, the harder it is to change course. Instead, make choices that are small enough that they're effectively temporary. When you make tiny decisions, you can't make big mistakes. These small decisions mean you can afford to change. There's no big penalty if you mess up. You just fix it.

Making tiny decisions doesn't mean you can't make big plans or think big ideas. It just means you believe the best way to achieve those big things is one tiny decision at a time. Polar explorer Ben Saunders said that during his solo North Pole expedition (thirty-one marathons back-to-back, seventy-two days alone) the "huge decision" was often so horrifically overwhelming to contemplate that his day-to-day decision making rarely extended beyond "getting to that bit of ice a few yards in front of me." Attainable goals like that are the best ones to have. Ones you can actually accomplish and build on. You get to say, "We nailed it. Done!" Then you get going on the next one. That's a lot more satisfying than some pie-in-the-sky fantasy goal you never meet.*Dave Demerjian, "Hustle & Flow," Fast Company, www.fastcompany.com/magazine/123/hustle-and-flow.html+"Maloof on Maloof: Quotations and Works of Sam Maloof," Smithsonian American Art Museum, americanart.si.edu/exhibitions/online/maloof/introduction CHAPTER COMPETITORS Don't copy Sometimes copying can be part of the learning process, like when you see an art student replicating a painting in a museum or a drummer playing along to John Bonham's solo on Led Zeppelin's "Moby Dick." When you're a student, this sort of imitation can be a helpful tool on the path to discovering your own voice. Unfortunately, copying in the business arena is usually more nefarious. Maybe it's because of the copy-and-paste world we live in these days. You can steal someone's words, images, or code instantly. And that means it's tempting to try to build a business by being a copycat. That's a formula for failure, though. The problem with this sort of copying is it skips understanding--and understanding is how you grow. You have to understand why something works or why something is the way it is. When you just copy and paste, you miss that. You just repurpose the last layer instead of understanding all the layers underneath. So much of the work an original creator puts into something is invisible. It's buried beneath the surface. The copycat doesn't really know why something looks the way it looks or feels the way it feels or reads the way it reads. The copy is a faux finish. It delivers no substance, no understanding, and nothing to base future decisions on. Plus, if you're a copycat, you can never keep up. You're always in a passive position. You never lead; you always follow. You give birth to something that's already behind the times--just a knockoff, an inferior version of the original. That's no way to live. How do you know if you're copying someone? If someone else is doing the bulk of the work, you're copying. Be influenced, but don't steal. Decommoditize your product If you're successful, people will try to copy what you do. It's just a fact of life. But there's a great way to protect yourself from copycats: Make you part of your product or service. Inject what's unique about the way you think into what you sell. Decommoditize your product. Make it something no one else can offer. Look at Zappos.com, a billion-dollar online shoe retailer. A pair of sneakers from Zappos is the same as a pair from Foot Locker or any other retailer. But Zappos sets itself apart by injecting CEO Tony Hsieh's obsession with customer service into everything it does. At Zappos, customer-service employees don't use scripts and are allowed to talk at length with customers. The call center and the company's headquarters are in the same place, not oceans apart. And all Zappos employees--even those who don't work in customer service or fulfillment--start out by spending four weeks answering phones and working in the warehouse. It's this devotion to customer service that makes Zappos unique among shoe sellers.* Another example is Polyface, an environmentally friendly Virginia farm owned by Joel Salatin. Salatin has a strong set of beliefs and runs his business accordingly. Polyface sells the idea that it does things a bigger agribusiness can't do. Even though it's more expensive to do so, it feeds cows grass instead of corn and never gives them antibiotics. It never ships food. Anyone is welcome to visit the farm anytime and go anywhere (try that at a typical meat-processing plant). Polyface doesn't just sell chickens, it sells a way of thinking. And customers love Polyface for it. Some customers routinely drive from 150 miles away to get "clean" meat for their families.* Pour yourself into your product and everything around your product too: how you sell it, how you support it, how you explain it, and how you deliver it. Competitors can never copy the you in your product. Pick a fight If you think a competitor sucks, say so. When you do that, you'll find that others who agree with you will rally to your side. Being the anti-_______ is a great way to differentiate yourself and attract followers. For example, Dunkin' Donuts likes to position itself as the anti-Starbucks. Its ads mock Starbucks for using "Fritalian" terms instead of small, medium, and large. Another Dunkin' campaign is centered on a taste test in which it beat Starbucks. There's even a site called DunkinBeatStarbucks.com where visitors can send e-cards with statements like "Friends don't let friends drink Starbucks." Audi is another example. It's been taking on the old guard of car manufacturers. It puts "old luxury" brands like Rolls-Royce and Mercedes "on notice" in ads touting Audi as the fresh luxury alternative. Audi takes on Lexus's automatic parking systems with ads that say Audi drivers know how to park their own cars. Another ad gives a side-by-side comparison of BMW and Audi owners: The BMW owner uses the rearview mirror to adjust his hair while the Audi driver uses the mirror to see what's behind him. Apple jabs at Microsoft with ads that compare Mac and PC owners, and 7UP bills itself as the Uncola. Under Armour positions itself as Nike for a new generation. All these examples show the power and direction you can gain by having a target in your sights. Who do you want to take a shot at? You can even pit yourself as the opponent of an entire industry. Dyson's Airblade starts with the premise that the hand-dryer industry is a failure and then sells itself as faster and more hygienic than the others. I Can't Believe It's Not Butter puts its enemy right there in its product name. Having an enemy gives you a great story to tell customers, too. Taking a stand always stands out. People get stoked by conflict. They take sides. Passions are ignited. And that's a good way to get people to take notice. Underdo your competition Conventional wisdom says that to beat your competitors, you need to one-up them. If they have four features, you need five (or fifteen, or twenty-five). If they're spending $20,000, you need to spend $30,000. If they have fifty employees, you need a hundred. This sort of one-upping, Cold War mentality is a dead end. When you get suckered into an arms race, you wind up in a never-ending battle that costs you massive amounts of money, time, and drive. And it forces you to constantly be on the defensive, too. Defensive companies can't think ahead; they can only think behind. They don't lead; they follow. So what do you do instead? Do less than your competitors to beat them. Solve the simple problems and leave the hairy, difficult, nasty problems to the competition. Instead of one-upping, try one-downing. Instead of outdoing, try underdoing. The bicycle world provides a great example. For years, major bicycle brands focused on the latest in hightech equipment: mountain bikes with suspension and ultrastrong disc brakes, or lightweight titanium road bikes with carbon-fiber everything. And it was assumed that bikes should have multiple gears: three, ten, or twenty-one. But recently, fixed-gear bicycles have boomed in popularity, despite being as low-tech as you can get. These bikes have just one gear. Some models don't have brakes. The advantage: They're simpler, lighter, cheaper, and don't require as much maintenance. Another great example of a product that is succeeding by underdoing the competition: the Flip--an ultrasimple, point-and-shoot, compact camcorder that's taken a significant percentage of the market in a short time. Look at all the things the Flip does not deliver: No big screen (and the tiny screen doesn't swing out for self-portraits either) No photo-taking ability No tapes or discs (you have to offload the videos to a computer) No menus No settings No video light No viewfinder No special effects No headphone jack No lens cap No memory card No optical zoom The Flip wins fans because it only does a few simple things and it does them well. It's easy and fun to use. It goes places a bigger camera would never go and gets used by people who would never use a fancier camera. Don't shy away from the fact that your product or service does less. Highlight it. Be proud of it. Sell it as aggressively as competitors sell their extensive feature lists. Who cares what they're doing? In the end, it's not worth paying much attention to the competition anyway. Why not? Because worrying about the competition quickly turns into an obsession. What are they doing right now? Where are they going next? How should we react? Every little move becomes something to be analyzed. And that's a terrible mindset. It leads to overwhelming stress and anxiety. That state of mind is bad soil for growing anything. It's a pointless exercise anyway. The competitive landscape changes all the time. Your competitor tomorrow may be completely different from your competitor today. It's out of your control. What's the point of worrying about things you can't control? Focus on yourself instead. What's going on in here is way more important than what's going on out there. When you spend time worrying about someone else, you can't spend that time improving yourself. Focus on competitors too much and you wind up diluting your own vision. Your chances of coming up with something fresh go way down when you keep feeding your brain other people's ideas. You become reactionary instead of visionary. You wind up offering your competitor's products with a different coat of paint. If you're planning to build "the iPod killer" or "the next Pokemon," you're already dead. You're allowing the competition to set the parameters. You're not going to outApple Apple. They're defining the rules of the game. And you can't beat someone who's making the rules. You need to redefine the rules, not just build something slightly better. Don't ask yourself whether you're "beating" Apple (or whoever the big boy is in your industry). That's the wrong question to ask. It's not a win-or-lose battle. Their profits and costs are theirs. Yours are yours. If you're just going to be like everyone else, why are you even doing this? If you merely replicate competitors, there's no point to your existence. Even if you wind up losing, it's better to go down fighting for what you believe in instead of just imitating others.*"A Shine on Their Shoes," Business Week, Dec. 5, 2005, www.businessweek.com/magazine/content/05_49/b3962118.htm*"The   Polyface   Story," www.polyfacefarms.com/story.aspx CHAPTER EVOLUTION Say no by defaultIf I'd listened to customers, I'd have given them a faster horse. -- HENRY FORD It's so easy to say yes. Yes to another feature, yes to an overly optimistic deadline, yes to a mediocre design. Soon, the stack of things you've said yes to grows so tall you can't even see the things you should really be doing. Start getting into the habit of saying no--even to many of your best ideas. Use the power of no to get your priorities straight. You rarely regret saying no. But you often wind up regretting saying yes. People avoid saying no because confrontation makes them uncomfortable. But the alternative is even worse. You drag things out, make things complicated, and work on ideas you don't believe in. It's like a relationship: Breaking one up is hard to do, but staying in it just because you're too chicken to drop the ax is even worse. Deal with the brief discomfort of confrontation up front and avoid the long-term regret. Don't believe that "customer is always right" stuff, either. Let's say you're a chef. If enough of your customers say your food is too salty or too hot, you change it. But if a few persnickety patrons tell you to add bananas to your lasagna, you're going to turn them down, and that's OK. Making a few vocal customers happy isn't worth it if it ruins the product for everyone else. ING Direct has built the fastest-growing bank in America by saying no. When customers ask for a credit card, the answer is no. When they ask for an online brokerage, the answer is no. When they ask if they can open an account with a million dollars in it, the answer is no (the bank has a strict deposit maximum). ING wants to keep things simple. That's why the bank offers just a few savings accounts, certificates of deposit, and mutual funds--and that's it. Don't be a jerk about saying no, though. Just be honest. If you're not willing to yield to a customer request, be polite and explain why. People are surprisingly understanding when you take the time to explain your point of view. You may even win them over to your way of thinking. If not, recommend a competitor if you think there's a better solution out there. It's better to have people be happy using someone else's product than disgruntled using yours. Your goal is to make sure your product stays right for you. You're the one who has to believe in it most. That way, you can say, "I think you'll love it because I love it." Let your customers outgrow you Maybe you've seen this scenario: There's a customer that's paying a company a lot of money. The company tries to please that customer in any way possible. It tweaks and changes the product per this one customer's requests and starts to alienate its general customer base. Then one day that big customer winds up leaving and the company is left holding the bag--and the bag is a product that's ideally suited to someone who's not there anymore. And now it's a bad fit for everyone else. When you stick with your current customers come hell or high water, you wind up cutting yourself off from new ones. Your product or service becomes so tailored to your current customers that it stops appealing to fresh blood. And that's how your company starts to die. After our first product had been around for a while, we started getting some heat from folks who had been with us from the beginning. They said they were starting to grow out of the application. Their businesses were changing and they wanted us to change our product to mirror their newfound complexity and requirements. We said no. Here's why: We'd rather our customers grow out of our products eventually than never be able to grow into them in the first place. Adding power-user features to satisfy some can intimidate those who aren't on board yet. Scaring away new customers is worse than losing old customers. When you let customers outgrow you, you'll most likely wind up with a product that's basic--and that's fine. Small, simple, basic needs are constant. There's an endless supply of customers who need exactly that. And there are always more people who are not using your product than people who are. Make sure you make it easy for these people to get on board. That's where your continued growth potential lies. People and situations change. You can't be everything to everyone. Companies need to be true to a type of customer more than a specific individual customer with changing needs. Don't confuse enthusiasm with priority Coming up with a great idea gives you a rush. You start imagining the possibilities and the benefits. And of course, you want all that right away. So you drop everything else you're working on and begin pursuing your latest, greatest idea. Bad move. The enthusiasm you have for a new idea is not an accurate indicator of its true worth. What seems like a sure-fire hit right now often gets downgraded to just a "nice to have" by morning. And "nice to have" isn't worth putting everything else on hold. We have ideas for new features all the time. On top of that, we get dozens of interesting ideas from customers every day too. Sure, it'd be fun to immediately chase all these ideas to see where they lead. But if we did that, we'd just wind up running on a treadmill and never get anywhere. So let your latest grand ideas cool off for a while first. By all means, have as many great ideas as you can. Get excited about them. Just don't act in the heat of the moment. Write them down and park them for a few days. Then, evaluate their actual priority with a calm mind. Be at-home good You know what it feels like. You go to a store. You're comparing a few different products, and you're sold on the one that sounds like it's the best deal. It's got the most features. It looks the coolest. The packaging looks hot. There's sensational copy on the box. Everything seems great. But then you get it home, and it doesn't deliver. It's not as easy to use as you thought it'd be. It has too many features you don't need. You end up feeling that you've been taken. You didn't really get what you needed and you realize you spent too much. You just bought an in-store-good product. That's a product you're more excited about in the store than you are after you've actually used it. Smart companies make the opposite: something that's at-home good. When you get the product home, you're actually more impressed with it than you were at the store. You live with it and grow to like it more and more. And you tell your friends, too. When you create an at-home-good product, you may have to sacrifice a bit of instore sizzle. A product that executes on the basics beautifully may not seem as sexy as competitors loaded with bells and whistles. Being great at a few things often doesn't look all that flashy from afar. That's OK. You're aiming for a long-term relationship, not a one-night stand. This is as true for advertising as it is for in-store packaging or displays. We've all seen a TV ad for some "revolutionary" gadget that will change your life. But when the actual product arrives in the mail, it turns out to be a disappointment. In-media good isn't nearly as important as at-home good. You can't paint over a bad experience with good advertising or marketing. Don't write it down How should you keep track of what customers want? Don't. Listen, but then forget what people said. Seriously. There's no need for a spreadsheet, database, or filing system. The requests that really matter are the ones you'll hear over and over. After a while, you won't be able to forget them. Your customers will be your memory. They'll keep reminding you. They'll show you which things you truly need to worry about. If there's a request that you keep forgetting, that's a sign that it isn't very important. The really important stuff doesn't go away. CHAPTER PROMOTION Welcome obscurity No one knows who you are right now. And that's just fine. Being obscure is a great position to be in. Be happy you're in the shadows. Use this time to make mistakes without the whole world hearing about them. Keep tweaking. Work out the kinks. Test random ideas. Try new things. No one knows you, so it's no big deal if you mess up. Obscurity helps protect your ego and preserve your confidence. Retailers experiment with test markets all the time for this reason. When Dunkin' Donuts thought about selling pizza, hot dogs, and other hot sandwiches, it test-marketed the products at just ten select locations. Broadway shows also provide a great example of testing ideas on a small stage first. They routinely do a trial run in a smaller city before coming to New York. Testing out of town lets actors get some reps in front of a live audience before the show goes up in front of harsher critics and tastemakers. Would you want the whole world to watch you the first time you do anything? If you've never given a speech before, do you want your first speech to be in front of ten thousand people or ten people? You don't want everyone to watch you starting your business. It makes no sense to tell everyone to look at you if you're not ready to be looked at yet. And keep in mind that once you do get bigger and more popular, you're inevitably going to take fewer risks. When you're a success, the pressure to maintain predictability and consistency builds. You get more conservative. It's harder to take risks. That's when things start to fossilize and change becomes difficult. If millions of people are using your product, every change you make will have a much bigger impact. Before, you might have upset a hundred people when you changed something. Now you might upset thousands. You can reason with a hundred people, but you need riot gear to deal with ten thousand angry customers. These early days of obscurity are something you'll miss later on, when you're really under the microscope. Now's the time to take risks without worrying about embarrassing yourself. Build an audience All companies have customers. Lucky companies have fans. But the most fortunate companies have audiences. An audience can be your secret weapon. A lot of businesses still spend big bucks to reach people. Every time they want to say something, they dip into their budgets, pull out a huge wad of cash, and place some ads. But this approach is both expensive and unreliable. As they say, you waste half of your ad budget-- you just don't know which half. Today's smartest companies know better. Instead of going out to reach people, you want people to come to you. An audience returns often--on its own--to see what you have to say. This is the most receptive group of customers and potential customers you'll ever have. Over the past ten years, we've built an audience of more than a hundred thousand daily readers for our Signal vs. Noise blog. Every day they come back to see what we have to say. We may talk about design or business or software or psychology or usability or our industry at large. Whatever it is, these people are interested enough to come back to hear more. And if they like what we have to say, they'll probably also like what we have to sell. How much would it cost us to reach those hundred thousand people every day the old-fashioned way? Hundreds of thousands? Millions? And how would we have done it? Running ads? Buying radio spots? Sending direct mail? When you build an audience, you don't have to buy people's attention--they give it to you. This is a huge advantage. So build an audience. Speak, write, blog, tweet, make videos--whatever. Share information that's valuable and you'll slowly but surely build a loyal audience. Then when you need to get the word out, the right people will already be listening. Out-teach your competition You can advertise. You can hire salespeople. You can sponsor events. But your competitors are doing the same things. How does that help you stand out? Instead of trying to outspend, outsell, or outsponsor competitors, try to out-teach them. Teaching probably isn't something your competitors are even thinking about. Most businesses focus on selling or servicing, but teaching never even occurs to them. The Hoefler Type Foundry teaches designers about type at Typography.com. Etsy, an online store for things handmade, holds entrepreneurial workshops that explain "best practices" and promotional ideas to people who sell at the site. Gary Vaynerchuk, who owns a large wine shop, teaches people about wine online at Wine Library TV, and tens of thousands of people watch every day. Teach and you'll form a bond you just don't get from traditional marketing tactics. Buying people's attention with a magazine or online banner ad is one thing. Earning their loyalty by teaching them forms a whole different connection. They'll trust you more. They'll respect you more. Even if they don't use your product, they can still be your fans. Teaching is something individuals and small companies can do that bigger competitors can't. Big companies can afford a Super Bowl ad; you can't. But you can afford to teach, and that's something they'll never do, because big companies are obsessed with secrecy. Everything at those places has to get filtered through a lawyer and go through layers of red tape. Teaching is your chance to outmaneuver them. Emulate chefs You've probably heard of Emeril Lagasse, Mario Batali, Bobby Flay, Julia Child, Paula Deen, Rick Bayless, or Jacques Pepin. They're great chefs, but there are a lot of great chefs out there. So why do you know these few better than others? Because they share everything they know. They put their recipes in cookbooks and show their techniques on cooking shows. As a business owner, you should share everything you know too. This is anathema to most in the business world. Businesses are usually paranoid and secretive. They think they have proprietary this and competitive advantage that. Maybe a rare few do, but most don't. And those that don't should stop acting like those that do. Don't be afraid of sharing. A recipe is much easier to copy than a business. Shouldn't that scare Mario Batali? Why would he go on TV and show you how he does what he does? Why would he put all his recipes in cookbooks where anyone can buy and replicate them? Because he knows those recipes and techniques aren't enough to beat him at his own game. No one's going to buy his cookbook, open a restaurant next door, and put him out of business. It just doesn't work like that. Yet this is what many in the business world think will happen if their competitors learn how they do things. Get over it. So emulate famous chefs. They cook, so they write cookbooks. What do you do? What are your "recipes"? What's your "cookbook"? What can you tell the world about how you operate that's informative, educational, and promotional? This book is our cookbook. What's yours? Go behind the scenes Give people a backstage pass and show them how your business works. Imagine that someone wanted to make a reality show about your business. What would they share? Now stop waiting for someone else and do it yourself. Think no one will care? Think again. Even seemingly boring jobs can be fascinating when presented right. What could be more boring than commercial fishing and trucking? Yet the Discovery Channel and History Channel have turned these professions into highly rated shows: Deadliest Catch and Ice Road Truckers. It doesn't need to be a dangerous job, either. People love finding out the little secrets of all kinds of businesses, even one that makes those tiny marshmallows in breakfast cereals. That's why the Food Network's Unwrapped--which explores the secrets behind lunch-box treats, soda pop, movie candy, and more--is such a popular program. People are curious about how things are made. It's why they like factory tours or behind-the-scenes footage on DVDs. They want to see how the sets are built, how the animation is done, how the director cast the film, etc. They want to know how and why other people make decisions. Letting people behind the curtain changes your relationship with them. They'll feel a bond with you and see you as human beings instead of a faceless company. They'll see the sweat and effort that goes into what you sell. They'll develop a deeper level of understanding and appreciation for what you do. Nobody likes plastic flowers The business world is full of "professionals" who wear the uniform and try to seem perfect. In truth, they just come off as stiff and boring. No one can relate to people like that. Don't be afraid to show your flaws. Imperfections are real and people respond to real. It's why we like real flowers that wilt, not perfect plastic ones that never change. Don't worry about how you're supposed to sound and how you're supposed to act. Show the world what you're really like, warts and all. There's a beauty to imperfection. This is the essence of the Japanese principle of wabi-sabi. Wabi-sabi values character and uniqueness over a shiny facade. It teaches that cracks and scratches in things should be embraced. It's also about simplicity. You strip things down and then use what you have. Leonard Koren, author of a book on wabi-sabi, gives this advice: Pare down to the essence, but don't remove the poetry. Keep things clean and unencumbered but don't sterilize. * It's a beautiful way to put it: Leave the poetry in what you make. When something becomes too polished, it loses its soul. It seems robotic. So talk like you really talk. Reveal things that others are unwilling to discuss. Be upfront about your shortcomings. Show the latest version of what you're working on, even if you're not done yet. It's OK if it's not perfect. You might not seem as professional, but you will seem a lot more genuine. Press releases are spam What do you call a generic pitch sent out to hundreds of strangers hoping that one will bite? Spam. That's what press releases are too: generic pitches for coverage sent out to hundreds of journalists you don't know, hoping that one will write about you. Let's dissect the purpose of a press release for a moment: It's something you send out because you want to be noticed. You want the press to pick up on your new company, product, service, announcement, or whatever. You want them to be excited enough to write a story about you. But press releases are a terrible way to accomplish that. They're tired and formulaic. There's nothing exciting about them. Journalists sift through dozens a day. They wind up buried under an avalanche of hyperbolic headlines and fake quotes from CEOs. Everything is labeled sensational, revolutionary, groundbreaking, and amazing. It's numbing. If you want to get someone's attention, it's silly to do exactly the same thing as everyone else. You need to stand out. So why issue press releases like everyone else does? Why spam journalists when their inbox is already filled with other people's spam? Furthermore, a press release is generic. You write it once and then send it to tons of reporters--people whom you don't know and who don't know you. And your first introduction is this vague, generic note you also send to everyone else? Is that the impression you want to make? Is that really going to get you the story? Instead, call someone. Write a personal note. If you read a story about a similar company or product, contact the journalist who wrote it. Pitch her with some passion, some interest, some life. Do something meaningful. Be remarkable. Stand out. Be unforgettable. That's how you'll get the best coverage. Forget about the Wall Street Journal Forget about

Time, Forbes, Newsweek, Business Week, the New York Times, and the Wall Street Journal. Pitching a reporter at one of these places is practically impossible. Good luck even getting ahold of that guy. And even if you do, he probably won't care anyway. You're not big enough to matter. You're better off focusing on getting your story into a trade publication or picked up by a niche blogger. With these outlets, the barrier is much lower. You can send an email and get a response (and maybe even a post) the same day. There's no editorial board or PR person involved. There's no pipeline your message has to go through. These guys are actually hungry for fresh meat. They thrive on being tastemakers, finding the new thing, and getting the ball rolling. That's why many big-time reporters now use these smaller sites to find new stories. Stories that start on the fringe can go mainstream quickly. We've been written up in big mainstream publications like Wired and Time, but we've found that we actually get more hits when we're profiled on sites like Daring Fireball, a site for Mac nerds, or Lifehacker, a productivity site. Links from these places result in notable spikes in our traffic and sales. Articles in big-time publications are nice, but they don't result in the same level of direct, instant activity. Drug dealers get it right Drug dealers are astute businesspeople. They know their product is so good they're willing to give a little away for free upfront. They know you'll be back for more-- with money. Emulate drug dealers. Make your product so good, so addictive, so "can't miss" that giving customers a small, free taste makes them come back with cash in hand. This will force you to make something about your product bite-size. You want an easily digestible introduction to what you sell. This gives people a way to try it without investing any money or a lot of time. Bakeries, restaurants, and ice cream shops have done this successfully for years. Car dealers let you test-drive cars before buying them. Software firms are also getting on board, with free trials or limited-use versions. How many other industries could benefit from the drug-dealer model? Don't be afraid to give a little away for free--as long as you've got something else to sell. Be confident in what you're offering. You should know that people will come back for more. If you're not confident about that, you haven't created a strong enough product. Marketing is not a department Do you have a marketing department? If not, good. If you do, don't think these are the only people responsible for marketing. Accounting is a department. Marketing isn't. Marketing is something everyone in your company is doing 24/7/365. Just as you cannot not communicate, you cannot not market: Every time you answer the phone, it's marketing. Every time you send an email, it's marketing. Every time someone uses your product, it's marketing. Every word you write on your Web site is marketing. If you build software, every error message is marketing. If you're in the restaurant business, the after-dinner mint is marketing. If you're in the retail business, the checkout counter is marketing. If you're in a service business, your invoice is marketing. Recognize that all of these little things are more important than choosing which piece of swag to throw into a conference goodie bag. Marketing isn't just a few individual events. It's the sum total of everything you do. The myth of the overnight sensation You will not be a big hit right away. You will not get rich quick. You are not so special that everyone else will instantly pay attention. No one cares about you. At least not yet. Get used to it. You know those overnight success stories you've heard about? It's not the whole story. Dig deeper and you'll usually find people who have busted their asses for years to get into a position where things could take off. And on the rare occasion that instant success does come along, it usually doesn't last--there's no foundation there to support it. Trade the dream of overnight success for slow, measured growth. It's hard, but you have to be patient. You have to grind it out. You have to do it for a long time before the right people notice. You may think you can speed up the process by hiring a PR firm. Don't bother. You're just not ready for that yet. For one thing, it's too expensive. Good PR firms can cost upward of $10,000 per month. That's a waste of money right now. Plus, you're still just a no-name with a product no one's ever heard about. Who's going to write about that? Once you have some customers and a history, you'll have a story to tell. But just launching isn't a good story. And remember, great brands launch without PR campaigns all the time. Starbucks, Apple, Nike, Amazon, Google, and Snapple all became great brands over time, not because of a big PR push upfront. Start building your audience today. Start getting people interested in what you have to say. And then keep at it. In a few years, you too will get to chuckle when people discuss your "overnight" success.*Pilar Viladas, "The Talk: The Slow Lane," New York Times Magazine, Oct. 9, 2005, www.tinyurl.com/ychqtup CHAPTER HIRING Do it yourself first Never hire anyone to do a job until you've tried to do it yourself first. That way, you'll understand the nature of the work. You'll know what a job well done looks like. You'll know how to write a realistic job description and which questions to ask in an interview. You'll know whether to hire someone full-time or part-time, outsource it, or keep doing it yourself (the last is preferable, if possible). You'll also be a much better manager, because you'll be supervising people who are doing a job you've done before. You'll know when to criticize and when to support. At 37signals, we didn't hire a system administrator until one of us had spent a whole summer setting up a bunch of servers on his own. For the first three years, one of us did all of our customer support. Then we hired a dedicated support person. We ran with the ball as far as we could before handing it off. That way, we knew what we were looking for once we did decide to hire. You may feel out of your element at times. You might even feel like you suck. That's all right. You can hire your way out of that feeling or you can learn your way out of it. Try learning first. What you give up in initial execution will be repaid many times over by the wisdom you gain. Plus, you should want to be intimately involved in all aspects of your business. Otherwise you'll wind up in the dark, putting your fate solely in the hands of others. That's dangerous. Hire when it hurts Don't hire for pleasure; hire to kill pain. Always ask yourself: What if we don't hire anyone? Is that extra work that's burdening us really necessary? Can we solve the problem with a slice of software or a change of practice instead? What if we just don't do it? Similarly, if you lose someone, don't replace him immediately. See how long you can get by without that person and that position. You'll often discover you don't need as many people as you think. The right time to hire is when there's more work than you can handle for a sustained period of time. There should be things you can't do anymore. You should notice the quality level slipping. That's when you're hurting. And that's when it's time to hire, not earlier. Pass on great people Some companies are addicted to hiring. Some even hire when they aren't hiring. They'll hear about someone great and invent a position or title just to lure them in. And there they'll sit-- parked in a position that doesn't matter, doing work that isn't important. Pass on hiring people you don't need, even if you think that person's a great catch. You'll be doing your company more harm than good if you bring in talented people who have nothing important to do. Problems start when you have more people than you need. You start inventing work to keep everyone busy. Artificial work leads to artificial projects. And those artificial projects lead to real costs and complexity. Don't worry about "the one that got away." It's much worse to have people on staff who aren't doing anything meaningful. There's plenty of talent out there. When you do have a real need, you'll find someone who fits well. Great has nothing to do with it. If you don't need someone, you don't need someone. Strangers at a cocktail party If you go to a cocktail party where everyone is a stranger, the conversation is dull and stiff. You make small talk about the weather, sports, TV shows, etc. You shy away from serious conversations and controversial opinions. A small, intimate dinner party among old friends is a different story, though. There are genuinely interesting conversations and heated debates. At the end of the night, you feel you actually got something out of it. Hire a ton of people rapidly and a "strangers at a cocktail party" problem is exactly what you end up with. There are always new faces around, so everyone is unfailingly polite. Everyone tries to avoid any conflict or drama. No one says, "This idea sucks." People appease instead of challenge. And that appeasement is what gets companies into trouble. You need to be able to tell people when they're full of crap. If that doesn't happen, you start churning out something that doesn't offend anyone but also doesn't make anyone fall in love. You need an environment where everyone feels safe enough to be honest when things get tough. You need to know how far you can push someone. You need to know what people really mean when they say something. So hire slowly. It's the only way to avoid winding up at a cocktail party of strangers. Resumes are ridiculous We all know resumes are a joke. They're exaggerations. They're filled with "action verbs" that don't mean anything. They list job titles and responsibilities that are vaguely accurate at best. And there's no way to verify most of what's on there. The whole thing is a farce. Worst of all, they're too easy. Anyone can create a decent-enough resume. That's why half-assed applicants love them so much. They can shotgun out hundreds at a time to potential employers. It's another form of spam. They don't care about landing your job; they just care about landing any job. If someone sends out a resume to three hundred companies, that's a huge red flag right there. There's no way that applicant has researched you. There's no way he knows what's different about your company. If you hire based on this garbage, you're missing the point of what hiring is about. You want a specific candidate who cares specifically about your company, your products, your customers, and your job. So how do you find these candidates? First step: Check the cover letter. In a cover letter, you get actual communication instead of a list of skills, verbs, and years of irrelevance. There's no way an applicant can churn out hundreds of personalized letters. That's why the cover letter is a much better test than a resume. You hear someone's actual voice and are able recognize if it's in tune with you and your company. Trust your gut reaction. If the first paragraph sucks, the second has to work that much harder. If there's no hook in the first three, it's unlikely there's a match there. On the other hand, if your gut is telling you there's a chance at a real match, then move on to the interview stage. Years of irrelevance We've all seen job ads that say, "Five years of experience required." That may give you a number, but it tells you nothing. Of course, requiring some baseline level of experience can be a good idea when hiring. It makes sense to go after candidates with six months to a year of experience. It takes that long to internalize the idioms, learn how things work, understand the relevant tools, etc. But after that, the curve flattens out. There's surprisingly little difference between a candidate with six months of experience and one with six years. The real difference comes from the individual's dedication, personality, and intelligence. How do you really measure this stuff anyway? What does five years of experience mean? If you spent a couple of weekends experimenting with something a few years back, can you count that as a year of experience? How is a company supposed to verify these claims? These are murky waters. How long someone's been doing it is overrated. What matters is how well they've been doing it. Forget about formal educationI have never let my schooling interfere with my education. --MARK TWAIN There are plenty of companies out there who have educational requirements. They'll only hire people with a college degree (sometimes in a specific field) or an advanced degree or a certain GPA or certification of some sort or some other requirement. Come on. There are plenty of intelligent people who don't excel in the classroom. Don't fall into the trap of thinking you need someone from one of the "best" schools in order to get results. Ninety percent of CEOs currently heading the top five hundred American companies did not receive undergraduate degrees from Ivy League colleges. In fact, more received their undergraduate degrees from the University of Wisconsin than from Harvard (the most heavily represented Ivy school, with nine CEOs).* Too much time in academia can actually do you harm. Take writing, for example. When you get out of school, you have to unlearn so much of the way they teach you to write there. Some of the misguided lessons you learn in academia: The longer a document is, the more it matters. Stiff, formal tone is better than being conversational. Using big words is impressive. You need to write a certain number of words or pages to make a point. The format matters as much (or more) than the content of what you write. It's no wonder so much business writing winds up dry, wordy, and dripping with nonsense. People are just continuing the bad habits they picked up in school. It's not just academic writing, either. There are a lot of skills that are useful in academia that aren't worth much outside of it. Bottom line: The pool of great candidates is far bigger than just people who completed college with a stellar GPA. Consider dropouts, people who had low GPAs, community-college students, and even those who just went to high school. Everybody works With a small team, you need people who are going to do work, not delegate work. Everyone's got to be producing. No one can be above the work. That means you need to avoid hiring delegators, those people who love telling others what to do. Delegators are dead weight for a small team. They clog the pipes for others by coming up with busywork. And when they run out of work to assign, they make up more--regardless of whether it needs to be done. Delegators love to pull people into meetings, too. In fact, meetings are a delegator's best friend. That's where he gets to seem important. Meanwhile, everyone else who attends is pulled away from getting real work done. Hire managers of one Managers of one are people who come up with their own goals and execute them. They don't need heavy direction. They don't need daily check-ins. They do what a manager would do--set the tone, assign items, determine what needs to get done, etc.--but they do it by themselves and for themselves. These people free you from oversight. They set their own direction. When you leave them alone, they surprise you with how much they've gotten done. They don't need a lot of hand-holding or supervision. How can you spot these people? Look at their backgrounds. They have set the tone for how they've worked at other jobs. They've run something on their own or launched some kind of project. You want someone who's capable of building something from scratch and seeing it through. Finding these people frees the rest of your team to work more and manage less. Hire great writers If you are trying to decide among a few people to fill a position, hire the best writer. It doesn't matter if that person is a marketer, salesperson, designer, programmer, or whatever; their writing skills will pay off. That's because being a good writer is about more than writing. Clear writing is a sign of clear thinking. Great writers know how to communicate. They make things easy to understand. They can put themselves in someone else's shoes. They know what to omit. And those are qualities you want in any candidate. Writing is making a comeback all over our society. Look at how much people email and text-message now rather than talk on the phone. Look at how much communication happens via instant messaging and blogging. Writing is today's currency for good ideas.Own your bad news When something goes wrong, someone is going to tell the story. You'll be better off if it's you. Otherwise, you create an opportunity for rumors, hearsay, and false information to spread. When something bad happens, tell your customers (even if they never noticed in the first place). Don't think you can just sweep it under the rug. You can't hide anymore. These days, someone else will call you on it if you don't do it yourself. They'll post about it online and everyone will know. There are no more secrets. People will respect you more if you are open, honest, public, and responsive during a crisis. Don't hide behind spin or try to keep your bad news on the down low. You want your customers to be as informed as possible. Back in 1989, the Exxon Valdez oil tanker spilled 11 million gallons of oil into Alaska's Prince William Sound. Exxon made the mistake of waiting a long time before responding to the spill and sending aid to Alaska. Exxon's chairman failed to go there until two weeks after the spill. The company held news briefings in Valdez, a remote Alaskan town that was difficult for the press to reach. The result: a PR disaster for Exxon that led the public to believe the company was either hiding something or didn't really care about what had happened. * Contrast that Exxon story to the rupture of an Ashland Oil storage tank that spilled oil into a river near Pittsburgh around the same time. Ashland Oil's chairman, John Hall, went to the scene of the Ashland spill and took charge. He pledged to clean everything up. He visited news bureaus to explain what the company would do and answer any questions. Within a day, he had shifted the story from a rotten-oil-companydoes-evil narrative to a good-oil-company-tries-to-clean-up story. + Here are some tips on how you can own the story: The message should come from the top. The highest-ranking person available should take control in a forceful way. Spread the message far and wide. Use whatever megaphone you have. Don't try to sweep it under the rug. "No comment" is not an option. Apologize the way a real person would and explain what happened in detail. Honestly be concerned about the fate of your customers--then prove it. Speed changes everything "Your call is very important to us. We appreciate your patience. The average hold time right now is sixteen minutes." Give me a fucking break. Getting back to people quickly is probably the most important thing you can do when it comes to customer service. It's amazing how much that can defuse a bad situation and turn it into a good one. Have you ever sent an e-mail and it took days or weeks for the company to get back to you? How did it make you feel? These days, that's what people have come to expect. They're used to being put on hold. They're used to platitudes about "caring" that aren't backed up. That's why so many support queries start off with an antagonistic tone. Some people may even make threats or call you names. Don't take it personally. They think that's the only way to be heard. They're only trying to be a squeaky wheel in hopes it'll get them a little grease. Once you answer quickly, they shift 180 degrees. They light up. They become extra polite. Often they thank you profusely. It's especially true if you offer a personal response. Customers are so used to canned answers, you can really differentiate yourself by answering thoughtfully and showing that you're listening. And even if you don't have a perfect answer, say something. "Let me do some research and get back to you" can work wonders. How to say you're sorry There's never really a great way to say you're sorry, but there are plenty of terrible ways. One of the worst ways is the non-apology apology, which sounds like an apology but doesn't really accept any blame. For example, "We're sorry if this upset you." Or "I'm sorry that you don't feel we lived up to your expectations." Whatever. A good apology accepts responsibility. It has no conditional if phrase attached. It shows people that the buck stops with you. And then it provides real details about what happened and what you're doing to prevent it from happening again. And it seeks a way to make things right. Here's another bad one: "We apologize for any inconvenience this may have caused." Oh, please. Let's break down why that's bad: "We apologize ..." If you spilled coffee on someone while riding the subway, would you say, "I apologize"? No, you'd say, "I'm so, so sorry!" Well, if your service is critical to your customers, an interruption to that service is like spilling hot coffee all over them. So use the appropriate tone and language to show that you understand the severity of what happened. Also, the person in charge should take personal responsibility. An "I" apology is a lot stronger than a "we" apology. "... any inconvenience ..." If customers depend on your service and can't get to it, it's not merely an inconvenience. It's a crisis. An inconvenience is a long line at the grocery store. This ain't that. "... this may have caused" The "may" here implies there might not be anything wrong at all. That's a classic non-apology apology move. It slights the very real problem(s) that customers are experiencing. If this didn't affect them, you don't really need to say anything. If it did affect them, then there's no need for "may" here. Stop wavering. So what's the perfect way to say you're sorry? There's no magic bullet. Any stock answer will sound generic and hollow. You're going to have to take it on a case-by-case basis. The number-one principle to keep in mind when you apologize: How would you feel about the apology if you were on the other end? If someone said those words to you, would you believe them? Keep in mind that you can't apologize your way out of being an ass. Even the best apology won't rescue you if you haven't earned people's trust. Everything you do before things go wrong matters far more than the actual words you use to apologize. If you've built rapport with customers, they'll cut you some slack and trust you when you say you're sorry. Put everyone on the front lines In the restaurant business, there's a world of difference between working in the kitchen and dealing with customers. Cooking schools and smart restaurateurs know it's important for both sides to understand and empathize with each other. That's why they often have chefs work out front as waiters for a stretch. That way, the kitchen staff can interact with customers and see what it's actually like on the front lines. A lot of companies have a similar front-of-house/back-of-house split. The people who make the product work in the "kitchen" while support handles the customers. Unfortunately, that means the product's chefs never get to directly hear what customers are saying. Too bad. Listening to customers is the best way to get in tune with a product's strengths and weaknesses. Think about the children's game Telephone. There are ten kids sitting in a circle. A message starts and is whispered from one child to another. By the time it gets all the way around, the message is completely distorted--to the point where it's usually hilarious. A sentence that makes sense at first comes out the other end as "Macaroni cantaloupe knows the future." And the more people you have in the circle, the more distorted the message gets. The same thing is true at your company. The more people you have between your customers' words and the people doing the work, the more likely it is that the message will get lost or distorted along the way. Everyone on your team should be connected to your customers--maybe not every day, but at least a few times throughout the year. That's the only way your team is going to feel the hurt your customers are experiencing. It's feeling the hurt that really motivates people to fix the problem. And the flip side is true too: The joy of happy customers or ones who have had a problem solved can also be wildly motivating. So don't protect the people doing the work from customer feedback. No one should be shielded from direct criticism. Maybe you think you don't have time to interact with customers. Then make time. Craigslist founder Craig Newmark still answers support e-mails today (often within minutes). He also deletes racist comments from the site's discussion boards and pesters New York City Realtors who post apartments for rent that don't exist.* If he can devote this kind of attention to customer service, you can too. Take a deep breath When you rock the boat, there will be waves.

After you introduce a new feature, change a policy, or remove something, knee-jerk reactions will pour in. Resist the urge to panic or make rapid changes in response. Passions flare in the beginning. That's normal. But if you ride out that first rocky week, things usually settle down. People are creatures of habit. That's why they react to change in such a negative way. They're used to using something in a certain way and any change upsets the natural order of things. So they push back. They complain. They demand that you revert to the way things were. But that doesn't mean you should act. Sometimes you need to go ahead with a decision you believe in, even if it's unpopular at first. People often respond before they give a change a fair chance. Sometimes that initial negative reaction is more of a primal response. That's why you'll sometimes hear things like, "It's the worst thing I've ever seen." No, it's not. It's a minor change. Come on. Also, remember that negative reactions are almost always louder and more passionate than positive ones. In fact, you may hear only negative voices even when the majority of your customers are happy about a change. Make sure you don't foolishly backpedal on a necessary but controversial decision. So when people complain, let things simmer for a while. Let them know you're listening. Show them you're aware of what they're saying. Let them know you understand their discontent. But explain that you're going to let it go for a while and see what happens. You'll probably find that people will adjust eventually. They may even wind up liking the change more than the old way, once they get used to it.*Reyna Susi, "The Exxon Crisis, 1989," Effective Crisis Management, iml.jou.ufl.edu/projects/Fall02/Susi/exxon.htm +John Holusha, "Exxon's PublicRelations Problem," New York Times, Apr. 21, 1989, www.tinyurl.com/yg2bgff*Scott Kirsner, "Craigslist's Unorthodox Path," Boston Globe, June 15, 2008, www.tinyurl.com/4vkg58 CHAPTER CULTURE You don't create a culture Instant cultures are artificial cultures. They're big bangs made of mission statements, declarations, and rules. They are obvious, ugly, and plastic. Artificial culture is paint. Real culture is patina. You don't create a culture. It happens. This is why new companies don't have a culture. Culture is the byproduct of consistent behavior. If you encourage people to share, then sharing will be built into your culture. If you reward trust, then trust will be built in. If you treat customers right, then treating customers right becomes your culture. Culture isn't a foosball table or trust falls. It isn't policy. It isn't the Christmas party or the company picnic. Those are objects and events, not culture. And it's not a slogan, either. Culture is action, not words. So don't worry too much about it. Don't force it. You can't install a culture. Like a fine scotch, you've got to give it time to develop. Decisions are temporary "But what if ...?" "What happens when ...?" "Don't we need to plan for ...?" Don't make up problems you don't have yet. It's not a problem until it's a real problem. Most of the things you worry about never happen anyway. Besides, the decisions you make today don't need to last forever. It's easy to shoot down good ideas, interesting policies, or worthwhile experiments by assuming that whatever you decide now needs to work for years on end. It's just not so, especially for a small business. If circumstances change, your decisions can change. Decisions are temporary. At this stage, it's silly to worry about whether or not your concept will scale from five to five thousand people (or from a hundred thousand to 100 million people). Getting a product or service off the ground is hard enough without inventing even more obstacles. Optimize for now and worry about the future later. The ability to change course is one of the big advantages of being small. Compared with larger competitors, you're way more capable of making quick, sweeping changes. Big companies just can't move that fast. So pay attention to today and worry about later when it gets here. Otherwise you'll waste energy, time, and money fixating on problems that may never materialize. Skip the rock stars A lot of companies post help-wanted ads seeking "rock stars" or "ninjas." Lame. Unless your workplace is filled with groupies and throwing stars, these words have nothing to do with your business. Instead of thinking about how you can land a roomful of rock stars, think about the room instead. We're all capable of bad, average, and great work. The environment has a lot more to do with great work than most people realize. That's not to say we're all created equal and you'll unlock star power in anyone with a rock star environment. But there's a ton of untapped potential trapped under lame policies, poor direction, and stifling bureaucracies. Cut the crap and you'll find that people are waiting to do great work. They just need to be given the chance. This isn't about casual Fridays or bring-your-dog-to-work day. (If those are such good things, then why aren't you doing them every day of the week?) Rockstar environments develop out of trust, autonomy, and responsibility. They're a result of giving people the privacy, workspace, and tools they deserve. Great environments show respect for the people who do the work and how they do it. They're not thirteen When you treat people like children, you get children's work. Yet that's exactly how a lot of companies and managers treat their employees. Employees need to ask permission before they can do anything. They need to get approval for every tiny expenditure. It's surprising they don't have to get a hall pass to go take a shit. When everything constantly needs approval, you create a culture of nonthinkers. You create a boss-versus-worker relationship that screams, "I don't trust you." What do you gain if you ban employees from, say, visiting a social-networking site or watching YouTube while at work? You gain nothing. That time doesn't magically convert to work. They'll just find some other diversion. And look, you're not going to get a full eight hours a day out of people anyway. That's a myth. They might be at the office for eight hours, but they're not actually working eight hours. People need diversions. It helps disrupt the monotony of the workday. A little YouTube or Facebook time never hurt anyone. Then there's all the money and time you spend policing this stuff. How much does it cost to set up surveillance software? How much time do IT employees waste on monitoring other employees instead of working on a project that's actually valuable? How much time do you waste writing rule books that never get read? Look at the costs and you quickly realize that failing to trust your employees is awfully expensive. Send people home at 5 The dream employee for a lot of companies is a twenty-something with as little of a life as possible outside of work--someone who'll be fine working fourteen-hour days and sleeping under his desk. But packing a room full of these burn-the-midnight-oil types isn't as great as it seems. It lets you get away with lousy execution. It perpetuates myths like "This is the only way we can compete against the big guys." You don't need more hours; you need better hours. When people have something to do at home, they get down to business. They get their work done at the office because they have somewhere else to be. They find ways to be more efficient because they have to. They need to pick up the kids or get to choir practice. So they use their time wisely. As the saying goes, "If you want something done, ask the busiest person you know." You want busy people. People who have a life outside of work. People who care about more than one thing. You shouldn't expect the job to be someone's entire life--at least not if you want to keep them around for a long time. Don't scar on the first cut The second something goes wrong, the natural tendency is to create a policy. "Someone's wearing shorts!? We need a dress code!" No, you don't. You just need to tell John not to wear shorts again. Policies are organizational scar tissue. They are codified overreactions to situations that are unlikely to happen again. They are collective punishment for the misdeeds of an individual. This is how bureaucracies are born. No one sets out to create a bureaucracy. They sneak up on companies slowly. They are created one policy--one scar--at a time. So don't scar on the first cut. Don't create a policy because one person did something wrong once. Policies are only meant for situations that come up over and over again. Sound like you What is it with businesspeople trying to sound big? The stiff language, the formal announcements, the artificial friendliness, the legalese, etc. You read this stuff and it sounds like a robot wrote it. These companies talk at you, not to you. This mask of professionalism is a joke. We all know this. Yet small companies still try to emulate it. They think sounding big makes them appear bigger and more "professional." But it really just makes them sound ridiculous. Plus, you sacrifice one of a small company's greatest assets: the ability to communicate simply and directly, without running every last word through a legal-and PR-department sieve. There's nothing wrong with sounding your own size. Being honest about who you are is smart business, too. Language is often your first impression--why start it off with a lie? Don't be afraid to be you. That applies to the language you use everywhere--in e-mail, packaging, interviews, blog posts, presentations, etc. Talk to customers the way you would to friends. Explain things as if you were sitting next to them. Avoid jargon or any sort of corporate-speak. Stay away from buzzwords when normal words will do just fine. Don't talk about "monetization" or being "transparent;" talk about making money and being honest. Don't use seven words when four will do. And don't force your employees to end e-mails with legalese like "This e-mail message is for the sole use of the intended recipient(s) and may contain confidential and privileged information." That's like ending all your company e-mails with a signature that says, "We don't trust you and we're ready to prove it in court." Good luck making friends that way. Write to be read, don't write just to write. Whenever you write something, read it out loud. Does it sound the way it would if you were actually talking to someone? If not, how can you make it more conversational? Who said writing needs to be formal? Who said you have to strip away your personality when putting words on paper? Forget rules. Communicate! And when you're writing, don't think about all the people who may read your words. Think of one person. Then write for that one person. Writing for a mob leads to generalities and awkwardness. When you write to a specific target, you're a lot more likely to hit the mark. Four-letter words There are four-letter words you should never use in business. They're not fuck or shit. They're need, must, can't, easy, just, only, and fast. These words get in the way of healthy communication. They are red flags that introduce animosity, torpedo good discussions, and cause projects to be late. When you use these four-letter words, you create a black-and-white situation. But the truth is rarely black and white. So people get upset and problems ensue. Tension and conflict are injected unnecessarily. Here's what's wrong with some of them:Need. Very few things actually need to get done. Instead of saying "need," you're better off saying "maybe" or "What do you think about this?" or "How does this sound?" or "Do you think we could get away with that?" Can't. When you say "can't," you probably can. Sometimes there are even opposing can'ts: "We can't launch it like that, because it's not quite right" versus "We can't spend any more time on this because we have to launch." Both of those statements can't be true. Or wait a minute, can they? Easy. Easy is a word that's used to describe other people's jobs. "That should be easy for you to do, right?" But notice how rarely people describe their own tasks as easy. For you, it's "Let me look into it"--but for others, it's "Get it done." These four-letter words often pop up during debates (and also watch out for their cousins: everyone, no one, always, and never). Once uttered, they make it tough to find a solution. They box you into a corner by pitting two absolutes against each other. That's when head-butting occurs. You squeeze out any middle ground. And these words are especially dangerous when you string them together: "We need to add this feature now. We can't launch without this feature. Everyone wants it. It's only one little thing so it will be easy. You should be able to get it in there fast!" Only thirty-six words, but a hundred assumptions. That's a recipe for disaster. ASAP is poison Stop saying ASAP. We get it. It's implied. Everyone wants things done as soon as they can be done. When you turn into one of these people who adds ASAP to the end of every request, you're saying everything is high priority. And when everything is high priority, nothing is. (Funny how everything is a top priority until you actually have to prioritize things.) ASAP is inflationary. It devalues any request that doesn't say ASAP. Before you know it, the only way to get anything done is by putting the ASAP sticker on it. Most things just don't warrant that kind of hysteria. If a task doesn't get done this very instant, nobody is going to die. Nobody's going to lose their job. It won't cost the company a ton of money. What it will do is create artificial stress, which leads to burnout and worse. So reserve your use of emergency language for true emergencies. The kind where there are direct, measurable consequences to inaction. For everything else, chill out.

CHAPTER THREE

HISTORY OF THE '90S

The 1990s have a good image. We tend to remember them as a prosperous, optimistic decade that happened to end with the internet boom and bust. But many of those years were not as cheerful as our nostalgia holds. We've long since forgotten the global context for the 18 months of dot-com mania at decade's end. The '90s started with a burst of euphoria when the Berlin Wall came down in November '89. It was short-lived. By mid-1990, the United States was in recession. Technically the downturn ended in March '91, but recovery was slow and unemployment continued to rise until July '92. Manufacturing never fully rebounded. The shift to a service economy was protracted and painful. 1992 through the end of 1994 was a time of general malaise. Images of dead American soldiers in Mogadishu looped on cable news. Anxiety about globalization and U.S. competitiveness intensified as jobs flowed to Mexico. This pessimistic undercurrent drove then-president Bush 41 out of office and won Ross Perot nearly 20% of the popular vote in '92—the best showing for a third-party candidate since Theodore Roosevelt in 1912. And whatever the cultural fascination with Nirvana, grunge, and heroin reflected, it wasn't hope or confidence. Silicon Valley felt sluggish, too. Japan seemed to be winning the semiconductor war. The internet had yet to take off, partly because its commercial use was restricted until late 1992 and partly due to the lack of user-friendly web browsers. It's telling that when I arrived at Stanford in 1985, economics, not computer science, was the most popular major. To most people on campus, the tech sector seemed idiosyncratic or even provincial. The internet changed all this. The Mosaic browser was officially released in November 1993, giving regular people a way to get online. Mosaic became Netscape, which released its Navigator browser in late 1994. Navigator's adoption grew so quickly—from about 20% of the browser market in January 1995 to almost 80% less than 12 months later—that Netscape was able to IPO in August '95 even though it wasn't yet profitable. Within five months, Netscape stock had shot up from $28 to $174 per share. Other tech companies were booming, too. Yahoo! went public in April '96 with an $848 million valuation. Amazon followed suit in May '97 at $438 million. By spring of '98, each company's stock had more than quadrupled. Skeptics questioned earnings and revenue multiples higher than those for any non-internet company. It was easy to conclude that the market had gone crazy. This conclusion was understandable but misplaced. In December '96—more than three years before the bubble actually burst—Fed chairman Alan Greenspan warned that "irrational exuberance" might have "unduly escalated asset values." Tech investors were exuberant, but it's not clear that they were so irrational. It is too easy to forget that things weren't going very well in the rest of the world at the time. The East Asian financial crises hit in July 1997. Crony capitalism and massive foreign debt brought the Thai, Indonesian, and South Korean economies to their knees. The ruble crisis followed in August '98 when Russia, hamstrung by chronic fiscal deficits, devalued its currency and defaulted on its debt. American investors grew nervous about a nation with 10,000 nukes and no money; the Dow Jones Industrial Average plunged more than 10% in a matter of days. People were right to worry. The ruble crisis set off a chain reaction that brought down Long-Term Capital Management, a highly leveraged U.S. hedge fund. LTCM managed to lose $4.6 billion in the latter half of 1998, and still had over $100 billion in liabilities when the Fed intervened with a massive bailout and slashed interest rates in order to prevent systemic disaster. Europe wasn't doing that much better. The euro launched in January 1999 to great skepticism and apathy. It rose to $1.19 on its first day of trading but sank to $0.83 within two years. In mid-2000, G7 central bankers had to prop it up with a multibillion-dollar intervention. So the backdrop for the short-lived dot-com mania that started in September 1998 was a world in which nothing else seemed to be working. The Old Economy couldn't handle the challenges of globalization. Something needed to work—and work in a big way—if the future was going to be better at all. By indirect proof, the New Economy of the internet was the only way forward. MANIA: SEPTEMBER 1998–MARCH 2000 Dot-com mania was intense but short—18 months of insanity from September 1998 to March 2000. It was a Silicon Valley gold rush: there was money everywhere, and no shortage of exuberant, often sketchy people to chase it. Every week, dozens of new startups competed to throw the most lavish launch party. (Landing parties were much more rare.)

Paper millionaires would rack up thousanddollar dinner bills and try to pay with shares of their startup's stock—sometimes it even worked. Legions of people decamped from their well-paying jobs to found or join startups. One 40-something grad student that I knew was running six different companies in 1999. (Usually, it's considered weird to be a 40-year-old graduate student. Usually, it's considered insane to start a half-dozen companies at once. But in the late '90s, people could believe that was a winning combination.) Everybody should have known that the mania was unsustainable; the most "successful" companies seemed to embrace a sort of anti-business model where they lost money as they grew. But it's hard to blame people for dancing when the music was playing; irrationality was rational given that appending ".com" to your name could double your value overnight. PAYPAL MANIA When I was running PayPal in late 1999, I was scared out of my wits—not because I didn't believe in our company, but because it seemed like everyone else in the Valley was ready to believe anything at all. Everywhere I looked, people were starting and flipping companies with alarming casualness. One acquaintance told me how he had planned an IPO from his living room before he'd even incorporated his company—and he didn't think that was weird. In this kind of environment, acting sanely began to seem eccentric. At least PayPal had a suitably grand mission—the kind that post-bubble skeptics would later describe as grandiose: we wanted to create a new internet currency to replace the U.S. dollar. Our first product let people beam money from one PalmPilot to another. However, nobody had any use for that product except the journalists who voted it one of the 10 worst business ideas of 1999. PalmPilots were still too exotic then, but email was already commonplace, so we decided to create a way to send and receive payments over email. By the fall of '99, our email payment product worked well—anyone could log in to our website and easily transfer money. But we didn't have enough customers, growth was slow, and expenses mounted. For PayPal to work, we needed to attract a critical mass of at least a million users. Advertising was too ineffective to justify the cost. Prospective deals with big banks kept falling through. So we decided to pay people to sign up. We gave new customers $10 for joining, and we gave them $10 more every time they referred a friend. This got us hundreds of thousands of new customers and an exponential growth rate. Of course, this customer acquisition strategy was unsustainable on its own—when you pay people to be your customers, exponential growth means an exponentially growing cost structure. Crazy costs were typical at that time in the Valley.

But we thought our huge costs were sane: given a large user base, PayPal had a clear path to profitability by taking a small fee on customers' transactions. We knew we'd need more funding to reach that goal. We also knew that the boom was going to end. Since we didn't expect investors' faith in our mission to survive the coming crash, we moved fast to raise funds while we could. On February 16, 2000, the Wall Street Journal ran a story lauding our viral growth and suggesting that PayPal was worth $500 million. When we raised $100 million the next month, our lead investor took the Journal's back-of-the-envelope valuation as authoritative. (Other investors were in even more of a hurry. A South Korean firm wired us $5 million without first negotiating a deal or signing any documents. When I tried to return the money, they wouldn't tell me where to send it.) That March 2000 financing round bought us the time we needed to make PayPal a success. Just as we closed the deal, the bubble popped.

The NASDAQ reached 5,048 at its peak in the middle of March 2000 and then crashed to 3,321 in the middle of April. By the time it bottomed out at 1,114 in October 2002, the country had long since interpreted the market's collapse as a kind of divine judgment against the technological optimism of the '90s. The era of cornucopian hope was relabeled as an era of crazed greed and declared to be definitely over. Everyone learned to treat the future as fundamentally indefinite, and to dismiss as an extremist anyone with plans big enough to be measured in years instead of quarters. Globalization replaced technology as the hope for the future. Since the '90s migration "from bricks to clicks" didn't work as hoped, investors went back to bricks (housing) and BRICs (globalization). The result was another bubble, this time in real estate. The entrepreneurs who stuck with Silicon Valley learned four big lessons from the dot-com crash that still guide business thinking today: 1. Make incremental advances Grand visions inflated the bubble, so they should not be indulged. Anyone who claims to be able to do something great is suspect, and anyone who wants to change the world should be more humble. Small, incremental steps are the only safe path forward. 2. Stay lean and flexible All companies must be "lean," which is code for "unplanned." You should not know what your business will do; planning is arrogant and inflexible. Instead you should try things out, "iterate," and treat entrepreneurship as agnostic experimentation. 3. Improve on the competition Don't try to create a new market prematurely. The only way to know you have a real business is to start with an already existing customer, so you should build your company by improving on recognizable products already offered by successful competitors. 4. Focus on product, not sales If your product requires advertising or salespeople to sell it, it's not good enough: technology is primarily about product development, not distribution. Bubble-era advertising was obviously wasteful, so the only sustainable growth is viral growth. These lessons have become dogma in the startup world; those who would ignore them are presumed to invite the justified doom visited upon technology in the great crash of 2000. And yet the opposite principles are probably more correct: 1. It is better to risk boldness than triviality. 2. A bad plan is better than no plan. 3. Competitive markets destroy profits. 4. Sales matters just as much as product. It's true that there was a bubble in technology. The late '90s was a time of hubris: people believed in going from 0 to 1. Too few startups were actually getting there, and many never went beyond talking about it. But people understood that we had no choice but to find ways to do more with less. The market high of March 2000 was obviously a peak of insanity; less obvious but more important, it was also a peak of clarity. People looked far into the future, saw how much valuable new technology we would need to get there safely, and judged themselves capable of creating it. We still need new technology, and we may even need some 1999-style hubris and exuberance to get it. To build the next generation of companies, we must abandon the dogmas created after the crash. That doesn't mean the opposite ideas are automatically true: you can't escape the madness of crowds by dogmatically rejecting them. Instead ask yourself: how much of what you know about business is shaped by mistaken reactions to past mistakes? The most contrarian thing of all is not to oppose the crowd but to think for yourself. 3 ALL HAPPY COMPANIES ARE DIFFERENT THE BUSINESS VERSION of our contrarian question is: what valuable company is nobody building? This question is harder than it looks, because your company could create a lot of value without becoming very valuable itself. Creating value is not enough—you also need to capture some of the value you create. This means that even very big businesses can be bad businesses. For example, U.S. airline companies serve millions of passengers and create hundreds of billions of dollars of value each year. But in 2012, when the average airfare each way was $178, the airlines made only 37 cents per passenger trip. Compare them to Google, which creates less value but captures far more. Google brought in $50 billion in 2012 (versus $160 billion for the airlines), but it kept 21% of those revenues as profits—more than 100 times the airline industry's profit margin that year. Google makes so much money that it's now worth three times more than every U.S. airline combined. The airlines compete with each other, but Google stands alone. Economists use two simplified models to explain the difference: perfect competition and monopoly. "Perfect competition" is considered both the ideal and the default state in Economics 101. Socalled perfectly competitive markets achieve equilibrium when producer supply meets consumer demand. Every firm in a competitive market is undifferentiated and sells the same homogeneous products. Since no firm has any market power, they must all sell at whatever price the market determines. If there is money to be made, new firms will enter the market, increase supply, drive prices down, and thereby eliminate the profits that attracted them in the first place. If too many firms enter the market, they'll suffer losses, some will fold, and prices will rise back to sustainable levels. Under perfect competition, in the long run no company makes an economic profit. The opposite of perfect competition is monopoly. Whereas a competitive firm must sell at the market price, a monopoly owns its market, so it can set its own prices. Since it has no competition, it produces at the quantity and price combination that maximizes its profits. To an economist, every monopoly looks the same, whether it deviously eliminates rivals, secures a license from the state, or innovates its way to the top. In this book, we're not interested in illegal bullies or government favorites: by "monopoly," we mean the kind of company that's so good at what it does that no other firm can offer a close substitute. Google is a good example of a company that went from 0 to 1: it hasn't competed in search since the early 2000s, when it definitively distanced itself from Microsoft and Yahoo! Americans mythologize competition and credit it with saving us from socialist bread lines. Actually, capitalism and competition are opposites. Capitalism is premised on the accumulation of capital, but under perfect competition all profits get competed away. The lesson for entrepreneurs is clear: if you want to create and capture lasting value, don't build an undif erentiated commodity business. LIES PEOPLE TELL How much of the world is actually monopolistic? How much is truly competitive? It's hard to say, because our common conversation about these matters is so confused. To the outside observer, all businesses can seem reasonably alike, so it's easy to perceive only small differences between them. But the reality is much more binary than that. There's an enormous difference between perfect competition and monopoly, and most businesses are much closer to one extreme than we commonly realize. The confusion comes from a universal bias for describing market conditions in self-serving ways: both monopolists and competitors are incentivized to bend the truth. Monopoly Lies Monopolists lie to protect themselves. They know that bragging about their great monopoly invites being audited, scrutinized, and attacked. Since they very much want their monopoly profits to continue unmolested, they tend to do whatever they can to conceal their monopoly—usually by exaggerating the power of their (nonexistent) competition. Think about how Google talks about its business. It certainly doesn't claim to be a monopoly. But is it one? Well, it depends: a monopoly in what? Let's say that Google is primarily a search engine. As of May 2014, it owns about 68% of the search market. (Its closest competitors, Microsoft and Yahoo!, have about 19% and 10%, respectively.) If that doesn't seem dominant enough, consider the fact that the word "google" is now an official entry in the Oxford English Dictionary—as a verb. Don't hold your breath waiting for that to happen to Bing. But suppose we say that Google is primarily an advertising company. That changes things. The U.S. search engine advertising market is $17 billion annually. Online advertising is $37 billion annually. The entire U.S. advertising market is $150 billion. And global advertising is a $495 billion market. So even if Google completely monopolized U.S. search engine advertising, it would own just 3.4% of the global advertising market. From this angle, Google looks like a small player in a competitive world. What if we frame Google as a multifaceted technology company instead? This seems reasonable enough; in addition to its search engine, Google makes dozens of other software products, not to mention robotic cars, Android phones, and wearable computers. But 95% of Google's revenue comes from search advertising; its other products generated just $2.35 billion in 2012, and its consumer tech products a mere fraction of that. Since consumer tech is a $964 billion market globally, Google owns less than 0.24% of it—a far cry from relevance, let alone monopoly. Framing itself as just another tech company allows Google to escape all sorts of unwanted attention. Competitive Lies Non-monopolists tell the opposite lie: "we're in a league of our own." Entrepreneurs are always biased to understate the scale of competition, but that is the biggest mistake a startup can make. The fatal temptation is to describe your market extremely narrowly so that you dominate it by definition. Suppose you want to start a restaurant that serves British food in Palo Alto. "No one else is doing it," you might reason. "We'll own the entire market." But that's only true if the relevant market is the market for British food specifically. What if the actual market is the Palo Alto restaurant market in general? And what if all the restaurants in nearby towns are part of the relevant market as well? These are hard questions, but the bigger problem is that you have an incentive not to ask them at all. When you hear that most new restaurants fail within one or two years, your instinct will be to come up with a story about how yours is different. You'll spend time trying to convince people that you are exceptional instead of seriously considering whether that's true. It would be better to pause and consider whether there are people in Palo Alto who would rather eat British food above all else. It's very possible they don't exist. In 2001, my co-workers at PayPal and I would often get lunch on Castro Street in Mountain View. We had our pick of restaurants, starting with obvious categories like Indian, sushi, and burgers. There were more options once we settled on a type: North Indian or South Indian, cheaper or fancier, and so on. In contrast to the competitive local restaurant market, PayPal was at that time the only email- based payments company in the world. We employed fewer people than the restaurants on Castro Street did, but our business was much more valuable than all of those restaurants combined. Starting a new South Indian restaurant is a really hard way to make money. If you lose sight of competitive reality and focus on trivial differentiating factors—maybe you think your naan is superior because of your great-grandmother's recipe—your business is unlikely to survive. Creative industries work this way, too. No screenwriter wants to admit that her new movie script simply rehashes what has already been done before. Rather, the pitch is: "This film will combine various exciting elements in entirely new ways." It could even be true. Suppose her idea is to have Jay-Z star in a cross between Hackers and Jaws: rap star joins elite group of hackers to catch the shark that killed his friend. That has definitely never been done before. But, like the lack of British restaurants in Palo Alto, maybe that's a good thing. Non-monopolists exaggerate their distinction by defining their market as the intersection of various smaller markets: British food ∩ restaurant ∩ Palo Alto Rap star ∩ hackers ∩ sharks Monopolists, by contrast, disguise their monopoly by framing their market as the union of several large markets: search engine ∪ mobile phones ∪ wearable computers ∪ self-driving cars What does a monopolist's union story look like in practice? Consider a statement from Google chairman Eric Schmidt's testimony at a 2011 congressional hearing: We face an extremely competitive landscape in which consumers have a multitude of options to access information. Or, translated from PR-speak to plain English: Google is a small fish in a big pond. We could be swallowed whole at any time. We are not the monopoly that the government is looking for.

RUTHLESS PEOPLE The problem with a competitive business goes beyond lack of profits. Imagine you're running one of those restaurants in Mountain View. You're not that different from dozens of your competitors, so you've got to fight hard to survive. If you offer affordable food with low margins, you can probably pay employees only minimum wage. And you'll need to squeeze out every efficiency: that's why small restaurants put Grandma to work at the register and make the kids wash dishes in the back. Restaurants aren't much better even at the very highest rungs, where reviews and ratings like Michelin's star system enforce a culture of intense competition that can drive chefs crazy. (French chef and winner of three Michelin stars Bernard Loiseau was quoted as saying, "If I lose a star, I will commit suicide." Michelin maintained his rating, but Loiseau killed himself anyway in 2003 when a competing French dining guide downgraded his restaurant.) The competitive ecosystem pushes people toward ruthlessness or death. A monopoly like Google is different. Since it doesn't have to worry about competing with anyone, it has wider latitude to care about its workers, its products, and its impact on the wider world. Google's motto—"Don't be evil"—is in part a branding ploy, but it's also characteristic of a kind of business that's successful enough to take ethics seriously without jeopardizing its own existence. In business, money is either an important thing or it is everything. Monopolists can afford to think about things other than making money; non-monopolists can't. In perfect competition, a business is so focused on today's margins that it can't possibly plan for a long-term future. Only one thing can allow a business to transcend the daily brute struggle for survival: monopoly profits.

MONOPOLY CAPITALISM So, a monopoly is good for everyone on the inside, but what about everyone on the outside? Do outsized profits come at the expense of the rest of society? Actually, yes: profits come out of customers' wallets, and monopolies deserve their bad reputation—but only in a world where nothing changes. In a static world, a monopolist is just a rent collector. If you corner the market for something, you can jack up the price; others will have no choice but to buy from you. Think of the famous board game: deeds are shuffled around from player to player, but the board never changes. There's no way to win by inventing a better kind of real estate development. The relative values of the properties are fixed for all time, so all you can do is try to buy them up. But the world we live in is dynamic: it's possible to invent new and better things. Creative monopolists give customers more choices by adding entirely new categories of abundance to the world. Creative monopolies aren't just good for the rest of society; they're powerful engines for making it better. Even the government knows this: that's why one of its departments works hard to create monopolies (by granting patents to new inventions) even though another part hunts them down (by prosecuting antitrust cases). It's possible to question whether anyone should really be awarded a legally enforceable monopoly simply for having been the first to think of something like a mobile software design. But it's clear that something like Apple's monopoly profits from designing, producing, and marketing the iPhone were the reward for creating greater abundance, not artificial scarcity: customers were happy to finally have the choice of paying high prices to get a smartphone that actually works. The dynamism of new monopolies itself explains why old monopolies don't strangle innovation. With Apple's iOS at the forefront, the rise of mobile computing has dramatically reduced Microsoft's decades-long operating system dominance. Before that, IBM's hardware monopoly of the '60s and '70s was overtaken by Microsoft's software monopoly. AT&T had a monopoly on telephone service for most of the 20th century, but now anyone can get a cheap cell phone plan from any number of providers. If the tendency of monopoly businesses were to hold back progress, they would be dangerous and we'd be right to oppose them. But the history of progress is a history of better monopoly businesses replacing incumbents. Monopolies drive progress because the promise of years or even decades of monopoly profits provides a powerful incentive to innovate. Then monopolies can keep innovating because profits enable them to make the long-term plans and to finance the ambitious research projects that firms locked in competition can't dream of. So why are economists obsessed with competition as an ideal state? It's a relic of history. Economists copied their mathematics from the work of 19th-century physicists: they see individuals and businesses as interchangeable atoms, not as unique creators. Their theories describe an equilibrium state of perfect competition because that's what's easy to model, not because it represents the best of business. But it's worth recalling that the long-run equilibrium predicted by 19th-century physics was a state in which all energy is evenly distributed and everything comes to rest—also known as the heat death of the universe. Whatever your views on thermodynamics, it's a powerful metaphor: in business, equilibrium means stasis, and stasis means death. If your industry is in a competitive equilibrium, the death of your business won't matter to the world; some other undifferentiated competitor will always be ready to take your place. Perfect equilibrium may describe the void that is most of the universe. It may even characterize many businesses. But every new creation takes place far from equilibrium. In the real world outside economic theory, every business is successful exactly to the extent that it does something others cannot. Monopoly is therefore not a pathology or an exception. Monopoly is the condition of every successful business. Tolstoy opens Anna Karenina by observing: "All happy families are alike; each unhappy family is unhappy in its own way." Business is the opposite. All happy companies are different: each one earns a monopoly by solving a unique problem. All failed companies are the same: they failed to escape competition. 4 THE IDEOLOGY OF COMPETITION CREATIVE MONOPOLY means new products that benefit everybody and sustainable profits for the creator. Competition means no profits for anybody, no meaningful differentiation, and a struggle for survival. So why do people believe that competition is healthy? The answer is that competition is not just an economic concept or a simple inconvenience that individuals and companies must deal with in the marketplace. More than anything else, competition is an ideology—the ideology—that pervades our society and distorts our thinking. We preach competition, internalize its necessity, and enact its commandments; and as a result, we trap ourselves within it—even though the more we compete, the less we gain. This is a simple truth, but we've all been trained to ignore it. Our educational system both drives and reflects our obsession with competition. Grades themselves allow precise measurement of each student's competitiveness; pupils with the highest marks receive status and credentials. We teach every young person the same subjects in mostly the same ways, irrespective of individual talents and preferences. Students who don't learn best by sitting still at a desk are made to feel somehow inferior, while children who excel on conventional measures like tests and assignments end up defining their identities in terms of this weirdly contrived academic parallel reality. And it gets worse as students ascend to higher levels of the tournament. Elite students climb confidently until they reach a level of competition sufficiently intense to beat their dreams out of them. Higher education is the place where people who had big plans in high school get stuck in fierce rivalries with equally smart peers over conventional careers like management consulting and investment banking.

For the privilege of being turned into conformists, students (or their families) pay hundreds of thousands of dollars in skyrocketing tuition that continues to outpace inflation. Why are we doing this to ourselves? I wish I had asked myself when I was younger. My path was so tracked that in my 8th-grade yearbook, one of my friends predicted—accurately—that four years later I would enter Stanford as a sophomore. And after a conventionally successful undergraduate career, I enrolled at Stanford Law School, where I competed even harder for the standard badges of success. The highest prize in a law student's world is unambiguous: out of tens of thousands of graduates each year, only a few dozen get a Supreme Court clerkship. After clerking on a federal appeals court for a year, I was invited to interview for clerkships with Justices Kennedy and Scalia. My meetings with the Justices went well. I was so close to winning this last competition. If only I got the clerkship, I thought, I would be set for life. But I didn't. At the time, I was devastated. In 2004, after I had built and sold PayPal, I ran into an old friend from law school who had helped me prepare my failed clerkship applications. We hadn't spoken in nearly a decade. His first question wasn't "How are you doing?" or "Can you believe it's been so long?" Instead, he grinned and asked: "So, Peter, aren't you glad you didn't get that clerkship?" With the benefit of hindsight, we both knew that winning that ultimate competition would have changed my life for the worse. Had I actually clerked on the Supreme Court, I probably would have spent my entire career taking depositions or drafting other people's business deals instead of creating anything new. It's hard to say how much would be different, but the opportunity costs were enormous. All Rhodes Scholars had a great future in their past. WAR AND PEACE Professors downplay the cutthroat culture of academia, but managers never tire of comparing business to war. MBA students carry around copies of Clausewitz and Sun Tzu. War metaphors invade our everyday business language: we use headhunters to build up a sales force that will enable us to take a captive market and make a killing. But really it's competition, not business, that is like war: allegedly necessary, supposedly valiant, but ultimately destructive. Why do people compete with each other? Marx and Shakespeare provide two models for understanding almost every kind of conflict. According to Marx, people fight because they are different. The proletariat fights the bourgeoisie because they have completely different ideas and goals (generated, for Marx, by their very different material circumstances). The greater the differences, the greater the conflict. To

Shakespeare, by contrast, all combatants look more or less alike. It's not at all clear why they should be fighting, since they have nothing to fight about. Consider the opening line from Romeo and Juliet: "Two households, both alike in dignity." The two houses are alike, yet they hate each other. They grow even more similar as the feud escalates. Eventually, they lose sight of why they started fighting in the first place. In the world of business, at least, Shakespeare proves the superior guide. Inside a firm, people become obsessed with their competitors for career advancement. Then the firms themselves become obsessed with their competitors in the marketplace. Amid all the human drama, people lose sight of what matters and focus on their rivals instead. Let's test the Shakespearean model in the real world. Imagine a production called Gates and Schmidt, based on Romeo and Juliet. Montague is Microsoft. Capulet is Google. Two great families, run by alpha nerds, sure to clash on account of their sameness. As with all good tragedy, the conflict seems inevitable only in retrospect. In fact it was entirely avoidable. These families came from very different places. The House of Montague built operating systems and office applications. The House of Capulet wrote a search engine. What was there to fight about? Lots, apparently. As a startup, each clan had been content to leave the other alone and prosper independently. But as they grew, they began to focus on each other. Montagues obsessed about Capulets obsessed about Montagues. The result? Windows vs. Chrome OS, Bing vs. Google Search, Explorer vs. Chrome, Office vs. Docs, and Surface vs. Nexus. Just as war cost the Montagues and Capulets their children, it cost Microsoft and Google their dominance: Apple came along and overtook them all. In January 2013, Apple's market capitalization was $500 billion, while Google and Microsoft combined were worth $467 billion. Just three years before, Microsoft and Google were each more valuable than Apple. War is costly business. Rivalry causes us to overemphasize old opportunities and slavishly copy what has worked in the past. Consider the recent proliferation of mobile credit card readers. In October 2010, a startup called Square released a small, white, square-shaped product that let anyone with an iPhone swipe and accept credit cards. It was the first good payment processing solution for mobile handsets. Imitators promptly sprang into action. A Canadian company called NetSecure launched its own card reader in a half-moon shape. Intuit brought a cylindrical reader to the geometric battle. In March 2012, eBay's PayPal unit launched its own copycat card reader. It was shaped like a triangle—a clear jab at Square, as three sides are simpler than four. One gets the sense that this Shakespearean saga won't end until the apes run out of shapes. The hazards of imitative competition may partially explain why individuals with an Asperger'slike social ineptitude seem to be at an advantage in Silicon Valley today. If you're less sensitive to social cues, you're less likely to do the same things as everyone else around you. If you're interested in making things or programming computers, you'll be less afraid to pursue those activities singlemindedly and thereby become incredibly good at them. Then when you apply your skills, you're a little less likely than others to give up your own convictions: this can save you from getting caught up in crowds competing for obvious prizes. Competition can make people hallucinate opportunities where none exist. The crazy '90s version of this was the fierce battle for the online pet store market. It was Pets.com vs. PetStore.com vs. Petopia.com vs. what seemed like dozens of others. Each company was obsessed with defeating its rivals, precisely because there were no substantive differences to focus on. Amid all the tactical questions—Who could price chewy dog toys most aggressively? Who could create the best Super Bowl ads?—these companies totally lost sight of the wider question of whether the online pet supply market was the right space to be in. Winning is better than losing, but everybody loses when the war isn't one worth fighting. When Pets.com folded after the dot-com crash, $300 million of investment capital disappeared with it. Other times, rivalry is just weird and distracting. Consider the Shakespearean conflict between Larry Ellison, co-founder and CEO of Oracle, and Tom Siebel, a top salesman at Oracle and Ellison's protégé before he went on to found Siebel Systems in 1993. Ellison was livid at what he thought was Siebel's betrayal. Siebel hated being in the shadow of his former boss. The two men were basically identical—hard-charging Chicagoans who loved to sell and hated to lose—so their hatred ran deep. Ellison and Siebel spent the second half of the '90s trying to sabotage each other. At one point, Ellison sent truckloads of ice cream sandwiches to Siebel's headquarters to try to convince Siebel employees to jump ship. The copy on the wrappers? "Summer is near. Oracle is here. To brighten your day and your career." Strangely, Oracle intentionally accumulated enemies. Ellison's theory was that it's always good to have an enemy, so long as it was large enough to appear threatening (and thus motivational to employees) but not so large as to actually threaten the company. So Ellison was probably thrilled when in 1996 a small database company called Informix put up a billboard near Oracle's Redwood Shores headquarters that read: CAUTION: DINOSAUR

CROSSING. Another Informix billboard on northbound Highway 101 read: YOU'VE JUST PASSED REDWOOD SHORES. SO DID WE. Oracle shot back with a billboard that implied that Informix's software was slower than snails. Then Informix CEO Phil White decided to make things personal. When White learned that Larry Ellison enjoyed Japanese samurai culture, he commissioned a new billboard depicting the Oracle logo along with a broken samurai sword. The ad wasn't even really aimed at Oracle as an entity, let alone the consuming public; it was a personal attack on Ellison. But perhaps White spent a little too much time worrying about the competition: while he was busy creating billboards, Informix imploded in a massive accounting scandal and White soon found himself in federal prison for securities fraud. If you can't beat a rival, it may be better to merge. I started Confinity with my co-founder Max Levchin in 1998. When we released the PayPal product in late 1999, Elon Musk's X.com was right on our heels: our companies' offices were four blocks apart on University Avenue in Palo Alto, and X's product mirrored ours feature-for-feature. By late 1999, we were in all-out war. Many of us at PayPal logged 100-hour workweeks. No doubt that was counterproductive, but the focus wasn't on objective productivity; the focus was defeating X.com. One of our engineers actually designed a bomb for this purpose; when he presented the schematic at a team meeting, calmer heads prevailed and the proposal was attributed to extreme sleep deprivation. But in February 2000, Elon and I were more scared about the rapidly inflating tech bubble than we were about each other: a financial crash would ruin us both before we could finish our fight. So in early March we met on neutral ground—a café almost exactly equidistant to our offices—and negotiated a 50-50 merger. De-escalating the rivalry post-merger wasn't easy, but as far as problems go, it was a good one to have. As a unified team, we were able to ride out the dot-com crash and then build a successful business. Sometimes you do have to fight. Where that's true, you should fight and win. There is no middle ground: either don't throw any punches, or strike hard and end it quickly. This advice can be hard to follow because pride and honor can get in the way. Hence Hamlet: Exposing what is mortal and unsure To all that fortune, death, and danger dare, Even for an eggshell. Rightly to be great Is not to stir without great argument, But greatly to find quarrel in a straw When honor's at the stake. For Hamlet, greatness means willingness to fight for reasons as thin as an eggshell: anyone would fight for things that matter; true heroes take their personal honor so seriously they will fight for things that don't matter. This twisted logic is part of human nature, but it's disastrous in business. If you can recognize competition as a destructive force instead of a sign of value, you're already more sane than most. The next chapter is about how to use a clear head to build a monopoly business. 5 LAST MOVER ADVANTAGE ESCAPING COMPETITION will give you a monopoly, but even a monopoly is only a great business if it can endure in the future. Compare the value of the New York Times Company with Twitter. Each employs a few thousand people, and each gives millions of people a way to get news. But when Twitter went public in 2013, it was valued at $24 billion—more than 12 times the Times's market capitalization —even though the Times earned $133 million in 2012 while Twitter lost money. What explains the huge premium for Twitter? The answer is cash flow. This sounds bizarre at first, since the Times was profitable while Twitter wasn't. But a great business is defined by its ability to generate cash flows in the future. Investors expect Twitter will be able to capture monopoly profits over the next decade, while newspapers' monopoly days are over. Simply stated, the value of a business today is the sum of all the money it will make in the future. (To properly value a business, you also have to discount those future cash flows to their present worth, since a given amount of money today is worth more than the same amount in the future.) Comparing discounted cash flows shows the difference between low-growth businesses and highgrowth startups at its starkest. Most of the value of low-growth businesses is in the near term. An Old Economy business (like a newspaper) might hold its value if it can maintain its current cash flows for five or six years. However, any firm with close substitutes will see its profits competed away. Nightclubs or restaurants are extreme examples: successful ones might collect healthy amounts today, but their cash flows will probably dwindle over the next few years when customers move on to newer and trendier alternatives. Technology companies follow the opposite trajectory. They often lose money for the first few years: it takes time to build valuable things, and that means delayed revenue. Most of a tech company's value will come at least 10 to 15 years in the future. In March 2001, PayPal had yet to make a profit but our revenues were growing 100% year-overyear. When I projected our future cash flows, I found that 75% of the company's present value would come from profits generated in 2011 and beyond—hard to believe for a company that had been in business for only 27 months. But even that turned out to be an underestimation. Today, PayPal continues to grow at about 15% annually, and the discount rate is lower than a decade ago. It now appears that most of the company's value will come from 2020 and beyond. LinkedIn is another good example of a company whose value exists in the far future. As of early 2014, its market capitalization was $24.5 billion—very high for a company with less than $1 billion in revenue and only $21.6 million in net income for 2012. You might look at these numbers and conclude that investors have gone insane. But this valuation makes sense when you consider LinkedIn's projected future cash flows. The overwhelming importance of future profits is counterintuitive even in Silicon Valley. For a company to be valuable it must grow and endure, but many entrepreneurs focus only on short-term growth. They have an excuse: growth is easy to measure, but durability isn't. Those who succumb to measurement mania obsess about weekly active user statistics, monthly revenue targets, and quarterly earnings reports. However, you can hit those numbers and still overlook deeper, harder-to-measure problems that threaten the durability of your business. For example, rapid short-term growth at both Zynga and Groupon distracted managers and investors from long-term challenges. Zynga scored early wins with games like Farmville and claimed to have a "psychometric engine" to rigorously gauge the appeal of new releases. But they ended up with the same problem as every Hollywood studio: how can you reliably produce a constant stream of popular entertainment for a fickle audience? (Nobody knows.) Groupon posted fast growth as hundreds of thousands of local businesses tried their product. But persuading those businesses to become repeat customers was harder than they thought. If you focus on near-term growth above all else, you miss the most important question you should be asking: will this business still be around a decade from now? Numbers alone won't tell you the answer; instead you must think critically about the qualitative characteristics of your business. CHARACTERISTICS OF MONOPOLY What does a company with large cash flows far into the future look like? Every monopoly is unique, but they usually share some combination of the following characteristics: proprietary technology, network effects, economies of scale, and branding. This isn't a list of boxes to check as you build your business—there's no shortcut to monopoly. However, analyzing your business according to these characteristics can help you think about how to make it durable. 1. Proprietary Technology Proprietary technology is the most substantive advantage a company can have because it makes your product difficult or impossible to replicate. Google's search algorithms, for example, return results better than anyone else's. Proprietary technologies for extremely short page load times and highly accurate query autocompletion add to the core search product's robustness and defensibility. It would be very hard for anyone to do to Google what Google did to all the other search engine companies in the early 2000s. As a good rule of thumb, proprietary technology must be at least 10 times better than its closest substitute in some important dimension to lead to a real monopolistic advantage. Anything less than an order of magnitude better will probably be perceived as a marginal improvement and will be hard to sell, especially in an already crowded market. The clearest way to make a 10x improvement is to invent something completely new. If you build something valuable where there was nothing before, the increase in value is theoretically infinite. A drug to safely eliminate the need for sleep, or a cure for baldness, for example, would certainly support a monopoly business. Or you can radically improve an existing solution: once you're 10x better, you escape competition. PayPal, for instance, made buying and selling on eBay at least 10 times better. Instead of mailing a check that would take 7 to 10 days to arrive, PayPal let buyers pay as soon as an auction ended. Sellers received their proceeds right away, and unlike with a check, they knew the funds were good. Amazon made its first 10x improvement in a particularly visible way: they offered at least 10 times as many books as any other bookstore. When it launched in 1995, Amazon could claim to be "Earth's largest bookstore" because, unlike a retail bookstore that might stock 100,000 books, Amazon didn't need to physically store any inventory—it simply requested the title from its supplier whenever a customer made an order. This quantum improvement was so effective that a very unhappy Barnes & Noble filed a lawsuit three days before Amazon's IPO, claiming that Amazon was unfairly calling itself a "bookstore" when really it was a "book broker." You can also make a 10x improvement through superior integrated design. Before 2010, tablet computing was so poor that for all practical purposes the market didn't even exist. "Microsoft Windows XP Tablet PC Edition" products first shipped in 2002, and Nokia released its own "Internet Tablet" in 2005, but they were a pain to use. Then Apple released the iPad. Design improvements are hard to measure, but it seems clear that Apple improved on anything that had come before by at least an order of magnitude: tablets went from unusable to useful. 2. Network Ef ects Network effects make a product more useful as more people use it. For example, if all your friends are on Facebook, it makes sense for you to join Facebook, too. Unilaterally choosing a different social network would only make you an eccentric. Network effects can be powerful, but you'll never reap them unless your product is valuable to its very first users when the network is necessarily small. For example, in 1960 a quixotic company called Xanadu set out to build a two-way communication network between all computers—a sort of early, synchronous version of the World Wide Web. After more than three decades of futile effort, Xanadu folded just as the web was becoming commonplace. Their technology probably would have worked at scale, but it could have worked only at scale: it required every computer to join the network at the same time, and that was never going to happen. Paradoxically, then, network effects businesses must start with especially small markets. Facebook started with just Harvard students—Mark Zuckerberg's first product was designed to get all his classmates signed up, not to attract all people of Earth. This is why successful network businesses rarely get started by MBA types: the initial markets are so small that they often don't even appear to be business opportunities at all. 3. Economies of Scale A monopoly business gets stronger as it gets bigger: the fixed costs of creating a product (engineering, management, office space) can be spread out over ever greater quantities of sales. Software startups can enjoy especially dramatic economies of scale because the marginal cost of producing another copy of the product is close to zero. Many businesses gain only limited advantages as they grow to large scale. Service businesses especially are difficult to make monopolies. If you own a yoga studio, for example, you'll only be able to serve a certain number of customers. You can hire more instructors and expand to more locations, but your margins will remain fairly low and you'll never reach a point where a core group of talented people can provide something of value to millions of separate clients, as software engineers are able to do. A good startup should have the potential for great scale built into its first design. Twitter already has more than 250 million users today. It doesn't need to add too many customized features in order to acquire more, and there's no inherent reason why it should ever stop growing. 4. Branding A company has a monopoly on its own brand by definition, so creating a strong brand is a powerful way to claim a monopoly. Today's strongest tech brand is Apple: the attractive looks and carefully chosen materials of products like the iPhone and MacBook, the Apple Stores' sleek minimalist design and close control over the consumer experience, the omnipresent advertising campaigns, the price positioning as a maker of premium goods, and the lingering nimbus of Steve Jobs's personal charisma all contribute to a perception that Apple offers products so good as to constitute a category of their own. Many have tried to learn from Apple's success: paid advertising, branded stores, luxurious materials, playful keynote speeches, high prices, and even minimalist design are all susceptible to imitation. But these techniques for polishing the surface don't work without a strong underlying substance. Apple has a complex suite of proprietary technologies, both in hardware (like superior touchscreen materials) and software (like touchscreen interfaces purpose-designed for specific materials). It manufactures products at a scale large enough to dominate pricing for the materials it buys. And it enjoys strong network effects from its content ecosystem: thousands of developers write software for Apple devices because that's where hundreds of millions of users are, and those users stay on the platform because it's where the apps are. These other monopolistic advantages are less obvious than Apple's sparkling brand, but they are the fundamentals that let the branding effectively reinforce Apple's monopoly. Beginning with brand rather than substance is dangerous. Ever since Marissa Mayer became CEO of Yahoo! in mid-2012, she has worked to revive the once-popular internet giant by making it cool again. In a single tweet, Yahoo! summarized Mayer's plan as a chain reaction of "people then products then traffic then revenue." The people are supposed to come for the coolness: Yahoo! demonstrated design awareness by overhauling its logo, it asserted youthful relevance by acquiring hot startups like Tumblr, and it has gained media attention for Mayer's own star power. But the big question is what products Yahoo! will actually create. When Steve Jobs returned to Apple, he didn't just make Apple a cool place to work; he slashed product lines to focus on the handful of opportunities for 10x improvements. No technology company can be built on branding alone. BUILDING A MONOPOLY Brand, scale, network effects, and technology in some combination define a monopoly; but to get them to work, you need to choose your market carefully and expand deliberately. Start Small and Monopolize Every startup is small at the start. Every monopoly dominates a large share of its market. Therefore, every startup should start with a very small market. Always err on the side of starting too small. The reason is simple: it's easier to dominate a small market than a large one. If you think your initial market might be too big, it almost certainly is. Small doesn't mean nonexistent. We made this mistake early on at PayPal. Our first product let people beam money to each other via PalmPilots. It was interesting technology and no one else was doing it. However, the world's millions of PalmPilot users weren't concentrated in a particular place, they had little in common, and they used their devices only episodically. Nobody needed our product, so we had no customers. With that lesson learned, we set our sights on eBay auctions, where we found our first success. In late 1999, eBay had a few thousand high-volume "PowerSellers," and after only three months of dedicated effort, we were serving 25% of them. It was much easier to reach a few thousand people who really needed our product than to try to compete for the attention of millions of scattered individuals. The perfect target market for a startup is a small group of particular people concentrated together and served by few or no competitors. Any big market is a bad choice, and a big market already served by competing companies is even worse. This is why it's always a red flag when entrepreneurs talk about getting 1% of a $100 billion market. In practice, a large market will either lack a good starting point or it will be open to competition, so it's hard to ever reach that 1%. And even if you do succeed in gaining a small foothold, you'll have to be satisfied with keeping the lights on: cutthroat competition means your profits will be zero. Scaling Up Once you create and dominate a niche market, then you should gradually expand into related and slightly broader markets. Amazon shows how it can be done. Jeff Bezos's founding vision was to dominate all of online retail, but he very deliberately started with books. There were millions of books to catalog, but they all had roughly the same shape, they were easy to ship, and some of the most rarely sold books—those least profitable for any retail store to keep in stock—also drew the most enthusiastic customers. Amazon became the dominant solution for anyone located far from a bookstore or seeking something unusual. Amazon then had two options: expand the number of people who read books, or expand to adjacent markets. They chose the latter, starting with the most similar markets: CDs, videos, and software. Amazon continued to add categories gradually until it had become the world's general store. The name itself brilliantly encapsulated the company's scaling strategy. The biodiversity of the Amazon rain forest reflected Amazon's first goal of cataloging every book in the world, and now it stands for every kind of thing in the world, period. eBay also started by dominating small niche markets. When it launched its auction marketplace in 1995, it didn't need the whole world to adopt it at once; the product worked well for intense interest groups, like Beanie Baby obsessives. Once it monopolized the Beanie Baby trade, eBay didn't jump straight to listing sports cars or industrial surplus: it continued to cater to small-time hobbyists until it became the most reliable marketplace for people trading online no matter what the item. Sometimes there are hidden obstacles to scaling—a lesson that eBay has learned in recent years. Like all marketplaces, the auction marketplace lent itself to natural monopoly because buyers go where the sellers are and vice versa. But eBay found that the auction model works best for individually distinctive products like coins and stamps. It works less well for commodity products: people don't want to bid on pencils or Kleenex, so it's more convenient just to buy them from Amazon. eBay is still a valuable monopoly; it's just smaller than people in 2004 expected it to be. Sequencing markets correctly is underrated, and it takes discipline to expand gradually. The most successful companies make the core progression—to first dominate a specific niche and then scale to adjacent markets—a part of their founding narrative. Don't Disrupt Silicon Valley has become obsessed with "disruption." Originally, "disruption" was a term of art to describe how a firm can use new technology to introduce a low-end product at low prices, improve the product over time, and eventually overtake even the premium products offered by incumbent companies using older technology. This is roughly what happened when the advent of PCs disrupted the market for mainframe computers: at first PCs seemed irrelevant, then they became dominant. Today mobile devices may be doing the same thing to PCs. However, disruption has recently transmogrified into a self-congratulatory buzzword for anything posing as trendy and new. This seemingly trivial fad matters because it distorts an entrepreneur's self-understanding in an inherently competitive way. The concept was coined to describe threats to incumbent companies, so startups' obsession with disruption means they see themselves through older firms' eyes. If you think of yourself as an insurgent battling dark forces, it's easy to become unduly fixated on the obstacles in your path. But if you truly want to make something new, the act of creation is far more important than the old industries that might not like what you create. Indeed, if your company can be summed up by its opposition to already existing firms, it can't be completely new and it's probably not going to become a monopoly. Disruption also attracts attention: disruptors are people who look for trouble and find it. Disruptive kids get sent to the principal's office. Disruptive companies often pick fights they can't win. Think of Napster: the name itself meant trouble. What kinds of things can one "nap"? Music ... Kids ... and perhaps not much else. Shawn Fanning and Sean Parker, Napster's then-teenage founders, credibly threatened to disrupt the powerful music recording industry in 1999. The next year, they made the cover of Time magazine. A year and a half after that, they ended up in bankruptcy court. PayPal could be seen as disruptive, but we didn't try to directly challenge any large competitor. It's true that we took some business away from Visa when we popularized internet payments: you might use PayPal to buy something online instead of using your Visa card to buy it in a store. But since we expanded the market for payments overall, we gave Visa far more business than we took. The overall dynamic was net positive, unlike Napster's negative-sum struggle with the U.S. recording industry. As you craft a plan to expand to adjacent markets, don't disrupt: avoid competition as much as possible. THE LAST WILL BE FIRST You've probably heard about "first mover advantage": if you're the first entrant into a market, you can capture significant market share while competitors scramble to get started. But moving first is a tactic, not a goal. What really matters is generating cash flows in the future, so being the first mover doesn't do you any good if someone else comes along and unseats you. It's much better to be the last mover—that is, to make the last great development in a specific market and enjoy years or even decades of monopoly profits. The way to do that is to dominate a small niche and scale up from there, toward your ambitious long-term vision. In this one particular at least, business is like chess. Grandmaster José Raúl Capablanca put it well: to succeed, "you must study the endgame before everything else.

CHAPTER FOUR

YOU ARE NOT A LOTTERY TICKET

THE MOST CONTENTIOUS question in business is whether success comes from luck or skill. What do successful people say? Malcolm Gladwell, a successful author who writes about successful people, declares in Outliers that success results from a "patchwork of lucky breaks and arbitrary advantages." Warren Buffett famously considers himself a "member of the lucky sperm club" and a winner of the "ovarian lottery." Jeff Bezos attributes Amazon's success to an "incredible planetary alignment" and jokes that it was "half luck, half good timing, and the rest brains." Bill Gates even goes so far as to claim that he "was lucky to be born with certain skills," though it's not clear whether that's actually possible. Perhaps these guys are being strategically humble. However, the phenomenon of serial entrepreneurship would seem to call into question our tendency to explain success as the product of chance. Hundreds of people have started multiple multimillion-dollar businesses. A few, like Steve Jobs, Jack Dorsey, and Elon Musk, have created several multibillion-dollar companies. If success were mostly a matter of luck, these kinds of serial entrepreneurs probably wouldn't exist. In January 2013, Jack Dorsey, founder of Twitter and Square, tweeted to his 2 million followers: "Success is never accidental." Most of the replies were unambiguously negative. Referencing the tweet in The Atlantic, reporter Alexis Madrigal wrote that his instinct was to reply: " 'Success is never accidental,' said all multimillionaire white men." It's true that already successful people have an easier time doing new things, whether due to their networks, wealth, or experience. But perhaps we've become too quick to dismiss anyone who claims to have succeeded according to plan. Is there a way to settle this debate objectively? Unfortunately not, because companies are not experiments. To get a scientific answer about Facebook, for example, we'd have to rewind to 2004, create 1,000 copies of the world, and start Facebook in each copy to see how many times it would succeed. But that experiment is impossible. Every company starts in unique circumstances, and every company starts only once. Statistics doesn't work when the sample size is one. From the Renaissance and the Enlightenment to the mid-20th century, luck was something to be mastered, dominated, and controlled; everyone agreed that you should do what you could, not focus on what you couldn't. Ralph Waldo Emerson captured this ethos when he wrote: "Shallow men believe in luck, believe in circumstances.... Strong men believe in cause and effect." In 1912, after he became the first explorer to reach the South Pole, Roald Amundsen wrote: "Victory awaits him who has everything in order—luck, people call it." No one pretended that misfortune didn't exist, but prior generations believed in making their own luck by working hard. If you believe your life is mainly a matter of chance, why read this book? Learning about startups is worthless if you're just reading stories about people who won the lottery. Slot Machines for Dummies can purport to tell you which kind of rabbit's foot to rub or how to tell which machines are "hot," but it can't tell you how to win. Did Bill Gates simply win the intelligence lottery? Was Sheryl Sandberg born with a silver spoon, or did she "lean in"? When we debate historical questions like these, luck is in the past tense. Far more important are questions about the future: is it a matter of chance or design? CAN YOU CONTROL YOUR FUTURE? You can expect the future to take a definite form or you can treat it as hazily uncertain. If you treat the future as something definite, it makes sense to understand it in advance and to work to shape it. But if you expect an indefinite future ruled by randomness, you'll give up on trying to master it. Indefinite attitudes to the future explain what's most dysfunctional in our world today. Process trumps substance: when people lack concrete plans to carry out, they use formal rules to assemble a portfolio of various options. This describes Americans today. In middle school, we're encouraged to start hoarding "extracurricular activities." In high school, ambitious students compete even harder to appear omnicompetent. By the time a student gets to college, he's spent a decade curating a bewilderingly diverse résumé to prepare for a completely unknowable future. Come what may, he's ready—for nothing in particular. A definite view, by contrast, favors firm convictions. Instead of pursuing many-sided mediocrity and calling it "well-roundedness," a definite person determines the one best thing to do and then does it. Instead of working tirelessly to make herself indistinguishable, she strives to be great at something substantive—to be a monopoly of one. This is not what young people do today, because everyone around them has long since lost faith in a definite world. No one gets into Stanford by excelling at just one thing, unless that thing happens to involve throwing or catching a leather ball. You can also expect the future to be either better or worse than the present. Optimists welcome the future; pessimists fear it. Combining these possibilities yields four views: Indefinite Pessimism Every culture has a myth of decline from some golden age, and almost all peoples throughout history have been pessimists. Even today pessimism still dominates huge parts of the world. An indefinite pessimist looks out onto a bleak future, but he has no idea what to do about it. This describes Europe since the early 1970s, when the continent succumbed to undirected bureaucratic drift. Today the whole Eurozone is in slow-motion crisis, and nobody is in charge. The European Central Bank doesn't stand for anything but improvisation: the U.S. Treasury prints "In God We Trust" on the dollar; the ECB might as well print "Kick the Can Down the Road" on the euro. Europeans just react to events as they happen and hope things don't get worse. The indefinite pessimist can't know whether the inevitable decline will be fast or slow, catastrophic or gradual. All he can do is wait for it to happen, so he might as well eat, drink, and be merry in the meantime: hence Europe's famous vacation mania. Definite Pessimism A definite pessimist believes the future can be known, but since it will be bleak, he must prepare for it. Perhaps surprisingly, China is probably the most definitely pessimistic place in the world today. When Americans see the Chinese economy grow ferociously fast (10% per year since 2000), we imagine a confident country mastering its future. But that's because Americans are still optimists, and we project our optimism onto China. From China's viewpoint, economic growth cannot come fast enough. Every other country is afraid that China is going to take over the world; China is the only country afraid that it won't. China can grow so fast only because its starting base is so low. The easiest way for China to grow is to relentlessly copy what has already worked in the West. And that's exactly what it's doing: executing definite plans by burning ever more coal to build ever more factories and skyscrapers. But with a huge population pushing resource prices higher, there's no way Chinese living standards can ever actually catch up to those of the richest countries, and the Chinese know it. This is why the Chinese leadership is obsessed with the way in which things threaten to get worse. Every senior Chinese leader experienced famine as a child, so when the Politburo looks to the future, disaster is not an abstraction. The Chinese public, too, knows that winter is coming. Outsiders are fascinated by the great fortunes being made inside China, but they pay less attention to the wealthy Chinese trying hard to get their money out of the country. Poorer Chinese just save everything they can and hope it will be enough. Every class of people in China takes the future deadly seriously. Definite Optimism To a definite optimist, the future will be better than the present if he plans and works to make it better. From the 17th century through the 1950s and '60s, definite optimists led the Western world. Scientists, engineers, doctors, and businessmen made the world richer, healthier, and more long-lived than previously imaginable. As Karl Marx and Friedrich Engels saw clearly, the 19th-century business class created more massive and more colossal productive forces than all preceding generations together. Subjection of Nature's forces to man, machinery, application of chemistry to industry and agriculture, steam-navigation, railways, electric telegraphs, clearing of whole continents for cultivation, canalisation of rivers, whole populations conjured out of the ground—what earlier century had even a presentiment that such productive forces slumbered in the lap of social labor? Each generation's inventors and visionaries surpassed their predecessors. In 1843, the London public was invited to make its first crossing underneath the River Thames by a newly dug tunnel. In 1869, the Suez Canal saved Eurasian shipping traffic from rounding the Cape of Good Hope. In 1914 the Panama Canal cut short the route from Atlantic to Pacific. Even the Great Depression failed to impede relentless progress in the United States, which has always been home to the world's most farseeing definite optimists. The Empire State Building was started in 1929 and finished in 1931. The Golden Gate Bridge was started in 1933 and completed in 1937. The Manhattan Project was started in 1941 and had already produced the world's first nuclear bomb by 1945. Americans continued to remake the face of the world in peacetime: the Interstate Highway System began construction in 1956, and the first 20,000 miles of road were open for driving by 1965. Definite planning even went beyond the surface of this planet: NASA's Apollo Program began in 1961 and put 12 men on the moon before it finished in 1972. Bold plans were not reserved just for political leaders or government scientists. In the late 1940s, a Californian named John Reber set out to reinvent the physical geography of the whole San Francisco Bay Area. Reber was a schoolteacher, an amateur theater producer, and a self-taught engineer. Undaunted by his lack of credentials, he publicly proposed to build two huge dams in the Bay, construct massive freshwater lakes for drinking water and irrigation, and reclaim 20,000 acres of land for development. Even though he had no personal authority, people took the Reber Plan seriously. It was endorsed by newspaper editorial boards across California. The U.S. Congress held hearings on its feasibility. The Army Corps of Engineers even constructed a 1.5-acre scale model of the Bay in a cavernous Sausalito warehouse to simulate it. These tests revealed technical shortcomings, so the plan wasn't executed. But would anybody today take such a vision seriously in the first place? In the 1950s, people welcomed big plans and asked whether they would work. Today a grand plan coming from a schoolteacher would be dismissed as crankery, and a long-range vision coming from anyone more powerful would be derided as hubris. You can still visit the Bay Model in that Sausalito warehouse, but today it's just a tourist attraction: big plans for the future have become archaic curiosities. In the 1950s, Americans thought big plans for the future were too important to be left to experts. Indefinite Optimism After a brief pessimistic phase in the 1970s, indefinite optimism has dominated American thinking ever since 1982, when a long bull market began and finance eclipsed engineering as the way to approach the future. To an indefinite optimist, the future will be better, but he doesn't know how exactly, so he won't make any specific plans. He expects to profit from the future but sees no reason to design it concretely. Instead of working for years to build a new product, indefinite optimists rearrange alreadyinvented ones. Bankers make money by rearranging the capital structures of already existing companies. Lawyers resolve disputes over old things or help other people structure their affairs. And private equity investors and management consultants don't start new businesses; they squeeze extra efficiency from old ones with incessant procedural optimizations. It's no surprise that these fields all attract disproportionate numbers of high-achieving Ivy League optionality chasers; what could be a more appropriate reward for two decades of résumé-building than a seemingly elite, process-oriented career that promises to "keep options open"? Recent graduates' parents often cheer them on the established path. The strange history of the Baby Boom produced a generation of indefinite optimists so used to effortless progress that they feel entitled to it. Whether you were born in 1945 or 1950 or 1955, things got better every year for the first 18 years of your life, and it had nothing to do with you. Technological advance seemed to accelerate automatically, so the Boomers grew up with great expectations but few specific plans for how to fulfill them. Then, when technological progress stalled in the 1970s, increasing income inequality came to the rescue of the most elite Boomers. Every year of adulthood continued to get automatically better and better for the rich and successful. The rest of their generation was left behind, but the wealthy Boomers who shape public opinion today see little reason to question their naïve optimism. Since tracked careers worked for them, they can't imagine that they won't work for their kids, too. Malcolm Gladwell says you can't understand Bill Gates's success without understanding his fortunate personal context: he grew up in a good family, went to a private school equipped with a computer lab, and counted Paul Allen as a childhood friend. But perhaps you can't understand Malcolm Gladwell without understanding his historical context as a Boomer (born in 1963). When Baby Boomers grow up and write books to explain why one or another individual is successful, they point to the power of a particular individual's context as determined by chance. But they miss the even bigger social context for their own preferred explanations: a whole generation learned from childhood to overrate the power of chance and underrate the importance of planning. Gladwell at first appears to be making a contrarian critique of the myth of the self-made businessman, but actually his own account encapsulates the conventional view of a generation. OUR INDEFINITELY OPTIMISTIC WORLD Indefinite Finance While a definitely optimistic future would need engineers to design underwater cities and settlements in space, an indefinitely optimistic future calls for more bankers and lawyers. Finance epitomizes indefinite thinking because it's the only way to make money when you have no idea how to create wealth. If they don't go to law school, bright college graduates head to Wall Street precisely because they have no real plan for their careers. And once they arrive at Goldman, they find that even inside finance, everything is indefinite. It's still optimistic—you wouldn't play in the markets if you expected to lose—but the fundamental tenet is that the market is random; you can't know anything specific or substantive; diversification becomes supremely important. The indefiniteness of finance can be bizarre. Think about what happens when successful entrepreneurs sell their company. What do they do with the money? In a financialized world, it unfolds like this: • The founders don't know what to do with it, so they give it to a large bank. • The bankers don't know what to do with it, so they diversify by spreading it across a portfolio of institutional investors. • Institutional investors don't know what to do with their managed capital, so they diversify by amassing a portfolio of stocks. • Companies try to increase their share price by generating free cash flows. If they do, they issue dividends or buy back shares and the cycle repeats. At no point does anyone in the chain know what to do with money in the real economy. But in an indefinite world, people actually prefer unlimited optionality; money is more valuable than anything you could possibly do with it. Only in a definite future is money a means to an end, not the end itself. Indefinite Politics Politicians have always been officially accountable to the public at election time, but today they are attuned to what the public thinks at every moment. Modern polling enables politicians to tailor their image to match preexisting public opinion exactly, so for the most part, they do. Nate Silver's election predictions are remarkably accurate, but even more remarkable is how big a story they become every four years. We are more fascinated today by statistical predictions of what the country will be thinking in a few weeks' time than by visionary predictions of what the country will look like 10 or 20 years from now. And it's not just the electoral process—the very character of government has become indefinite, too. The government used to be able to coordinate complex solutions to problems like atomic weaponry and lunar exploration. But today, after 40 years of indefinite creep, the government mainly just provides insurance; our solutions to big problems are Medicare, Social Security, and a dizzying array of other transfer payment programs. It's no surprise that entitlement spending has eclipsed discretionary spending every year since 1975. To increase discretionary spending we'd need definite plans to solve specific problems. But according to the indefinite logic of entitlement spending, we can make things better just by sending out more checks. Indefinite Philosophy You can see the shift to an indefinite attitude not just in politics but in the political philosophers whose ideas underpin both left and right. The philosophy of the ancient world was pessimistic: Plato, Aristotle, Epicurus, and Lucretius all accepted strict limits on human potential. The only question was how best to cope with our tragic fate. Modern philosophers have been mostly optimistic. From Herbert Spencer on the right and Hegel in the center to Marx on the left, the 19th century shared a belief in progress. (Remember Marx and Engels's encomium to the technological triumphs of capitalism from this page.) These thinkers expected material advances to fundamentally change human life for the better: they were definite optimists. In the late 20th century, indefinite philosophies came to the fore.

The two dominant political thinkers, John Rawls and Robert Nozick, are usually seen as stark opposites: on the egalitarian left, Rawls was concerned with questions of fairness and distribution; on the libertarian right, Nozick focused on maximizing individual freedom. They both believed that people could get along with each other peacefully, so unlike the ancients, they were optimistic. But unlike Spencer or Marx, Rawls and Nozick were indefinite optimists: they didn't have any specific vision of the future. Their indefiniteness took different forms. Rawls begins A Theory of Justice with the famous "veil of ignorance": fair political reasoning is supposed to be impossible for anyone with knowledge of the world as it concretely exists. Instead of trying to change our actual world of unique people and real technologies, Rawls fantasized about an "inherently stable" society with lots of fairness but little dynamism. Nozick opposed Rawls's "patterned" concept of justice. To Nozick, any voluntary exchange must be allowed, and no social pattern could be noble enough to justify maintenance by coercion. He didn't have any more concrete ideas about the good society than Rawls: both of them focused on process. Today, we exaggerate the differences between left-liberal egalitarianism and libertarian individualism because almost everyone shares their common indefinite attitude. In philosophy, politics, and business, too, arguing over process has become a way to endlessly defer making concrete plans for a better future. Indefinite Life Our ancestors sought to understand and extend the human lifespan. In the 16th century, conquistadors searched the jungles of Florida for a Fountain of Youth. Francis Bacon wrote that "the prolongation of life" should be considered its own branch of medicine—and the noblest. In the 1660s, Robert Boyle placed life extension (along with "the Recovery of Youth") atop his famous wish list for the future of science. Whether through geographic exploration or laboratory research, the best minds of the Renaissance thought of death as something to defeat. (Some resisters were killed in action: Bacon caught pneumonia and died in 1626 while experimenting to see if he could extend a chicken's life by freezing it in the snow.) We haven't yet uncovered the secrets of life, but insurers and statisticians in the 19th century successfully revealed a secret about death that still governs our thinking today: they discovered how to reduce it to a mathematical probability. "Life tables" tell us our chances of dying in any given year, something previous generations didn't know. However, in exchange for better insurance contracts, we seem to have given up the search for secrets about longevity. Systematic knowledge of the current range of human lifespans has made that range seem natural. Today our society is permeated by the twin ideas that death is both inevitable and random. Meanwhile, probabilistic attitudes have come to shape the agenda of biology itself. In 1928, Scottish scientist Alexander Fleming found that a mysterious antibacterial fungus had grown on a petri dish he'd forgotten to cover in his laboratory: he discovered penicillin by accident. Scientists have sought to harness the power of chance ever since. Modern drug discovery aims to amplify Fleming's serendipitous circumstances a millionfold: pharmaceutical companies search through combinations of molecular compounds at random, hoping to find a hit. But it's not working as well as it used to. Despite dramatic advances over the past two centuries, in recent decades biotechnology hasn't met the expectations of investors—or patients. Eroom's law— that's Moore's law backward—observes that the number of new drugs approved per billion dollars spent on R&D has halved every nine years since 1950. Since information technology accelerated faster than ever during those same years, the big question for biotech today is whether it will ever see similar progress. Compare biotech startups to their counterparts in computer software: Biotech startups are an extreme example of indefinite thinking. Researchers experiment with things that just might work instead of refining definite theories about how the body's systems operate. Biologists say they need to work this way because the underlying biology is hard. According to them, IT startups work because we created computers ourselves and designed them to reliably obey our commands. Biotech is difficult because we didn't design our bodies, and the more we learn about them, the more complex they turn out to be. But today it's possible to wonder whether the genuine difficulty of biology has become an excuse for biotech startups' indefinite approach to business in general. Most of the people involved expect some things to work eventually, but few want to commit to a specific company with the level of intensity necessary for success. It starts with the professors who often become part-time consultants instead of full-time employees—even for the biotech startups that begin from their own research. Then everyone else imitates the professors' indefinite attitude. It's easy for libertarians to claim that heavy regulation holds biotech back—and it does—but indefinite optimism may pose an even greater challenge for the future of biotech. IS INDEFINITE OPTIMISM EVEN POSSIBLE? What kind of future will our indefinitely optimistic decisions bring about? If American households were saving, at least they could expect to have money to spend later. And if

American companies were investing, they could expect to reap the rewards of new wealth in the future. But U.S. households are saving almost nothing. And U.S. companies are letting cash pile up on their balance sheets without investing in new projects because they don't have any concrete plans for the future. The other three views of the future can work. Definite optimism works when you build the future you envision. Definite pessimism works by building what can be copied without expecting anything new. Indefinite pessimism works because it's self-fulfilling: if you're a slacker with low expectations, they'll probably be met. But indefinite optimism seems inherently unsustainable: how can the future get better if no one plans for it? Actually, most everybody in the modern world has already heard an answer to this question: progress without planning is what we call "evolution." Darwin himself wrote that life tends to "progress" without anybody intending it. Every living thing is just a random iteration on some other organism, and the best iterations win. Darwin's theory explains the origin of trilobites and dinosaurs, but can it be extended to domains that are far removed? Just as Newtonian physics can't explain black holes or the Big Bang, it's not clear that Darwinian biology should explain how to build a better society or how to create a new business out of nothing. Yet in recent years Darwinian (or pseudo-Darwinian) metaphors have become common in business. Journalists analogize literal survival in competitive ecosystems to corporate survival in competitive markets. Hence all the headlines like "Digital Darwinism," "Dotcom Darwinism," and "Survival of the Clickiest." Even in engineering-driven Silicon Valley, the buzzwords of the moment call for building a "lean startup" that can "adapt" and "evolve" to an ever-changing environment. Would-be entrepreneurs are told that nothing can be known in advance: we're supposed to listen to what customers say they want, make nothing more than a "minimum viable product," and iterate our way to success. But leanness is a methodology, not a goal. Making small changes to things that already exist might lead you to a local maximum, but it won't help you find the global maximum. You could build the best version of an app that lets people order toilet paper from their iPhone. But iteration without a bold plan won't take you from 0 to 1. A company is the strangest place of all for an indefinite optimist: why should you expect your own business to succeed without a plan to make it happen? Darwinism may be a fine theory in other contexts, but in startups, intelligent design works best. THE RETURN OF DESIGN What would it mean to prioritize design over chance? Today, "good design" is an aesthetic imperative, and everybody from slackers to yuppies carefully "curates" their outward appearance. It's true that every great entrepreneur is first and foremost a designer. Anyone who has held an iDevice or a smoothly machined MacBook has felt the result of Steve Jobs's obsession with visual and experiential perfection. But the most important lesson to learn from Jobs has nothing to do with aesthetics. The greatest thing Jobs designed was his business. Apple imagined and executed definite multi-year plans to create new products and distribute them effectively. Forget "minimum viable products"—ever since he started Apple in 1976, Jobs saw that you can change the world through careful planning, not by listening to focus group feedback or copying others' successes. Long-term planning is often undervalued by our indefinite short-term world. When the first iPod was released in October 2001, industry analysts couldn't see much more than "a nice feature for Macintosh users" that "doesn't make any difference" to the rest of the world. Jobs planned the iPod to be the first of a new generation of portable post-PC devices, but that secret was invisible to most people. One look at the company's stock chart shows the harvest of this multi-year plan: The power of planning explains the difficulty of valuing private companies. When a big company makes an offer to acquire a successful startup, it almost always offers too much or too little: founders only sell when they have no more concrete visions for the company, in which case the acquirer probably overpaid; definite founders with robust plans don't sell, which means the offer wasn't high enough. When Yahoo! offered to buy Facebook for $1 billion in July 2006, I thought we should at least consider it. But Mark Zuckerberg walked into the board meeting and announced: "Okay, guys, this is just a formality, it shouldn't take more than 10 minutes. We're obviously not going to sell here." Mark saw where he could take the company, and Yahoo! didn't. A business with a good definite plan will always be underrated in a world where people see the future as random. YOU ARE NOT A LOTTERY TICKET We have to find our way back to a definite future, and the Western world needs nothing short of a cultural revolution to do it. Where to start? John Rawls will need to be displaced in philosophy departments. Malcolm Gladwell must be persuaded to change his theories. And pollsters have to be driven from politics. But the philosophy professors and the Gladwells of the world are set in their ways, to say nothing of our politicians. It's extremely hard to make changes in those crowded fields, even with brains and good intentions. A startup is the largest endeavor over which you can have definite mastery. You can have agency not just over your own life, but over a small and important part of the world. It begins by rejecting the unjust tyranny of Chance. You are not a lottery ticket. 7 FOLLOW THE MONEY MONEY MAKES MONEY. "For whoever has will be given more, and they will have an abundance. Whoever does not have, even what they have will be taken from them" (Matthew 25:29). Albert Einstein made the same observation when he stated that compound interest was "the eighth wonder of the world," "the greatest mathematical discovery of all time," or even "the most powerful force in the universe." Whichever version you prefer, you can't miss his message: never underestimate exponential growth. Actually, there's no evidence that Einstein ever said any of those things—the quotations are all apocryphal. But this very misattribution reinforces the message: having invested the principal of a lifetime's brilliance, Einstein continues to earn interest on it from beyond the grave by receiving credit for things he never said. Most sayings are forgotten. At the other extreme, a select few people like Einstein and Shakespeare are constantly quoted and ventriloquized. We shouldn't be surprised, since small minorities often achieve disproportionate results. In 1906, economist Vilfredo Pareto discovered what became the "Pareto principle," or the 80-20 rule, when he noticed that 20% of the people owned 80% of the land in Italy—a phenomenon that he found just as natural as the fact that 20% of the peapods in his garden produced 80% of the peas. This extraordinarily stark pattern, in which a small few radically outstrip all rivals, surrounds us everywhere in the natural and social world. The most destructive earthquakes are many times more powerful than all smaller earthquakes combined. The biggest cities dwarf all mere towns put together. And monopoly businesses capture more value than millions of undifferentiated competitors. Whatever Einstein did or didn't say, the power law—so named because exponential equations describe severely unequal distributions—is the law of the universe. It defines our surroundings so completely that we usually don't even see it. This chapter shows how the power law becomes visible when you follow the money: in venture capital, where investors try to profit from exponential growth in early-stage companies, a few companies attain exponentially greater value than all others. Most businesses never need to deal with venture capital, but everyone needs to know exactly one thing that even venture capitalists struggle to understand: we don't live in a normal world; we live under a power law. THE POWER LAW OF VENTURE CAPITAL Venture capitalists aim to identify, fund, and profit from promising early-stage companies. They raise money from institutions and wealthy people, pool it into a fund, and invest in technology companies that they believe will become more valuable. If they turn out to be right, they take a cut of the returns —usually 20%. A venture fund makes money when the companies in its portfolio become more valuable and either go public or get bought by larger companies. Venture funds usually have a 10-year lifespan since it takes time for successful companies to grow and "exit." But most venture-backed companies don't IPO or get acquired; most fail, usually soon after they start. Due to these early failures, a venture fund typically loses money at first. VCs hope the value of the fund will increase dramatically in a few years' time, to break-even and beyond, when the successful portfolio companies hit their exponential growth spurts and start to scale. The big question is when this takeoff will happen. For most funds, the answer is never. Most startups fail, and most funds fail with them. Every VC knows that his task is to find the companies that will succeed. However, even seasoned investors understand this phenomenon only superficially. They know companies are different, but they underestimate the degree of difference. The error lies in expecting that venture returns will be normally distributed: that is, bad companies will fail, mediocre ones will stay flat, and good ones will return 2x or even 4x. Assuming this bland pattern, investors assemble a diversified portfolio and hope that winners counterbalance losers. But this "spray and pray" approach usually produces an entire portfolio of flops, with no hits at all. This is because venture returns don't follow a normal distribution overall. Rather, they follow a power law: a small handful of companies radically outperform all others. If you focus on diversification instead of single-minded pursuit of the very few companies that can become overwhelmingly valuable, you'll miss those rare companies in the first place. This graph shows the stark reality versus the perceived relative homogeneity: Our results at Founders Fund illustrate this skewed pattern: Facebook, the best investment in our 2005 fund, returned more than all the others combined. Palantir, the second-best investment, is set to return more than the sum of every other investment aside from Facebook. This highly uneven pattern is not unusual: we see it in all our other funds as well. The biggest secret in venture capital is that the best investment in a successful fund equals or outperforms the entire rest of the fund combined. This implies two very strange rules for VCs. First, only invest in companies that have the potential to return the value of the entire fund. This is a scary rule, because it eliminates the vast majority of possible investments. (Even quite successful companies usually succeed on a more humble scale.) This leads to rule number two: because rule number one is so restrictive, there can't be any other rules. Consider what happens when you break the first rule. Andreessen Horowitz invested $250,000 in Instagram in 2010. When Facebook bought Instagram just two years later for $1 billion, Andreessen netted $78 million—a 312x return in less than two years. That's a phenomenal return, befitting the firm's reputation as one of the Valley's best. But in a weird way it's not nearly enough, because Andreessen Horowitz has a $1.5 billion fund: if they only wrote $250,000 checks, they would need to find 19 Instagrams just to break even. This is why investors typically put a lot more money into any company worth funding. (And to be fair, Andreessen would have invested more in Instagram's later rounds had it not been conflicted out by a previous investment.) VCs must find the handful of companies that will successfully go from 0 to 1 and then back them with every resource. Of course, no one can know with certainty ex ante which companies will succeed, so even the best VC firms have a "portfolio." However, every single company in a good venture portfolio must have the potential to succeed at vast scale. At Founders Fund, we focus on five to seven companies in a fund, each of which we think could become a multibillion-dollar business based on its unique fundamentals. Whenever you shift from the substance of a business to the financial question of whether or not it fits into a diversified hedging strategy, venture investing starts to look a lot like buying lottery tickets. And once you think that you're playing the lottery, you've already psychologically prepared yourself to lose. WHY PEOPLE DON'T SEE THE POWER LAW Why would professional VCs, of all people, fail to see the power law? For one thing, it only becomes clear over time, and even technology investors too often live in the present. Imagine a firm invests in 10 companies with the potential to become monopolies—already an unusually disciplined portfolio. Those companies will look very similar in the early stages before exponential growth. Over the next few years, some companies will fail while others begin to succeed; valuations will diverge, but the difference between exponential growth and linear growth will be unclear. After 10 years, however, the portfolio won't be divided between winners and losers; it will be split between one dominant investment and everything else. But no matter how unambiguous the end result of the power law, it doesn't reflect daily experience. Since investors spend most of their time making new investments and attending to companies in their early stages, most of the companies they work with are by definition average. Most of the differences that investors and entrepreneurs perceive every day are between relative levels of success, not between exponential dominance and failure. And since nobody wants to give up on an investment, VCs usually spend even more time on the most problematic companies than they do on the most obviously successful.

If even investors specializing in exponentially growing startups miss the power law, it's not surprising that most everyone else misses it, too. Power law distributions are so big that they hide in plain sight. For example, when most people outside Silicon Valley think of venture capital, they might picture a small and quirky coterie—like ABC's Shark Tank, only without commercials. After all, less than 1% of new businesses started each year in the U.S. receive venture funding, and total VC investment accounts for less than 0.2% of GDP. But the results of those investments disproportionately propel the entire economy. Venture-backed companies create 11% of all private sector jobs. They generate annual revenues equivalent to an astounding 21% of GDP. Indeed, the dozen largest tech companies were all venture-backed. Together those 12 companies are worth more than $2 trillion, more than all other tech companies combined. WHAT TO DO WITH THE POWER LAW The power law is not just important to investors; rather, it's important to everybody because everybody is an investor. An entrepreneur makes a major investment just by spending her time working on a startup. Therefore every entrepreneur must think about whether her company is going to succeed and become valuable. Every individual is unavoidably an investor, too. When you choose a career, you act on your belief that the kind of work you do will be valuable decades from now. The most common answer to the question of future value is a diversified portfolio: "Don't put all your eggs in one basket," everyone has been told. As we said, even the best venture investors have a portfolio, but investors who understand the power law make as few investments as possible. The kind of portfolio thinking embraced by both folk wisdom and financial convention, by contrast, regards diversified betting as a source of strength. The more you dabble, the more you are supposed to have hedged against the uncertainty of the future. But life is not a portfolio: not for a startup founder, and not for any individual. An entrepreneur cannot "diversify" herself: you cannot run dozens of companies at the same time and then hope that one of them works out well. Less obvious but just as important, an individual cannot diversify his own life by keeping dozens of equally possible careers in ready reserve. Our schools teach the opposite: institutionalized education traffics in a kind of homogenized, generic knowledge. Everybody who passes through the American school system learns not to think in power law terms. Every high school course period lasts 45 minutes whatever the subject. Every student proceeds at a similar pace. At college, model students obsessively hedge their futures by assembling a suite of exotic and minor skills. Every university believes in "excellence," and hundredpage course catalogs arranged alphabetically according to arbitrary departments of knowledge seem designed to reassure you that "it doesn't matter what you do, as long as you do it well." That is completely false. It does matter what you do. You should focus relentlessly on something you're good at doing, but before that you must think hard about whether it will be valuable in the future. For the startup world, this means you should not necessarily start your own company, even if you are extraordinarily talented. If anything, too many people are starting their own companies today. People who understand the power law will hesitate more than others when it comes to founding a new venture: they know how tremendously successful they could become by joining the very best company while it's growing fast. The power law means that differences between companies will dwarf the differences in roles inside companies. You could have 100% of the equity if you fully fund your own venture, but if it fails you'll have 100% of nothing. Owning just 0.01% of Google, by contrast, is incredibly valuable (more than $35 million as of this writing). If you do start your own company, you must remember the power law to operate it well. The most important things are singular: One market will probably be better than all others, as we discussed in Chapter 5. One distribution strategy usually dominates all others, too—for that see Chapter 11. Time and decision-making themselves follow a power law, and some moments matter far more than others —see Chapter 9. However, you can't trust a world that denies the power law to accurately frame your decisions for you, so what's most important is rarely obvious. It might even be secret. But in a power law world, you can't afford not to think hard about where your actions will fall on the curve. 8 SECRETS EVERY ONE OF TODAY 'S most famous and familiar ideas was once unknown and unsuspected. The mathematical relationship between a triangle's sides, for example, was secret for millennia. Pythagoras had to think hard to discover it. If you wanted in on Pythagoras's new discovery, joining his strange vegetarian cult was the best way to learn about it. Today, his geometry has become a convention—a simple truth we teach to grade schoolers. A conventional truth can be important—it's essential to learn elementary mathematics, for example—but it won't give you an edge. It's not a secret. Remember our contrarian question: what important truth do very few people agree with you on? If we already understand as much of the natural world as we ever will—if all of today's conventional ideas are already enlightened, and if everything has already been done—then there are no good answers. Contrarian thinking doesn't make any sense unless the world still has secrets left to give up. Of course, there are many things we don't yet understand, but some of those things may be impossible to figure out—mysteries rather than secrets. For example, string theory describes the physics of the universe in terms of vibrating one-dimensional objects called "strings." Is string theory true? You can't really design experiments to test it. Very few people, if any, could ever understand all its implications. But is that just because it's difficult? Or is it an impossible mystery? The difference matters. You can achieve difficult things, but you can't achieve the impossible. Recall the business version of our contrarian question: what valuable company is nobody building? Every correct answer is necessarily a secret: something important and unknown, something hard to do but doable. If there are many secrets left in the world, there are probably many worldchanging companies yet to be started. This chapter will help you think about secrets and how to find them. WHY AREN'T PEOPLE LOOKING FOR SECRETS? Most people act as if there were no secrets left to find. An extreme representative of this view is Ted Kaczynski, infamously known as the Unabomber. Kaczynski was a child prodigy who enrolled at Harvard at 16. He went on to get a PhD in math and become a professor at UC Berkeley. But you've only ever heard of him because of the 17-year terror campaign he waged with pipe bombs against professors, technologists, and businesspeople. In late 1995, the authorities didn't know who or where the Unabomber was. The biggest clue was a 35,000-word manifesto that Kaczynski had written and anonymously mailed to the press. The FBI asked some prominent newspapers to publish it, hoping for a break in the case. It worked: Kaczynski's brother recognized his writing style and turned him in. You might expect that writing style to have shown obvious signs of insanity, but the manifesto is eerily cogent. Kaczynski claimed that in order to be happy, every individual "needs to have goals whose attainment requires effort, and needs to succeed in attaining at least some of his goals." He divided human goals into three groups: 1. Goals that can be satisfied with minimal effort; 2. Goals that can be satisfied with serious effort; and 3. Goals that cannot be satisfied, no matter how much effort one makes. This is the classic trichotomy of the easy, the hard, and the impossible.

Kaczynski argued that modern people are depressed because all the world's hard problems have already been solved. What's left to do is either easy or impossible, and pursuing those tasks is deeply unsatisfying. What you can do, even a child can do; what you can't do, even Einstein couldn't have done. So Kaczynski's idea was to destroy existing institutions, get rid of all technology, and let people start over and work on hard problems anew. Kaczynski's methods were crazy, but his loss of faith in the technological frontier is all around us. Consider the trivial but revealing hallmarks of urban hipsterdom: faux vintage photography, the handlebar mustache, and vinyl record players all hark back to an earlier time when people were still optimistic about the future. If everything worth doing has already been done, you may as well feign an allergy to achievement and become a barista. Hipster or Unabomber? All fundamentalists think this way, not just terrorists and hipsters. Religious fundamentalism, for example, allows no middle ground for hard questions: there are easy truths that children are expected to rattle off, and then there are the mysteries of God, which can't be explained. In between—the zone of hard truths—lies heresy. In the modern religion of environmentalism, the easy truth is that we must protect the environment. Beyond that, Mother Nature knows best, and she cannot be questioned. Free marketeers worship a similar logic. The value of things is set by the market. Even a child can look up stock quotes. But whether those prices make sense is not to be second-guessed; the market knows far more than you ever could. Why has so much of our society come to believe that there are no hard secrets left? It might start with geography. There are no blank spaces left on the map anymore. If you grew up in the 18th century, there were still new places to go. After hearing tales of foreign adventure, you could become an explorer yourself. This was probably true up through the 19th and early 20th centuries; after that point photography from National Geographic showed every Westerner what even the most exotic, underexplored places on earth look like. Today, explorers are found mostly in history books and children's tales. Parents don't expect their kids to become explorers any more than they expect them to become pirates or sultans. Perhaps there are a few dozen uncontacted tribes somewhere deep in the Amazon, and we know there remains one last earthly frontier in the depths of the oceans. But the unknown seems less accessible than ever. Along with the natural fact that physical frontiers have receded, four social trends have conspired to root out belief in secrets. First is incrementalism. From an early age, we are taught that the right way to do things is to proceed one very small step at a time, day by day, grade by grade. If you overachieve and end up learning something that's not on the test, you won't receive credit for it. But in exchange for doing exactly what's asked of you (and for doing it just a bit better than your peers), you'll get an A. This process extends all the way up through the tenure track, which is why academics usually chase large numbers of trivial publications instead of new frontiers. Second is risk aversion. People are scared of secrets because they are scared of being wrong. By definition, a secret hasn't been vetted by the mainstream. If your goal is to never make a mistake in your life, you shouldn't look for secrets. The prospect of being lonely but right—dedicating your life to something that no one else believes in—is already hard. The prospect of being lonely and wrong can be unbearable. Third is complacency. Social elites have the most freedom and ability to explore new thinking, but they seem to believe in secrets the least. Why search for a new secret if you can comfortably collect rents on everything that has already been done? Every fall, the deans at top law schools and business schools welcome the incoming class with the same implicit message: "You got into this elite institution. Your worries are over. You're set for life." But that's probably the kind of thing that's true only if you don't believe it. Fourth is "flatness." As globalization advances, people perceive the world as one homogeneous, highly competitive marketplace: the world is "flat." Given that assumption, anyone who might have had the ambition to look for a secret will first ask himself: if it were possible to discover something new, wouldn't someone from the faceless global talent pool of smarter and more creative people have found it already? This voice of doubt can dissuade people from even starting to look for secrets in a world that seems too big a place for any individual to contribute something unique. There's an optimistic way to describe the result of these trends: today, you can't start a cult. Forty years ago, people were more open to the idea that not all knowledge was widely known. From the Communist Party to the Hare Krishnas, large numbers of people thought they could join some enlightened vanguard that would show them the Way. Very few people take unorthodox ideas seriously today, and the mainstream sees that as a sign of progress. We can be glad that there are fewer crazy cults now, yet that gain has come at great cost: we have given up our sense of wonder at secrets left to be discovered. THE WORLD ACCORDING TO CONVENTION How must you see the world if you don't believe in secrets? You'd have to believe we've already solved all great questions. If today's conventions are correct, we can afford to be smug and complacent: "God's in His heaven, All's right with the world." For example, a world without secrets would enjoy a perfect understanding of justice. Every injustice necessarily involves a moral truth that very few people recognize early on: in a democratic society, a wrongful practice persists only when most people don't perceive it to be unjust. At first, only a small minority of abolitionists knew that slavery was evil; that view has rightly become conventional, but it was still a secret in the early 19th century. To say that there are no secrets left today would mean that we live in a society with no hidden injustices. In economics, disbelief in secrets leads to faith in efficient markets. But the existence of financial bubbles shows that markets can have extraordinary inefficiencies. (And the more people believe in efficiency, the bigger the bubbles get.) In 1999, nobody wanted to believe that the internet was irrationally overvalued. The same was true of housing in 2005: Fed chairman Alan Greenspan had to acknowledge some "signs of froth in local markets" but stated that "a bubble in home prices for the nation as a whole does not appear likely." The market reflected all knowable information and couldn't be questioned. Then home prices fell across the country, and the financial crisis of 2008 wiped out trillions. The future turned out to hold many secrets that economists could not make vanish simply by ignoring them. What happens when a company stops believing in secrets? The sad decline of Hewlett-Packard provides a cautionary tale. In 1990, the company was worth $9 billion. Then came a decade of invention. In 1991, HP released the DeskJet 500C, the world's first affordable color printer. In 1993, it launched the OmniBook, one of the first "superportable" laptops. The next year, HP released the OfficeJet, the world's first all-in-one printer/fax/copier. This relentless product expansion paid off: by mid-2000, HP was worth $135 billion. But starting in late 1999, when HP introduced a new branding campaign around the imperative to "invent," it stopped inventing things. In 2001, the company launched HP Services, a glorified consulting and support shop. In 2002, HP merged with Compaq, presumably because it didn't know what else to do. By 2005, the company's market cap had plunged to $70 billion—roughly half of what it had been just five years earlier. HP's board was a microcosm of the dysfunction: it split into two factions, only one of which cared about new technology. That faction was led by Tom Perkins, an engineer who first came to HP in 1963 to run the company's research division at the personal request of Bill Hewlett and Dave Packard. At 73 years old in 2005, Perkins may as well have been a time-traveling visitor from a bygone age of optimism: he thought the board should identify the most promising new technologies and then have HP build them. But Perkins's faction lost out to its rival, led by chairwoman Patricia Dunn. A banker by trade, Dunn argued that charting a plan for future technology was beyond the board's competence. She thought the board should restrict itself to a night watchman's role: Was everything proper in the accounting department? Were people following all the rules? Amid this infighting, someone on the board started leaking information to the press. When it was exposed that Dunn arranged a series of illegal wiretaps to identify the source, the backlash was worse than the original dissension, and the board was disgraced. Having abandoned the search for technological secrets, HP obsessed over gossip. As a result, by late 2012 HP was worth just $23 billion—not much more than it was worth in 1990, adjusting for inflation. THE CASE FOR SECRETS You can't find secrets without looking for them. Andrew Wiles demonstrated this when he proved Fermat's Last Theorem after 358 years of fruitless inquiry by other mathematicians—the kind of sustained failure that might have suggested an inherently impossible task. Pierre de Fermat had conjectured in 1637 that no integers a, b, and c could satisfy the equation a n + b n = c n for any integer n greater than 2. He claimed to have a proof, but he died without writing it down, so his conjecture long remained a major unsolved problem in mathematics. Wiles started working on it in 1986, but he kept it a secret until 1993, when he knew he was nearing a solution. After nine years of hard work, Wiles proved the conjecture in 1995. He needed brilliance to succeed, but he also needed a faith in secrets. If you think something hard is impossible, you'll never even start trying to achieve it. Belief in secrets is an effective truth. The actual truth is that there are many more secrets left to find, but they will yield only to relentless searchers. There is more to do in science, medicine, engineering, and in technology of all kinds. We are within reach not just of marginal goals set at the competitive edge of today's conventional disciplines, but of ambitions so great that even the boldest minds of the Scientific Revolution hesitated to announce them directly. We could cure cancer, dementia, and all the diseases of age and metabolic decay. We can find new ways to generate energy that free the world from conflict over fossil fuels. We can invent faster ways to travel from place to place over the surface of the planet; we can even learn how to escape it entirely and settle new frontiers. But we will never learn any of these secrets unless we demand to know them and force ourselves to look. The same is true of business. Great companies can be built on open but unsuspected secrets about how the world works. Consider the Silicon Valley startups that have harnessed the spare capacity that is all around us but often ignored. Before Airbnb, travelers had little choice but to pay high prices for a hotel room, and property owners couldn't easily and reliably rent out their unoccupied space. Airbnb saw untapped supply and unaddressed demand where others saw nothing at all. The same is true of private car services Lyft and Uber. Few people imagined that it was possible to build a billion-dollar business by simply connecting people who want to go places with people willing to drive them there. We already had state-licensed taxicabs and private limousines; only by believing in and looking for secrets could you see beyond the convention to an opportunity hidden in plain sight. The same reason that so many internet companies, including Facebook, are often underestimated— their very simplicity—is itself an argument for secrets. If insights that look so elementary in retrospect can support important and valuable businesses, there must remain many great companies still to start. HOW TO FIND SECRETS There are two kinds of secrets: secrets of nature and secrets about people. Natural secrets exist all around us; to find them, one must study some undiscovered aspect of the physical world. Secrets about people are different: they are things that people don't know about themselves or things they hide because they don't want others to know. So when thinking about what kind of company to build, there are two distinct questions to ask: What secrets is nature not telling you? What secrets are people not telling you? It's easy to assume that natural secrets are the most important: the people who look for them can sound intimidatingly authoritative. This is why physics PhDs are notoriously difficult to work with— because they know the most fundamental truths, they think they know all truths. But does understanding electromagnetic theory automatically make you a great marriage counselor? Does a gravity theorist know more about your business than you do? At PayPal, I once interviewed a physics PhD for an engineering job. Halfway through my first question, he shouted, "Stop! I already know what you're going to ask!" But he was wrong. It was the easiest no-hire decision I've ever made. Secrets about people are relatively underappreciated. Maybe that's because you don't need a dozen years of higher education to ask the questions that uncover them: What are people not allowed to talk about? What is forbidden or taboo? Sometimes looking for natural secrets and looking for human secrets lead to the same truth. Consider the monopoly secret again: competition and capitalism are opposites. If you didn't already know it, you could discover it the natural, empirical way: do a quantitative study of corporate profits and you'll see they're eliminated by competition. But you could also take the human approach and ask: what are people running companies not allowed to say? You would notice that monopolists downplay their monopoly status to avoid scrutiny, while competitive firms strategically exaggerate their uniqueness. The differences between firms only seem small on the surface; in fact, they are enormous. The best place to look for secrets is where no one else is looking. Most people think only in terms of what they've been taught; schooling itself aims to impart conventional wisdom. So you might ask: are there any fields that matter but haven't been standardized and institutionalized? Physics, for example, is a real major at all major universities, and it's set in its ways. The opposite of physics might be astrology, but astrology doesn't matter. What about something like nutrition? Nutrition matters for everybody, but you can't major in it at Harvard. Most top scientists go into other fields. Most of the big studies were done 30 or 40 years ago, and most are seriously flawed. The food pyramid that told us to eat low fat and enormous amounts of grains was probably more a product of lobbying by Big Food than real science; its chief impact has been to aggravate our obesity epidemic. There's plenty more to learn: we know more about the physics of faraway stars than we know about human nutrition. It won't be easy, but it's not obviously impossible: exactly the kind of field that could yield secrets. WHAT TO DO WITH SECRETS If you find a secret, you face a choice: Do you tell anyone? Or do you keep it to yourself? It depends on the secret: some are more dangerous than others. As Faust tells Wagner: The few who knew what might be learned, Foolish enough to put their whole heart on show, And reveal their feelings to the crowd below, Mankind has always crucified and burned. Unless you have perfectly conventional beliefs, it's rarely a good idea to tell everybody everything that you know. So who do you tell? Whoever you need to, and no more. In practice, there's always a golden mean between telling nobody and telling everybody—and that's a company. The best entrepreneurs know this: every great business is built around a secret that's hidden from the outside. A great company is a conspiracy to change the world; when you share your secret, the recipient becomes a fellow conspirator. As Tolkien wrote in The Lord of the Rings: The Road goes ever on and on Down from the door where it began. Life is a long journey; the road marked out by the steps of previous travelers has no end in sight. But later on in the tale, another verse appears: Still round the corner there may wait A new road or a secret gate, And though we pass them by today, Tomorrow we may come this way And take the hidden paths that run Towards the Moon or to the Sun. The road doesn't have to be infinite after all. Take the hidden paths. 9 FOUNDATIONS EVERY GREAT COMPANY is unique, but there are a few things that every business must get right at the beginning. I stress this so often that friends have teasingly nicknamed it "Thiel's law": a startup messed up at its foundation cannot be fixed. Beginnings are special. They are qualitatively different from all that comes afterward. This was true 13.8 billion years ago, at the founding of our cosmos: in the earliest microseconds of its existence, the universe expanded by a factor of 10 30—a million trillion trillion. As cosmogonic epochs came and went in those first few moments, the very laws of physics were different from those we know today. It was also true 227 years ago at the founding of our country: fundamental questions were open for debate by the Framers during the few months they spent together at the Constitutional Convention. How much power should the central government have? How should representation in Congress be apportioned? Whatever your views on the compromises reached that summer in Philadelphia, they've been hard to change ever since: after ratifying the Bill of Rights in 1791, we've amended the Constitution only 17 times. Today, California has the same representation in the Senate as Alaska, even though it has more than 50 times as many people. Maybe that's a feature, not a bug. But we're probably stuck with it as long as the United States exists. Another constitutional convention is unlikely; today we debate only smaller questions. Companies are like countries in this way. Bad decisions made early on—if you choose the wrong partners or hire the wrong people, for example—are very hard to correct after they are made. It may take a crisis on the order of bankruptcy before anybody will even try to correct them. As a founder, your first job is to get the first things right, because you cannot build a great company on a flawed foundation. FOUNDING MATRIMONY When you start something, the first and most crucial decision you make is whom to start it with. Choosing a co-founder is like getting married, and founder conflict is just as ugly as divorce. Optimism abounds at the start of every relationship. It's unromantic to think soberly about what could go wrong, so people don't. But if the founders develop irreconcilable differences, the company becomes the victim. In 1999, Luke Nosek was one of my co-founders at PayPal, and I still work with him today at Founders Fund. But a year before

PayPal, I invested in a company Luke started with someone else. It was his first startup; it was one of my first investments. Neither of us realized it then, but the venture was doomed to fail from the beginning because Luke and his co-founder were a terrible match. Luke is a brilliant and eccentric thinker; his co-founder was an MBA type who didn't want to miss out on the '90s gold rush. They met at a networking event, talked for a while, and decided to start a company together. That's no better than marrying the first person you meet at the slot machines in Vegas: you might hit the jackpot, but it probably won't work. Their company blew up and I lost my money. Now when I consider investing in a startup, I study the founding teams. Technical abilities and complementary skill sets matter, but how well the founders know each other and how well they work together matter just as much. Founders should share a prehistory before they start a company together —otherwise they're just rolling dice. OWNERSHIP, POSSESSION, AND CONTROL It's not just founders who need to get along. Everyone in your company needs to work well together. A Silicon Valley libertarian might say you could solve this problem by restricting yourself to a sole proprietorship. Freud, Jung, and every other psychologist has a theory about how every individual mind is divided against itself, but in business at least, working for yourself guarantees alignment. Unfortunately, it also limits what kind of company you can build. It's very hard to go from 0 to 1 without a team. A Silicon Valley anarchist might say you could achieve perfect alignment as long as you hire just the right people, who will flourish peacefully without any guiding structure. Serendipity and even free-form chaos at the workplace are supposed to help "disrupt" all the old rules made and obeyed by the rest of the world. And indeed, "if men were angels, no government would be necessary." But anarchic companies miss what James Madison saw: men aren't angels. That's why executives who manage companies and directors who govern them have separate roles to play; it's also why founders' and investors' claims on a company are formally defined. You need good people who get along, but you also need a structure to help keep everyone aligned for the long term. To anticipate likely sources of misalignment in any company, it's useful to distinguish between three concepts: • Ownership: who legally owns a company's equity? • Possession: who actually runs the company on a day-to-day basis? • Control: who formally governs the company's affairs? A typical startup allocates ownership among founders, employees, and investors. The managers and employees who operate the company enjoy possession. And a board of directors, usually comprising founders and investors, exercises control. In theory, this division works smoothly. Financial upside from part ownership attracts and rewards investors and workers. Effective possession motivates and empowers founders and employees—it means they can get stuff done. Oversight from the board places managers' plans in a broader perspective. In practice, distributing these functions among different people makes sense, but it also multiplies opportunities for misalignment. To see misalignment at its most extreme, just visit the DMV. Suppose you need a new driver's license. Theoretically, it should be easy to get one. The DMV is a government agency, and we live in a democratic republic. All power resides in "the people," who elect representatives to serve them in government. If you're a citizen, you're a part owner of the DMV and your representatives control it, so you should be able to walk in and get what you need. Of course, it doesn't work like that. We the people may "own" the DMV's resources, but that ownership is merely fictional. The clerks and petty tyrants who operate the DMV, however, enjoy very real possession of their small-time powers. Even the governor and the legislature charged with nominal control over the DMV can't change anything. The bureaucracy lurches ever sideways of its own inertia no matter what actions elected officials take. Accountable to nobody, the DMV is misaligned with everybody. Bureaucrats can make your licensing experience pleasurable or nightmarish at their sole discretion. You can try to bring up political theory and remind them that you are the boss, but that's unlikely to get you better service. Big corporations do better than the DMV, but they're still prone to misalignment, especially between ownership and possession. The CEO of a huge company like General Motors, for example, will own some of the company's stock, but only a trivial portion of the total. Therefore he's incentivized to reward himself through the power of possession rather than the value of ownership. Posting good quarterly results will be enough for him to keep his high salary and corporate jet. Misalignment can creep in even if he receives stock compensation in the name of "shareholder value." If that stock comes as a reward for short-term performance, he will find it more lucrative and much easier to cut costs instead of investing in a plan that might create more value for all shareholders far in the future. Unlike corporate giants, early-stage startups are small enough that founders usually have both ownership and possession. Most conflicts in a startup erupt between ownership and control—that is, between founders and investors on the board. The potential for conflict increases over time as interests diverge: a board member might want to take a company public as soon as possible to score a win for his venture firm, while the founders would prefer to stay private and grow the business. In the boardroom, less is more. The smaller the board, the easier it is for the directors to communicate, to reach consensus, and to exercise effective oversight. However, that very effectiveness means that a small board can forcefully oppose management in any conflict. This is why it's crucial to choose wisely: every single member of your board matters. Even one problem director will cause you pain, and may even jeopardize your company's future. A board of three is ideal. Your board should never exceed five people, unless your company is publicly held. (Government regulations effectively mandate that public companies have larger boards —the average is ninc members.) By far the worst you can do is to make your board extra large. When unsavvy observers see a nonprofit organization with dozens of people on its board, they think: "Look how many great people are committed to this organization! It must be extremely well run." Actually, a huge board will exercise no effective oversight at all; it merely provides cover for whatever microdictator actually runs the organization. If you want that kind of free rein from your board, blow it up to giant size. If you want an effective board, keep it small. ON THE BUS OR OFF THE BUS As a general rule, everyone you involve with your company should be involved full-time. Sometimes you'll have to break this rule; it usually makes sense to hire outside lawyers and accountants, for example. However, anyone who doesn't own stock options or draw a regular salary from your company is fundamentally misaligned. At the margin, they'll be biased to claim value in the near term, not help you create more in the future. That's why hiring consultants doesn't work. Part-time employees don't work. Even working remotely should be avoided, because misalignment can creep in whenever colleagues aren't together full-time, in the same place, every day. If you're deciding whether to bring someone on board, the decision is binary. Ken Kesey was right: you're either on the bus or off the bus. CASH IS NOT KING For people to be fully committed, they should be properly compensated. Whenever an entrepreneur asks me to invest in his company, I ask him how much he intends to pay himself. A company does better the less it pays the CEO—that's one of the single clearest patterns I've noticed from investing in hundreds of startups. In no case should a CEO of an early-stage, venture-backed startup receive more than $150,000 per year in salary. It doesn't matter if he got used to making much more than that at Google or if he has a large mortgage and hefty private school tuition bills. If a CEO collects $300,000 per year, he risks becoming more like a politician than a founder. High pay incentivizes him to defend the status quo along with his salary, not to work with everyone else to surface problems and fix them aggressively. A cash-poor executive, by contrast, will focus on increasing the value of the company as a whole. Low CEO pay also sets the standard for everyone else. Aaron Levie, the CEO of Box, was always careful to pay himself less than everyone else in the company—four years after he started Box, he was still living two blocks away from HQ in a one-bedroom apartment with no furniture except a mattress. Every employee noticed his obvious commitment to the company's mission and emulated it. If a CEO doesn't set an example by taking the lowest salary in the company, he can do the same thing by drawing the highest salary. So long as that figure is still modest, it sets an effective ceiling on cash compensation. Cash is attractive. It offers pure optionality: once you get your paycheck, you can do anything you want with it. However, high cash compensation teaches workers to claim value from the company as it already exists instead of investing their time to create new value in the future. A cash bonus is slightly better than a cash salary—at least it's contingent on a job well done. But even so-called incentive pay encourages short-term thinking and value grabbing. Any kind of cash is more about the present than the future. VESTED INTERESTS Startups don't need to pay high salaries because they can offer something better: part ownership of the company itself. Equity is the one form of compensation that can effectively orient people toward creating value in the future. However, for equity to create commitment rather than conflict, you must allocate it very carefully. Giving everyone equal shares is usually a mistake: every individual has different talents and responsibilities as well as different opportunity costs, so equal amounts will seem arbitrary and unfair from the start. On the other hand, granting different amounts up front is just as sure to seem unfair. Resentment at this stage can kill a company, but there's no ownership formula to perfectly avoid it. This problem becomes even more acute over time as more people join the company. Early employees usually get the most equity because they take more risk, but some later employees might be even more crucial to a venture's success. A secretary who joined eBay in 1996 might have made 200 times more than her industry-veteran boss who joined in 1999. The graffiti artist who painted Facebook's office walls in 2005 got stock that turned out to be worth $200 million, while a talented engineer who joined in 2010 might have made only $2 million. Since it's impossible to achieve perfect fairness when distributing ownership, founders would do well to keep the details secret. Sending out a company-wide email that lists everyone's ownership stake would be like dropping a nuclear bomb on your office. Most people don't want equity at all. At PayPal, we once hired a consultant who promised to help us negotiate lucrative business development deals. The only thing he ever successfully negotiated was a $5,000 daily cash salary; he refused to accept stock options as payment. Stories of startup chefs becoming millionaires notwithstanding, people often find equity unattractive. It's not liquid like cash. It's tied to one specific company. And if that company doesn't succeed, it's worthless. Equity is a powerful tool precisely because of these limitations. Anyone who prefers owning a part of your company to being paid in cash reveals a preference for the long term and a commitment to increasing your company's value in the future. Equity can't create perfect incentives, but it's the best way for a founder to keep everyone in the company broadly aligned. EXTENDING THE FOUNDING Bob Dylan has said that he who is not busy being born is busy dying. If he's right, being born doesn't happen at just one moment—you might even continue to do it somehow, poetically at least. The founding moment of a company, however, really does happen just once: only at the very start do you have the opportunity to set the rules that will align people toward the creation of value in the future. The most valuable kind of company maintains an openness to invention that is most characteristic of beginnings. This leads to a second, less obvious understanding of the founding: it lasts as long as a company is creating new things, and it ends when creation stops. If you get the founding moment right, you can do more than create a valuable company: you can steer its distant future toward the creation of new things instead of the stewardship of inherited success. You might even extend its founding indefinitely. 10 THE MECHANICS OF MAFIA START WITH A THOUGHT EXPERIMENT: what would the ideal company culture look like? Employees should love their work. They should enjoy going to the office so much that formal business hours become obsolete and nobody watches the clock. The workspace should be open, not cubicled, and workers should feel at home: beanbag chairs and Ping-Pong tables might outnumber file cabinets. Free massages, on-site sushi chefs, and maybe even yoga classes would sweeten the scene. Pets should be welcome, too: perhaps employees' dogs and cats could come and join the office's tankful of tropical fish as unofficial company mascots. What's wrong with this picture? It includes some of the absurd perks Silicon Valley has made famous, but none of the substance—and without substance perks don't work. You can't accomplish anything meaningful by hiring an interior decorator to beautify your office, a "human resources" consultant to fix your policies, or a branding specialist to hone your buzzwords. "Company culture" doesn't exist apart from the company itself: no company has a culture; every company is a culture. A startup is a team of people on a mission, and a good culture is just what that looks like on the inside. BEYOND PROFESSIONALISM The first team that I built has become known in Silicon Valley as the "PayPal Mafia" because so many of my former colleagues have gone on to help each other start and invest in successful tech companies. We sold PayPal to eBay for $1.5 billion in 2002. Since then, Elon Musk has founded SpaceX and co-founded Tesla Motors; Reid Hoffman co-founded LinkedIn; Steve Chen, Chad Hurley, and Jawed Karim together founded YouTube; Jeremy Stoppelman and Russel Simmons founded Yelp; David Sacks co-founded Yammer; and I co-founded Palantir. Today all seven of those companies are worth more than $1 billion each. PayPal's office amenities never got much press, but the team has done extraordinarily well, both together and individually: the culture was strong enough to transcend the original company. We didn't assemble a mafia by sorting through résumés and simply hiring the most talented people. I had seen the mixed results of that approach firsthand when I worked at a New York law firm. The lawyers I worked with ran a valuable business, and they were impressive individuals one by one. But the relationships between them were oddly thin. They spent all day together, but few of them seemed to have much to say to each other outside the office. Why work with a group of people who don't even like each other? Many seem to think it's a sacrifice necessary for making money. But taking a merely professional view of the workplace, in which free agents check in and out on a transactional basis, is worse than cold: it's not even rational. Since time is your most valuable asset, it's odd to spend it working with people who don't envision any long-term future together. If you can't count durable relationships among the fruits of your time at work, you haven't invested your time well— even in purely financial terms. From the start, I wanted PayPal to be tightly knit instead of transactional. I thought stronger relationships would make us not just happier and better at work but also more successful in our careers even beyond PayPal. So we set out to hire people who would actually enjoy working together. They had to be talented, but even more than that they had to be excited about working specifically with us. That was the start of the PayPal Mafia. RECRUITING CONSPIRATORS Recruiting is a core competency for any company. It should never be outsourced. You need people who are not just skilled on paper but who will work together cohesively after they're hired. The first four or five might be attracted by large equity stakes or high-profile responsibilities. More important than those obvious offerings is your answer to this question: Why should the 20th employee join your company? Talented people don't need to work for you; they have plenty of options. You should ask yourself a more pointed version of the question: Why would someone join your company as its 20th engineer when she could go work at Google for more money and more prestige? Here are some bad answers: "Your stock options will be worth more here than elsewhere." "You'll get to work with the smartest people in the world." "You can help solve the world's most challenging problems." What's wrong with valuable stock, smart people, or pressing problems? Nothing—but every company makes these same claims, so they won't help you stand out. General and undifferentiated pitches don't say anything about why a recruit should join your company instead of many others. The only good answers are specific to your company, so you won't find them in this book. But there are two general kinds of good answers: answers about your mission and answers about your team. You'll attract the employees you need if you can explain why your mission is compelling: not why it's important in general, but why you're doing something important that no one else is going to get done. That's the only thing that can make its importance unique. At PayPal, if you were excited by the idea of creating a new digital currency to replace the U.S. dollar, we wanted to talk to you; if not, you weren't the right fit. However, even a great mission is not enough. The kind of recruit who would be most engaged as an employee will also wonder: "Are these the kind of people I want to work with?" You should be able to explain why your company is a unique match for him personally. And if you can't do that, he's probably not the right match. Above all, don't fight the perk war. Anybody who would be more powerfully swayed by free laundry pickup or pet day care would be a bad addition to your team. Just cover the basics like health insurance and then promise what no others can: the opportunity to do irreplaceable work on a unique problem alongside great people. You probably can't be the Google of 2014 in terms of compensation or perks, but you can be like the Google of 1999 if you already have good answers about your mission and team.

AS MATURE INDUSTRIES stagnate, information technology has advanced so rapidly that it has now become synonymous with "technology" itself. Today, more than 1.5 billion people enjoy instant access to the world's knowledge using pocket-sized devices. Every one of today's smartphones has thousands of times more processing power than the computers that guided astronauts to the moon. And if Moore's law continues apace, tomorrow's computers will be even more powerful. Computers already have enough power to outperform people in activities we used to think of as distinctively human. In 1997, IBM's Deep Blue defeated world chess champion Garry Kasparov. Jeopardy!'s best-ever contestant, Ken Jennings, succumbed to IBM's Watson in 2011. And Google's self-driving cars are already on California roads today. Dale Earnhardt Jr. needn't feel threatened by them, but the Guardian worries (on behalf of the millions of chauffeurs and cabbies in the world) that self-driving cars "could drive the next wave of unemployment." Everyone expects computers to do more in the future—so much more that some wonder: 30 years from now, will there be anything left for people to do? "Software is eating the world," venture capitalist Marc Andreessen has announced with a tone of inevitability. VC Andy Kessler sounds almost gleeful when he explains that the best way to create productivity is "to get rid of people." Forbes captured a more anxious attitude when it asked readers: Will a machine replace you? Futurists can seem like they hope the answer is yes. Luddites are so worried about being replaced that they would rather we stop building new technology altogether. Neither side questions the premise that better computers will necessarily replace human workers. But that premise is wrong: computers are complements for humans, not substitutes. The most valuable businesses of coming decades will be built by entrepreneurs who seek to empower people rather than try to make them obsolete. SUBSTITUTION VS. COMPLEMENTARITY Fifteen years ago, American workers were worried about competition from cheaper Mexican substitutes. And that made sense, because humans really can substitute for each other. Today people think they can hear Ross Perot's "giant sucking sound" once more, but they trace it back to server farms somewhere in Texas instead of cut-rate factories in Tijuana. Americans fear technology in the near future because they see it as a replay of the globalization of the near past. But the situations are very different: people compete for jobs and for resources; computers compete for neither. Globalization Means Substitution When Perot warned about foreign competition, both George H. W. Bush and Bill Clinton preached the gospel of free trade: since every person has a relative strength at some particular job, in theory the economy maximizes wealth when people specialize according to their advantages and then trade with each other. In practice, it's not unambiguously clear how well free trade has worked, for many workers at least. Gains from trade are greatest when there's a big discrepancy in comparative advantage, but the global supply of workers willing to do repetitive tasks for an extremely small wage is extremely large. People don't just compete to supply labor; they also demand the same resources. While American consumers have benefited from access to cheap toys and textiles from China, they've had to pay higher prices for the gasoline newly desired by millions of Chinese motorists. Whether people eat shark fins in Shanghai or fish tacos in San Diego, they all need food and they all need shelter. And desire doesn't stop at subsistence—people will demand ever more as globalization continues. Now that millions of Chinese peasants can finally enjoy a secure supply of basic calories, they want more of them to come from pork instead of just grain. The convergence of desire is even more obvious at the top: all oligarchs have the same taste in Cristal, from Petersburg to Pyongyang. Technology Means Complementarity Now think about the prospect of competition from computers instead of competition from human workers. On the supply side, computers are far more different from people than any two people are different from each other: men and machines are good at fundamentally different things. People have intentionality—we form plans and make decisions in complicated situations. We're less good at making sense of enormous amounts of data. Computers are exactly the opposite: they excel at efficient data processing, but they struggle to make basic judgments that would be simple for any human. To understand the scale of this variance, consider another of Google's computer-for-human substitution projects. In 2012, one of their supercomputers made headlines when, after scanning 10 million thumbnails of YouTube videos, it learned to identify a cat with 75% accuracy. That seems impressive—until you remember that an average four-year-old can do it flawlessly. When a cheap laptop beats the smartest mathematicians at some tasks but even a supercomputer with 16,000 CPUs can't beat a child at others, you can tell that humans and computers are not just more or less powerful than each other—they're categorically different. The stark differences between man and machine mean that gains from working with computers are much higher than gains from trade with other people. We don't trade with computers any more than we trade with livestock or lamps. And that's the point: computers are tools, not rivals. The differences are even deeper on the demand side. Unlike people in industrializing countries, computers don't yearn for more luxurious foods or beachfront villas in Cap Ferrat; all they require is a nominal amount of electricity, which they're not even smart enough to want. When we design new computer technology to help solve problems, we get all the efficiency gains of a hyperspecialized trading partner without having to compete with it for resources. Properly understood, technology is the one way for us to escape competition in a globalizing world. As computers become more and more powerful, they won't be substitutes for humans: they'll be complements. COMPLEMENTARY BUSINESSES Complementarity between computers and humans isn't just a macro-scale fact. It's also the path to building a great business. I came to understand this from my experience at PayPal. In mid-2000, we had survived the dot-com crash and we were growing fast, but we faced one huge problem: we were losing upwards of $10 million to credit card fraud every month. Since we were processing hundreds or even thousands of transactions per minute, we couldn't possibly review each one—no human quality control team could work that fast. So we did what any group of engineers would do: we tried to automate a solution. First, Max Levchin assembled an elite team of mathematicians to study the fraudulent transfers in detail. Then we took what we learned and wrote software to automatically identify and cancel bogus transactions in real time. But it quickly became clear that this approach wouldn't work either: after an hour or two, the thieves would catch on and change their tactics. We were dealing with an adaptive enemy, and our software couldn't adapt in response. The fraudsters' adaptive evasions fooled our automatic detection algorithms, but we found that they didn't fool our human analysts as easily. So Max and his engineers rewrote the software to take a hybrid approach: the computer would flag the most suspicious transactions on a well-designed user interface, and human operators would make the final judgment as to their legitimacy. Thanks to this hybrid system—we named it "Igor," after the Russian fraudster who bragged that we'd never be able to stop him—we turned our first quarterly profit in the first quarter of 2002 (as opposed to a quarterly loss of $29.3 million one year before). The FBI asked us if we'd let them use Igor to help detect financial crime. And Max was able to boast, grandiosely but truthfully, that he was "the Sherlock Holmes of the Internet Underground." This kind of man-machine symbiosis enabled PayPal to stay in business, which in turn enabled hundreds of thousands of small businesses to accept the payments they needed to thrive on the internet. None of it would have been possible without the man-machine solution—even though most people would never see it or even hear about it. I continued to think about this after we sold PayPal in 2002: if humans and computers together could achieve dramatically better results than either could attain alone, what other valuable businesses could be built on this core principle? The next year, I pitched Alex Karp, an old Stanford classmate, and Stephen Cohen, a software engineer, on a new startup idea: we would use the humancomputer hybrid approach from PayPal's security system to identify terrorist networks and financial fraud. We already knew the FBI was interested, and in 2004 we founded Palantir, a software company that helps people extract insight from divergent sources of information. The company is on track to book sales of $1 billion in 2014, and Forbes has called Palantir's software the "killer app" for its rumored role in helping the government locate Osama bin Laden. We have no details to share from that operation, but we can say that neither human intelligence by itself nor computers alone will be able to make us safe. America's two biggest spy agencies take opposite approaches: The Central Intelligence Agency is run by spies who privilege humans. The National Security Agency is run by generals who prioritize computers. CIA analysts have to wade through so much noise that it's very difficult to identify the most serious threats. NSA computers can process huge quantities of data, but machines alone cannot authoritatively determine whether someone is plotting a terrorist act. Palantir aims to transcend these opposing biases: its software analyzes the data the government feeds it—phone records of radical clerics in Yemen or bank accounts linked to terror cell activity, for instance—and flags suspicious activities for a trained analyst to review. In addition to helping find terrorists, analysts using Palantir's software have been able to predict where insurgents plant IEDs in Afghanistan; prosecute high-profile insider trading cases; take down the largest child pornography ring in the world; support the Centers for Disease Control and Prevention in fighting foodborne disease outbreaks; and save both commercial banks and the government hundreds of millions of dollars annually through advanced fraud detection. Advanced software made this possible, but even more important were the human analysts, prosecutors, scientists, and financial professionals without whose active engagement the software would have been useless. Think of what professionals do in their jobs today. Lawyers must be able to articulate solutions to thorny problems in several different ways—the pitch changes depending on whether you're talking to a client, opposing counsel, or a judge. Doctors need to marry clinical understanding with an ability to communicate it to non-expert patients. And good teachers aren't just experts in their disciplines: they must also understand how to tailor their instruction to different individuals' interests and learning styles. Computers might be able to do some of these tasks, but they can't combine them effectively. Better technology in law, medicine, and education won't replace professionals; it will allow them to do even more. LinkedIn has done exactly this for recruiters. When LinkedIn was founded in 2003, they didn't poll recruiters to find discrete pain points in need of relief. And they didn't try to write software that would replace recruiters outright. Recruiting is part detective work and part sales: you have to scrutinize applicants' history, assess their motives and compatibility, and persuade the most promising ones to join you. Effectively replacing all those functions with a computer would be impossible. Instead, LinkedIn set out to transform how recruiters did their jobs. Today, more than 97% of recruiters use LinkedIn and its powerful search and filtering functionality to source job candidates, and the network also creates value for the hundreds of millions of professionals who use it to manage their personal brands. If LinkedIn had tried to simply replace recruiters with technology, they wouldn't have a business today. The Ideology of Computer Science Why do so many people miss the power of complementarity? It starts in school. Software engineers tend to work on projects that replace human efforts because that's what they're trained to do. Academics make their reputations through specialized research; their primary goal is to publish papers, and publication means respecting the limits of a particular discipline. For computer scientists, that means reducing human capabilities into specialized tasks that computers can be trained to conquer one by one. Just look at the trendiest fields in computer science today. The very term "machine learning" evokes imagery of replacement, and its boosters seem to believe that computers can be taught to perform almost any task, so long as we feed them enough training data. Any user of Netflix or Amazon has experienced the results of machine learning firsthand: both companies use algorithms to recommend products based on your viewing and purchase history. Feed them more data and the recommendations get ever better. Google Translate works the same way, providing rough but serviceable translations into any of the 80 languages it supports—not because the software understands human language, but because it has extracted patterns through statistical analysis of a huge corpus of text. The other buzzword that epitomizes a bias toward substitution is "big data." Today's companies have an insatiable appetite for data, mistakenly believing that more data always creates more value. But big data is usually dumb data. Computers can find patterns that elude humans, but they don't know how to compare patterns from different sources or how to interpret complex behaviors. Actionable insights can only come from a human analyst (or the kind of generalized artificial intelligence that exists only in science fiction). We have let ourselves become enchanted by big data only because we exoticize technology. We're impressed with small feats accomplished by computers alone, but we ignore big achievements from complementarity because the human contribution makes them less uncanny. Watson, Deep Blue, and ever-better machine learning algorithms are cool. But the most valuable companies in the future won't ask what problems can be solved with computers alone. Instead, they'll ask: how can computers help humans solve hard problems? EVER-SMARTER COMPUTERS: FRIEND OR FOE? The future of computing is necessarily full of unknowns. It's become conventional to see ever-smarter anthropomorphized robot intelligences like Siri and Watson as harbingers of things to come; once computers can answer all our questions, perhaps they'll ask why they should remain subservient to us at all. The logical endpoint to this substitutionist thinking is called "strong AI": computers that eclipse humans on every important dimension. Of course, the Luddites are terrified by the possibility. It even makes the futurists a little uneasy; it's not clear whether strong AI would save humanity or doom it. Technology is supposed to increase our mastery over nature and reduce the role of chance in our lives; building smarter-than-human computers could actually bring chance back with a vengeance. Strong AI is like a cosmic lottery ticket: if we win, we get utopia; if we lose, Skynet substitutes us out of existence. But even if strong AI is a real possibility rather than an imponderable mystery, it won't happen anytime soon: replacement by computers is a worry for the 22nd century. Indefinite fears about the far future shouldn't stop us from making definite plans today. Luddites claim that we shouldn't build the computers that might replace people someday; crazed futurists argue that we should. These two positions are mutually exclusive but they are not exhaustive: there is room in between for sane people to build a vastly better world in the decades ahead. As we find new ways to use computers, they won't just get better at the kinds of things people already do; they'll help us to do what was previously unimaginable.

THE FOUNDER'S PARADOX OF THE SIX PEOPLE who started PayPal, four had built bombs in high school. Five were just 23 years old—or younger. Four of us had been born outside the United States. Three had escaped here from communist countries: Yu Pan from China, Luke Nosek from Poland, and Max Levchin from Soviet Ukraine. Building bombs was not what kids normally did in those countries at that time. The six of us could have been seen as eccentric. My first-ever conversation with Luke was about how he'd just signed up for cryonics, to be frozen upon death in hope of medical resurrection. Max claimed to be without a country and proud of it: his family was put into diplomatic limbo when the USSR collapsed while they were escaping to the U.S. Russ Simmons had escaped from a trailer park to the top math and science magnet school in Illinois. Only Ken Howery fit the stereotype of a privileged American childhood: he was PayPal's sole Eagle Scout. But Kenny's peers thought he was crazy to join the rest of us and make just one-third of the salary he had been offered by a big bank. So even he wasn't entirely normal. The PayPal Team in 1999 Are all founders unusual people? Or do we just tend to remember and exaggerate whatever is most unusual about them? More important, which personal traits actually matter in a founder? This chapter is about why it's more powerful but at the same time more dangerous for a company to be led by a distinctive individual instead of an interchangeable manager. THE DIFFERENCE ENGINE Some people are strong, some are weak, some are geniuses, some are dullards—but most people are in the middle. Plot where everyone falls and you'll see a bell curve: Since so many founders seem to have extreme traits, you might guess that a plot showing only founders' traits would have fatter tails with more people at either end. But that doesn't capture the strangest thing about founders. Normally we expect opposite traits to be mutually exclusive: a normal person can't be both rich and poor at the same time, for instance. But it happens all the time to founders: startup CEOs can be cash poor but millionaires on paper. They may oscillate between sullen jerkiness and appealing charisma. Almost all successful entrepreneurs are simultaneously insiders and outsiders. And when they do succeed, they attract both fame and infamy. When you plot them out, founders' traits appear to follow an inverse normal distribution: Where does this strange and extreme combination of traits come from? They could be present from birth (nature) or acquired from an individual's environment (nurture). But perhaps founders aren't really as extreme as they appear. Might they strategically exaggerate certain qualities? Or is it possible that everyone else exaggerates them? All of these effects can be present at the same time, and whenever present they powerfully reinforce each other. The cycle usually starts with unusual people and ends with them acting and seeming even more unusual: As an example, take Sir Richard Branson, the billionaire founder of the Virgin Group. He could be described as a natural entrepreneur: Branson started his first business at age 16, and at just 22 he founded Virgin Records. But other aspects of his renown—the trademark lion's mane hairstyle, for example—are less natural: one suspects he wasn't born with that exact look. As Branson has cultivated his other extreme traits (Is kiteboarding with naked supermodels a PR stunt? Just a guy having fun? Both?), the media has eagerly enthroned him: Branson is "The Virgin King," "The Undisputed King of PR," "The King of Branding," and "The King of the Desert and Space." When Virgin Atlantic Airways began serving passengers drinks with ice cubes shaped like Branson's face, he became "The Ice King." Is Branson just a normal businessman who happens to be lionized by the media with the help of a good PR team? Or is he himself a born branding genius rightly singled out by the journalists he is so good at manipulating? It's hard to tell—maybe he's both. Another example is Sean Parker, who started out with the ultimate outsider status: criminal. Sean was a careful hacker in high school. But his father decided that Sean was spending too much time on the computer for a 16-year-old, so one day he took away Sean's keyboard mid-hack. Sean couldn't log out; the FBI noticed; soon federal agents were placing him under arrest. Sean got off easy since he was a minor; if anything, the episode emboldened him. Three years later, he co-founded Napster. The peer-to-peer file sharing service amassed 10 million users in its first year, making it one of the fastest-growing businesses of all time. But the record companies sued and a federal judge ordered it shut down 20 months after opening. After a whirlwind period at the center, Sean was back to being an outsider again. Then came Facebook. Sean met Mark Zuckerberg in 2004, helped negotiate Facebook's first funding, and became the company's founding president. He had to step down in 2005 amid allegations of drug use, but this only enhanced his notoriety. Ever since Justin Timberlake portrayed him in The Social Network, Sean has been perceived as one of the coolest people in America. JT is still more famous, but when he visits Silicon Valley, people ask if he's Sean Parker. The most famous people in the world are founders, too: instead of a company, every celebrity founds and cultivates a personal brand. Lady Gaga, for example, became one of the most influential living people. But is she even a real person? Her real name isn't a secret, but almost no one knows or cares what it is. She wears costumes so bizarre as to put any other wearer at risk of an involuntary psychiatric hold. Gaga would have you believe that she was "born this way"—the title of both her second album and its lead track. But no one is born looking like a zombie with horns coming out of her head: Gaga must therefore be a self-manufactured myth. Then again, what kind of person would do this to herself? Certainly nobody normal. So perhaps Gaga really was born that way. WHERE KINGS COME FROM Extreme founder figures are not new in human affairs. Classical mythology is full of them. Oedipus is the paradigmatic insider/outsider: he was abandoned as an infant and ended up in a foreign land, but he was a brilliant king and smart enough to solve the riddle of the Sphinx. Romulus and Remus were born of royal blood and abandoned as orphans. When they discovered their pedigree, they decided to found a city. But they couldn't agree on where to put it. When Remus crossed the boundary that Romulus had decided was the edge of Rome, Romulus killed him, declaring: "So perish every one that shall hereafter leap over my wall." Law-maker and law-breaker, criminal outlaw and king who defined Rome, Romulus was a self-contradictory insider/outsider. Normal people aren't like Oedipus or Romulus. Whatever those individuals were actually like in life, the mythologized versions of them remember only the extremes. But why was it so important for archaic cultures to remember extraordinary people? The famous and infamous have always served as vessels for public sentiment: they're praised amid prosperity and blamed for misfortune. Primitive societies faced one fundamental problem above all: they would be torn apart by conflict if they didn't have a way to stop it. So whenever plagues, disasters, or violent rivalries threatened the peace, it was beneficial for the society to place the entire blame on a single person, someone everybody could agree on: a scapegoat. Who makes an effective scapegoat? Like founders, scapegoats are extreme and contradictory figures. On the one hand, a scapegoat is necessarily weak; he is powerless to stop his own victimization. On the other hand, as the one who can defuse conflict by taking the blame, he is the most powerful member of the community. Before execution, scapegoats were often worshipped like deities. The Aztecs considered their victims to be earthly forms of the gods to whom they were sacrificed. You would be dressed in fine clothes and feast royally until your brief reign ended and they cut your heart out. These are the roots of monarchy: every king was a living god, and every god a murdered king. Perhaps every modern king is just a scapegoat who has managed to delay his own execution.THE RETURN OF THE KING Just as the legal attack on Microsoft was ending Bill Gates's dominance, Steve Jobs's return to Apple demonstrated the irreplaceable value of a company's founder. In some ways, Steve Jobs and Bill Gates were opposites. Jobs was an artist, preferred closed systems, and spent his time thinking about great products above all else; Gates was a businessman, kept his products open, and wanted to run the world. But both were insider/outsiders, and both pushed the companies they started to achievements that nobody else would have been able to match. A college dropout who walked around barefoot and refused to shower, Jobs was also the insider of his own personality cult. He could act charismatic or crazy, perhaps according to his mood or perhaps according to his calculations; it's hard to believe that such weird practices as apple-only diets weren't part of a larger strategy. But all this eccentricity backfired on him in 1985: Apple's board effectively kicked Jobs out of his own company when he clashed with the professional CEO brought in to provide adult supervision. Jobs's return to Apple 12 years later shows how the most important task in business—the creation of new value—cannot be reduced to a formula and applied by professionals. When he was hired as interim CEO of Apple in 1997, the impeccably credentialed executives who preceded him had steered the company nearly to bankruptcy. That year Michael Dell famously said of Apple, "What would I do? I'd shut it down and give the money back to the shareholders." Instead Jobs introduced the iPod (2001), the iPhone (2007), and the iPad (2010) before he had to resign in 2011 because of poor health. By the following year Apple was the single most valuable company in the world. Apple's value crucially depended on the singular vision of a particular person. This hints at the strange way in which the companies that create new technology often resemble feudal monarchies rather than organizations that are supposedly more "modern." A unique founder can make authoritative decisions, inspire strong personal loyalty, and plan ahead for decades. Paradoxically, impersonal bureaucracies staffed by trained professionals can last longer than any lifetime, but they usually act with short time horizons. The lesson for business is that we need founders. If anything, we should be more tolerant of founders who seem strange or extreme; we need unusual individuals to lead companies beyond mere incrementalism. The lesson for founders is that individual prominence and adulation can never be enjoyed except on the condition that it may be exchanged for individual notoriety and demonization at any moment— so be careful. Above all, don't overestimate your own power as an individual. Founders are important not because they are the only ones whose work has value, but rather because a great founder can bring out the best work from everybody at his company. That we need individual founders in all their peculiarity does not mean that we are called to worship Ayn Randian "prime movers" who claim to be independent of everybody around them. In this respect Rand was a merely half-great writer: her villains were real, but her heroes were fake. There is no Galt's Gulch. There is no secession from society. To believe yourself invested with divine self-sufficiency is not the mark of a strong individual, but of a person who has mistaken the crowd's worship—or jeering—for the truth. The single greatest danger for a founder is to become so certain of his own myth that he loses his mind. But an equally insidious danger for every business is to lose all sense of myth and mistake disenchantment for wisdom.

9 Steps To Help You Start A Startup

If you've never started a business, the first time can be a little scary. Especially because it takes a lot of hard work and planning. On top of this, only about half of all businesses survive five years or longer.1

Luckily, there are 9 basic strategies for startups you can follow to help get your company up and running:

1. Start with a Great Idea

Your first step in learning how to start a business is to identify a problem and solution. This is because successful startups begin from business ideas that fill the needs of a group of customers. But your idea doesn't always have to be a new one. You can update existing products or services in a way that's better for the consumer. This can be as simple as:

Changing the product's appearance

Adding a new feature

Finding a new use for a product that customers already love

For instance, Apple started from Steve Jobs' original idea for a computer and has since created enhanced versions that better fit the market. They've also continued to evolve newer products like iPhones and iPads, making them more useful with each update. One example is how they're adding a keyboard for iPads that'll make them easier to use like a laptop.2 All these innovations by Apple led to them being worth of over a billion dollars.

2. Make a Business Plan

Once you have an idea, you'll want to start building a business plan that describes your products and services in detail. It should include information on your industry, operations, finances and a market analysis.

Writing a business plan is also important for getting financing for your startup. Banks are more likely to give loans to companies that can clearly explain how they're going to use the money and why they need it.

3. Secure Funding for Your Startup

The cost of a startup is different for every business owner. However, no matter what your costs are, you'll likely need to get startup financing from:

Friends and family

Angel investors

Venture capitalists

Bank loans

You can also apply for a business credit card. Many companies offer 0% APR promotions, which means you won't pay interest on your purchases if you pay off the balance before the end of the offer period. We've partnered with Fundera, which put together a list of the top credit cards offering 0% interest rates.

If you don't get the right amount of funding or can't raise money for your business, you'll risk not being able to pay your operating costs. This may cause you to close your doors. In fact, it's estimated that 29% of startups fail because they run out of money.3

To make sure you get the right amount, you'll want to estimate your costs and cash flow, including the interest rates on your loans. Once you do that, you can use QuickBooks or FreshBooks to track your expenses and help you stick to a budget.

4. Surround Yourself With the Right People

There can be a lot of risk in starting a business. That's why you'll need essential business advisors to help guide you along the way, like:

Attorneys

Certified Public Accountants (CPAs)

Insurance professionals

Bankers

Building the right startup team is especially important in the early stages of small businesses. This means you'll want to carefully select your:

Co-founders

Contractors

Initial employees, including remote workers

5. Make Sure You're Following All the Legal Steps

From designing your product to setting up your workplace, opening your dream startup can be a lot of fun. But before you officially enter the market, you'll want to take the right legal steps to give you the best chance at success, including:

Applying for a business license

Registering your business name

Getting a federal tax ID number

Filing for a trademark

Creating a separate bank account

Familiarizing yourself with industry regulations

Building contracts for clients and others you plan to work with

6. Establish a Location (Physical and Online)

Whether you need to establish a manufacturing facility, set up an office space or open a storefront, you'll want to determine if leasing or buying a property is right for you. In many cases, you can get tax deductions for managing a commercial space, which is a benefit to owning your own place. You'll also be able to rent it out to make extra income.

However, one reason startups lease in the beginning is so they can invest their money into other aspects of the company. Leasing can also be a cheaper way to get your startup in a prime location. Keep in mind that rent prices can spike unexpectedly, which can force you to spend more or move. You also won't build any equity while you lease.

In today's digital era, it's important to set up an online presence and e-commerce platform. In fact, you'll have trouble being successful without it. This is because customers are increasingly shopping online and using google to find out more information on your products. On top of this, websites offer advantages like:

Keeping your store open 24 hours a day, on weekends and on holidays, which increases sales.

Helping you reach customers around the world.

Allowing customers to read reviews about your products, which can raise your brand's credibility.

You can enhance your online presence even more by starting a blog. This can help you establish yourself as an expert in your field. You can also use search engine optimization (SEO) to increase your brand's visibility on Google searches. And it's always a good idea to post on social media platforms, where your audience visits frequently.

7. Develop a Marketing Plan

Every startup needs to spend different amounts of money and time on marketing. It's an important expense, because it helps you:

Establish a brand identity

Stand out from competition

Create customer relationships and build loyalty

Increase visibility, which attracts new customers

Strengthen your company's reputation

Some startup marketing activities you should look into include:

Using social media to engage customers and promote coupons or deals

Giving rewards out for referrals, which brings in more business

Offering free samples or demos in your store

Sponsoring events to get your name out there in local communities

8. Build a Customer Base

In order for your startup business to have long-term success, you'll want to build a customer base. These loyal customers can help with:

Boosting your sales, because they're willing to keep spending at your company

Sending a message to new customers that your brand is trustworthy

Gaining referrals, which saves you time and effort with finding new customers

Some ways you can attract and retain customers include:

Regularly offering a great product or service

Launching loyalty programs to keep them coming in

Using affiliate marketing on social media, which involves paying influencers to promote products to your target audience

Focusing on great customer service

Using market research to understand your customers' expectations better

Asking for feedback directly from the customer

On top of this, the International Council of Shopping Centers (ICSC) found that 92% of consumers said their loyalty to specific retailers was because they offered prices that were fair and matched the value of their product, while 79% said it was because of product quality.4

9. Plan to Change

Startups change drastically within their first few years in operation. A key to success is to evolve and adapt your business model to your market and industry.

Some strategies to make sure you're prepared to adapt are:

Hiring forward thinkers so you know your team is adaptable

Listening to feedback from customers, suppliers and others that you work with

Staying updated on trends in your industry

Remember, it's businesses that are willing to evolve with consumer expectations that are able to establish themselves for years to come.

FOR MORE UNDERSTANDING ANY BUSINESS READ MY BOOK HOW TO START A COMPANY. AND

WHY ENTREPRENEURSHIP